brary

The Enviro

In memory of James Clarke (1921–2006), a gentleman

The Environment

A Sociological Introduction

PHILIP W. SUTTON

polity

First published in 2007 by Polity Press

Polity Press
65 Bridge Street
Cambridge CB2 1UR, UK

Polity Press
350 Main Street
Malden, MA 02148, USA

ISBN-10: 0-7456-3432-X
ISBN-13: 978-07456-3432-6
ISBN-10: 0-7456-3433-8 (pb)
ISBN-13: 978-07456-3433-3 (pb)

A catalogue record for this book is available from the British
Library.

Typeset in 9.5 on 12pt Utopia
by Servis Filmsetting Ltd, Longsight, Manchester
Printed and bound in Malaysia by Alden Press, Malaysia

The publisher has used its best endeavours to ensure that
the URLs for external websites referred to in this book are
correct and active at the time of going to press. However, the
publisher has no responsibility for the websites and can
make no guarantee that a site will remain live or that the
content is or will remain appropriate.

Every effort has been made to trace all copyright holders,
but if any have been inadvertently overlooked the
publishers will be pleased to include any necessary credits
in any subsequent reprint or edition.

For further information on Polity, visit our website:
www.polity.co.uk

Contents

Acknowledgements   vii
Preface   ix

1   Natural Environments   1
    Defining Nature and Environment   1
    Humans in Natural Environments   7
    Natural and Artificial Environments   14
    Conclusion   16

2   Knowing the Environment   18
    Involvement and Detachment   18
    The Scientific Revolution   22
    Social Constructions of Nature   26
    Critical Realism   32
    Conclusion   36

3   Experiencing the Environment   38
    An Environment of the Senses   38
    Experiencing Environments   41
    Ecological Identifications   44
    Ecological Citizenship   52

4   Transforming the Environment   55
    Social Development and the Environment   55
    Industrialization   59
    Urbanization   64
    The Treadmill of Production and Consumption   67

5   Polluting the Environment   72
    Types of Pollution   72
    Awareness and Significance of Pollution   74
    Sensitivity to Risks   80
    Conclusion   88

6   Defending the Environment   91
    Changing Attitudes   91
    The Modern Origins of Nature Conservation   95

The Development of Environmentalism   99
Conclusion   107

7 Politicizing the Environment   109
   A Politics of Nature   109
   Ecologism: A New Political Ideology   113
   The Emergence of Green Parties   116
   Conclusion   124

8 Sustaining the Environment   126
   The Idea of Sustainable Development   126
   A Brief History of Sustainable Development   130
   Sustainable Development in Practice   135
   Can Societies Become Sustainable?   139
   Conclusion   142

9 A Global Environment   144
   What is Globalization?   144
   The Biosphere as Environment   148
   Global Problems, Global Solutions?   150
   Conclusion   161

Glossary   164
References and Further Reading   170
Index   178

Acknowledgements

This book did not begin life as a great idea looking for an outlet, but gradually evolved into an idea and book project over the last four years or so. Once I began teaching environmental sociology, or the sociology of the environment, I came to realize that 'introductory' textbooks (now including my own) didn't really 'introduce' the subject matter, but rather discussed and debated it, assuming a knowledge base that many of my new students simply did not have. Sociologists came rather late to the study of environmental issues and, as a result, the latter have just not been a part of the staple diet of sociology students. Therefore, what seemed to be missing was a fairly concise, reliable and welcoming invitation to the sociological study of environmental issues for all of those with little if any familiarity with sociology, environmental issues or both. A suggestion by Emma Longstaff, my editor at Polity, that I should consider writing my own was the start of the process, which led, eventually, to this book. A special thank-you is due to Emma, as, without her knowledge of the publication needs of the discipline, I would probably have waited for someone else to do it. She also managed the project sympathetically and was a constant source of good advice. After becoming convinced that a brief introduction would be useful for a range of 'Environment and Society' courses, a proposal went out for review. I would like to thank David Held and the Editorial Board at Polity, but especially the independent reviewers for their extraordinarily detailed and constructive comments, suggestions and sound advice on the draft manuscript. Stephen Vertigans also read parts of the book and made some helpful suggestions for improvement. I am sure the book is better for these interventions, though obviously I remain solely responsible for any shortcomings that remain.

At The Robert Gordon University, Joyce Lishman has been extremely supportive over a number of years and, importantly for this book, enabled the help of a research assistant over the summer of 2004. A special thank-you to Helen White, who did a brilliant job digging out documentary materials and international examples for the book. I hope that Helen feels a spark of recognition in some of the examples I've used, though I guess she will also wonder whatever happened to all the rest! Another time perhaps. Thanks also to Roddy Hamilton for invaluable technical advice in sorting out the book's image files. A debt of gratitude is again owed to Julian Bell for his usual but inimitable understanding, support and interest, which are always much appreciated. I also acknowledge the contribution of all the students on my Environment and Society course for alerting me to the kind of material that would be most helpfully included in such an introductory-level text.

Lastly, heartfelt thanks to Pat for making the book possible and patiently enduring my seemingly endless revisions to it.

Preface

I make a basic assumption at the outset that anyone picking up this book has an interest in knowing something about the environment, sociology or both. For those interested in the environment, the book will cover some key environmental issues and problems, but will also show them how sociologists think about and carry out research in this area. I will try to convince them that understanding, explaining and solving environmental problems will require sociological knowledge. For those already interested in sociology, the book will try to convince them that they should take environmental issues and problems seriously and that sociologists should be prepared to make the effort to understand evidence from the natural sciences if they are to make their necessary contribution. Of course, should anyone already be interested in both the environment and sociology, they will need no convincing of any of this, but should still find the presentation of material and specific examples helpful.

The book has been written with two specific audiences in mind, namely the (possibly mythical) 'intelligent layperson' and the (hopefully real) new undergraduate student. Some of the former may even metamorphose into the latter before, after or possibly during the reading of this book, though this is by no means necessary. Still, self-evidently the book is sociological and contains some of the staple concerns of the discipline. Most of the time, the sociological content, and particularly the theory, is embedded within the discussions of evidence or delivered with a fairly light touch. In this way the sociological contribution builds gradually and is not separated out from the evidence. My hope therefore is that it will be possible for people with no, a little, or some knowledge of sociology to get something useful from the book. New students of sociology, politics, international relations, geography and environmental science should be able to read it without feeling too overwhelmed by social theory, a fair bit of which I readily admit is unnecessarily verbose.

What led to a textbook of this kind was my gradual realization that despite the existence of many introductions to 'environmental sociology' and the 'sociology of the environment', all of them have been written for the higher levels of undergraduate or postgraduate study. That means anyone approaching sociology to find out what it might be able to add to their existing knowledge of the environment and environmental issues would probably not find the existing literature that useful, simply because it is written at too high a level and makes the assumption of prior sociological knowledge. This book does not make that assumption. To a lesser extent, teaching my own Environment and Society course has also convinced me that a more basic introduction might even provide a service to higher-level students of sociology. This is because, apart from some brief material on risk, environmental politics and the general rubbishing of all things biological or natural, there really isn't much 'environment' in sociology degree schemes. Even though higher-level environmental sociology students may get along perfectly well with the sociology, their previous lack of acquaintance with environmental issues may have left a gap in knowledge which this book should help to fill. Such a lack of acquaintance does not entirely explain a former student who tried to convince us that genetically modified crops might be part of an extra-terrestrial alien conspiracy to wipe out the human species, but it probably didn't help.

None of this means that the book is undemanding or easy. The issues it deals with require a genuine interest and desire to understand wide-ranging environmental debates, which cross the science of global warming, the history of environmental movements and the long-term development of human societies. But I suggest that this is an entirely worthwhile and rewarding challenge. As many other sociologists have found, trying to make sense of environmental issues and problems takes us all into distinctly 'alien' territory. As an undergraduate sociology student seeking out information for my dissertation on the society–environment relationship, I was often found wandering and browsing in parts of the library previously considered no-go areas: general biology, physics, geography (human and physical), economics, history, history of science, anthropology and even theology and religious studies. This was absolutely necessary because the library's own categorizing of 'environment' books was determined by existing disciplinary divisions. In reality, the knowledge and information these books contained not only often failed to match the category, but were also of interest in themselves to a sociological project covering environmental issues. In fact, all of the above library sections have things to offer those who are fascinated by nature, environment and society. I strongly recommend my own research strategy – 'wandering' and 'browsing' as a way of seeking out implausible connections across disciplines, sadly an under-used research method in the age of qualitative software packages and electronic databases.

Two more important things to note. First, the text uses examples and illustrative materials, drawing on my own 'local' knowledge of the British situation and research literature. That means there will be many British examples throughout the text. However, I have drawn on the wider literature whenever possible and particularly when doing so makes for a stronger argument or makes a point especially well. Hence, environmental issues in post-communist Eastern Europe have a place, as do those in India, China, North America, Africa and many more. One pleasing and very satisfying aspect of environmental studies is the recognition that there is no point in restricting the focus to one country or region. The entire natural and human worlds are part of our subject matter and we just have to pursue issues wherever they may take us, both geographically and intellectually. Fascinating stuff! But also, necessarily demanding.

Secondly, the book does not provide another review of sociological ideas on environmental issues, at least not in the conventional way. That is because I have tried to keep the referencing of authors and their work to a minimum so as to distil their key contributions into a coherent and readable whole. One benefit of this method is that it allows the text to concentrate on illustrating theories and arguments with illustrative examples and evidence without the need to fill the book with streams of names and dates. There is nothing wrong with the latter, of course: adopting academic conventions is an essential part of what we do. But not at this level. The focus is also on presenting clear expositions of some central ideas and debates rather than engaging in an extended critique of the field. After all, that is what all of those higher-level introductory books aim to achieve. This book is therefore intended to serve as an entry point into sociological approaches to the environment which will guide readers towards the wider literature should they choose to take matters further. The Bibliography should help with this, and key readings can be found at the ends of chapters. I have also provided a glossary of keywords for practical assistance and keywords are identified **thus** on first use within each chapter. Of course, readers may not find the answers they are seeking here, but the book will hopefully give them a better idea of where to look.

Structure of the Book

As a whole, the book adopts a long-term perspective which sets current environmental issues into a wider social and historical context. The text also covers as much of the field of society–environment relations as would reasonably fit an entry-level text, though others will no doubt find that some things have been omitted or not covered in enough detail. The separate chapters are parts of what is really a closely intertwined whole, and at times the relatively discrete parts may raise issues which are not adequately dealt with until a later chapter. This is unavoidable, though I have tried to flag upcoming matters whenever possible and readers are advised to hold onto all their unanswered queries until they are discussed more fully in the relevant chapter. For those with an interest in structure, the book is roughly and invisibly divided into three sections, dealing with the socio-historical and cultural, the economic and political, followed by two chapters which work towards a higher level synthesis of all of these at an increasingly global level. To explore this a little further, the chapter breakdown is as follows.

Chapters 1–3 look at ways in which people gain knowledge about the natural environment. Much knowledge can be gained about the environment from academic books, television documentaries, fiction, film and from personal experience. Quite often, some of this knowledge is contested and we have to reach our own conclusions about it. Is the planet really steadily warming or not, for instance? These chapters raise some significant questions about the way that ideas about nature have changed over time. What is 'nature' and how might it be studied? Evidently, scientific knowledge has a privileged place amongst the possible knowledge sources, but even though science has displaced and marginalized many other types of knowledge, it has not entirely eliminated them. One issue that continues to trouble modern societies is the question of where human beings fit into the natural environment. Are they part of nature or do they stand outside? The book brings a typically sociological approach to this question, in that sociology sees human beings as naturally evolved and, at the same time, socially developed. The implications of this view are pursued throughout. Finally, sociological methods of gaining knowledge of environmental issues are introduced. These are presented in a polarized form simply because that is the way they have developed chronologically. However, it should be borne in mind that ways around these disagreements are emerging and some of these are included here. Ways of knowing the environment remain a crucially important matter because we act on the basis of what we know about the environment. If global warming really is happening but we are convinced that it is not, then the consequences could hardly be more serious. However, should we be convinced that global warming is real when it is not, then we may spend enormous amounts of the world's time, effort and money on trying to prevent it at the expense of other genuinely serious problems.

Chapters 4 and 5 examine the transformation of the natural environment by human activities. Again, a long-term view is adopted because we need to have in mind a 'history of the present', as it were, if we are to avoid misunderstandings. A brief review of human social development is included before the focus falls on industrialization, urban development and capitalistic production and consumption patterns. The combination of these is shown to have had revolutionary consequences for both human life and the natural environment on which they depend. The incalculable consequences of these transformations are then explored alongside current debates on risk and risk-awareness. Over recent years, people do seem to have become more aware of the risks of living in the modern world. These are not all to do with the environment of course, though many of the more serious and hard-to-tackle hazards have been defined in environmental terms. For example, one central environmental issue is industrial pollution and its effects on the health of human beings and the environment. This section outlines some important questions and introduces some of the ways in which pollution levels might be reduced.

Chapters 6 and 7 take stock of environmental politics, looking at the development of conservation and environmental groups, Green political parties, environmental ideologies and the greening of party political systems. Environmental politics is part of a much wider environmental movement that can be studied alongside other social movements such as feminism, disabled people's movements, peace and anti-nuclear movements and so on. Sociologists have to take social movements seriously because they have been and still are the source of new ideas, activities and values in societies. It is hard to imagine that 'the environment' would be quite such a widely recognized political issue without the relentless campaigning of environmental organizations such as Greenpeace or the commitment of environmental activists and supporters. Nevertheless, it is the case that more than this is required to bring the state of the natural environment into people's conscious awareness. Wider social and economic changes can affect and shape attitudes and beliefs in ways that are more or less conducive to environmentalist arguments and protests, so we have to be sensitive to this. If we are not, then we could run away with the (false) idea that the activities of a few people can change societies at any time of their own choosing. They cannot. Karl Marx once told us that of course 'people make history', people bring about revolutions or prevent them. But they do not do this under conditions they have freely chosen. They are simply born into a particular moment in the stream of historical development. For environmentalists, it took over a century for their ideas to gain widespread currency and be taken seriously.

Chapters 8 and 9 then tackle the thorny issue of how to align economic development with environmental protection through the concept of sustainable development; the global aspects of environmental issues complete the book. The dominant framework of sustainable development is discussed, and some examples of this show why it has become so central to international environmentalism. A notable feature of sustainable development is the way that it has tried to connect environmental problems with social justice and poverty in the developing countries. Although separate matters on the face of it, sustainable development advocates believe that unless global social justice issues are tackled, there is no hope for a sustainable future. This argument is outline and debated. Global warming is also introduced here as a global environmental issue *par excellence*, and a survey of the science and social debate on the issue attempts to assess its potential significance for the future. Chapter 9 also introduces some constructive solutions to global problems under the name of 'ecological modernization'.

By the end of the book my hope is that readers will understand better some of the distinctively sociological approaches to environmental issues and appreciate why these have to be part of all attempts to grasp and tackle the environmental problems of the future. More than this however, I hope that those who came along with an interest in the environment go away with an emerging sociological imagination, and those whose sociological interest brought them here leave with a clearer sense of the vital significance of environmental issues for the future of the discipline.

1 Natural Environments

Defining Nature and Environment

A good place to start any enquiry is simply with dictionary definitions of key words, which will hopefully give us an insight into their currently dominant meanings as well as previous usage. In my own dictionary, I see that 'environment' is defined as, 'external conditions or surroundings', but 'particularly those in which people live or work'. Obviously this is a human-centred definition of environment, taking *people* as its central concern and starting point. Environments, then, are those external conditions or surroundings *around people*. This is a reasonable start, though this definition, in itself and without further elaboration, could refer to a whole series of very different environments. For example, it could refer to the working environment of factories and office buildings within which people earn their living. It could mean the wider economic environment of wages, interest rates, mortgages and trade which influence the opportunities for people to make a living and whether they prosper or struggle. There is also the urban environment, sometimes pejoratively described in literature as the 'concrete jungle', and in which the majority of the world's people now live. It could also refer to the political environment of parties, interest groups and decision-making, which affects every aspect of people's existence. These are all environments – things that surround people – of varying kinds.

However, when people think about and discuss the state of *the* environment today, I think they are unlikely to have any of these specific meanings in mind. What was your own assumption about the environment as described in this book's title? What were you expecting from the book and what kind of information did you expect to find within its pages? I hope (for the sake of the book's sales figures) that you were looking for discussions of pollution, the science of climate change, animals and animal welfare, flora and fauna, environmental organizations such as Greenpeace, Green political parties and much more. If so, then not only will you not be disappointed, but we can conclude that for many, if not most, people in today's modern world, the environment has a very special and specific meaning, namely *non-human natural* conditions and surroundings. This meaning comes close to another key word that we all use regularly without too much reflection – namely, 'nature'. Do these two words then simply have the same meaning?

Again, I consult my dictionary for advice. But this time the answer is much more complicated, as I find that there are no fewer than twelve distinct meanings attached to the word 'nature'. This shows that nature is one of the most complex and difficult to explain words in the English language, in large part because its dominant meaning has changed several times alongside major periods of social change in the development of societies. We have been left, therefore, with multiple meanings of nature, three of which stand out as being the most significant and most widely used.

First, nature can mean something that is essential to a person or a thing. 'Why did she do that?' we might ask of a person's action that we don't understand. Well, we may be told, it's just 'in her nature'. That is, her behaviour is something that flows from her *essential* being and she just couldn't help doing it. This meaning can also be applied to animals and plants. Why do some birds build their nests at the same time every year? Again, we will be told that it is an essential part of their being and it is therefore entirely proper for them to do so and we should not expect them to build nests at any other time of year. This particular meaning of nature was still very widespread well into the seventeenth century. Of course, explanations that are rooted in this definition of nature tell us very little *as explanations* of the phenomena in question. How do we know what is and is not 'essential' to the nature of people and birds? More investigation than this would clearly be required to find out exactly what makes nest-building such an essential attribute of bird species. And for people, it seems to underestimate their capacity to change what they do and to make choices that alter their behaviour.

During the fourteenth century in Europe, the meaning of nature was undergoing change and a relatively new meaning emerged as the dominant one. People came to see nature as a series of forces, or indeed the force, that directed the world and ultimately explained why things happen when they do. This meaning is of course still with us whenever we talk about natural forces being at work in the direction of human affairs. Many people still consult astrological charts looking for their birth date-based 'star sign', which promises guidance on life strategies and what to expect in the coming days, weeks and months. Astrologers observe the movement of celestial bodies through patterns of stars called constellations, in order to forecast the most favourable and unfavourable times for certain actions. In doing so, they implicitly draw on the same basic idea that natural forces really do ultimately direct human life. Of course, many people do not believe everything that astrologers tell them and some undoubtedly pore over their own daily charts as a bit of fun to make a boring day at work pass more quickly. Nevertheless, astrology remains rooted in the idea that natural forces ultimately hold the key to understanding why events occur when they do and, as such, even in the twenty-first century, the fourteenth-century meaning of nature is still with us. As far as it is possible to tell, this is no longer the most significant meaning within modern societies.

By the seventeenth century, the dominant meaning of nature was in flux yet again. Gradually, nature was coming to be defined in terms of the *whole material world of things* rather than as an ultimate directing force. It would not be inaccurate to say that this change represented the movement away from seeing nature as a process (natural forces) towards the view that nature was much more 'thing-like' (the natural world). Defining nature as the whole material world meant that people came to see nature as a world full of fairly static *natural things* – fields, mountains, beaches and so on – rather than a world of moving natural forces and processes. We can see this emerging meaning in the trend towards seeing and describing nature as 'scenery' and in many artistic works, which literally 'framed' nature in a series of landscapes and pictorials. For some people, these pictorial landscapes were in many ways even preferable to the real natural world: they were less dirty, much neater and more pleasurable to look at. Humanly created representations could now be seen as in many ways better than the natural reality on which they were based. In addition, the farmed countryside and rural life came to be seen as more natural when compared to the artificial world which humans lived amongst in the growing towns and cities. Wild places untouched by humans, living wild plants and creatures other than humans were seen as genuinely natural, whilst human creations and constructions, however impressive they might be, were still somewhat less than authentic. Nature was coming to be defined in oppositional terms; as in many ways opposed to human society and culture. Of course, if nature was the opposition and an obstacle to society, then it also had to be overcome and its obstacles cleared to make way for human progress.

The majority view at the time was that nature was clearly deficient compared to culture and society. Nature 'in the raw' and nature 'red in tooth and claw' needed to be tamed and cultivated by people rather than left wild, uncultivated and barren. In 1850, Britain's Prince Albert gave a speech that represented this latest interpretation of 'nature'. He said:

> Man is approaching a more complete fulfilment of that great and sacred mission which he has to perform in this world. His reason being created after the image of God, he has to use it to discover the laws by which the Almighty governs his creation, and, by making these laws his standard of action, to conquer nature to his use; himself a divine instrument.   (Cited in Golby 1986: 2)

'Man' has 'reason' and is a creation in the 'image of God'. He must therefore use this gift to discover nature's 'laws' as a prelude to 'conquering nature' to his own ends. By today's standards, this is a very strong statement and may strike you as optimistic, even somewhat arrogant, though if we think of some of the environmental problems currently afflicting the world then the power of human societies to affect the rest of nature is evident.

For a significant minority of people in the nineteenth century though, nature was in many ways better than human society and culture. In its natural (that is pre-human) state, nature was clean, pure and inherently beautiful. It did not need to be conquered, nor was Man a 'divine instrument' of God. For this vocal minority, human societies polluted and wasted nature to feed their increasingly overly civilized urban lifestyles. Rather than yet more economic and urban 'development', people actually had much to learn from the natural world if only they would treat it with more respect.

Notice though, that for both groups of people, nature and society had come increasingly to be seen as separate things, and in philosophical language they continue to form a basic modern dualism. That is, despite their opposition, they have come to be defined in terms of each other. *Nature* is that which society is not, and *society* is that which nature is not. This meaning probably remains the dominant one today, though one difference is that more people would now agree with the nature-lovers and fewer people would support the nature-conquerors.

Time to return to the dictionary! As it confirms, then, today nature is a word of many meanings, some of which are more widely used than others. More importantly, the dominant oppositional meaning of nature is now itself being challenged in a variety of ways. For our purposes in this book, environmental issues pose a serious challenge to such an opposition because they demand that nature and society are understood together, rather than holding them separate. By now, it should be easier to see just why nature is such a complicated word.

The natural environment

In order to be as clear as possible about my own use of these difficult terms, throughout the book I will use a phrase which combines them – the natural environment. The term 'natural environment' is chosen to avoid some of the possible misunderstandings when using 'environment' or 'nature' separately. The natural environment refers to *the non-human world within which human societies and their products exist*. At the local level, a natural environment can be a particular and identifiable area such as a park or a beach. In its most expansive interpretation, the natural environment is simply planet Earth itself. I use this very much as a working definition, not an absolute or fixed one, but the meaning in use should be evident from the context of use.

All this should not be taken as implying that human beings and human societies are somehow not natural. My assumption is that they are just as natural as any other animals or animal groups; it is merely that this book is written from the standpoint of the discipline of sociology, the science of specifically *human* societies. In practice, this means that I will be particularly concerned to explore the *human* consequences of environmental issues and the things that people in human societies can do to resolve environmental problems and dilemmas.

For sociologists, human beings are an animal species that has evolved and developed over time, as have all others. But the human species remains the only one so far identified in which the balance between behaviour based on *inherited instincts* and behaviour based on *learning* has been tilted decisively towards the latter. Of course, many other animals learn, but for humans, learned behaviour is not optional or an addition to their basic inherited behavioural pattern. Human beings not only *can* learn, but also *have* to learn how to behave in order to survive and thrive within societies. This basic fact makes human individuals in some ways more vulnerable, as they are very dependent on other people for transmitting knowledge and behaviour. At the same time, though, it has also given humans the collective capacity to adapt to changing natural environments and social events without any need for a corresponding transformation in their biological structure. People can learn from each other and transmit their successful knowledge and practices over long distances, thereby sharing it across almost the entire human species. If people in other societies then use it to transform their own behaviour and social life, this has little to do with biologically inherited behavioural patterns, but is, rather, a social process of development based on learning from a shared fund of knowledge.

The long-term development of human societies has therefore been shaped by both biological evolution and social development. This crucial difference between human societies and most other animal groups is often misunderstood as demonstrating the superiority of humans. However, it is not really superiority but *difference*. And this clear difference makes the study of human societies a distinctly *socio-logical* enterprise, because we need to understand the distinctively social-developmental as well as the biological-evolutionary history of human beings – that is, how societies have changed and developed in different ways as well as how the human species has evolved. Without the sociological analysis of long-term social development, we can seriously misunderstand the nature of human nature, as it were.

Industrialization, urbanization and natural environments

Changes in the dominant meaning of nature in society take a long time to become established and are best seen as part of the long-term process of social change, closely connected to the transformation of people's ways of living. The historian Keith Thomas (1984) investigated changes in social life and people's attitudes in England between 1500 and 1800, the key period when dominant ideas of nature were in flux. The conclusions he arrived at are not restricted to England, as many of the same social changes were also spreading to many other national societies, first in Europe and later across the world. By examining literary and documentary sources, including personal diaries, Thomas showed that attitudes towards the natural environment and the treatment of animals slowly changed during this period. The change was not random, though, but in a clear direction moving away from perceiving nature as something to be used and exploited by people with no regard for the damage caused, towards attitudes of respect for natural environments, leading people to enjoy natural scenes and things. Appreciation of nature's wildness and heightened feelings of sympathy for animals were the result. Rather than continuing to see nature as God's creation *for* humans, which they could therefore legitimately use at will, a concern for the well-being of non-human animals gradually came to be expressed, along with a growing interest in the effects of human actions on the integrity of the natural environment.

Thomas says that there is a connection between the processes of industrialization and urbanization and people's attitudes to natural environments. As more people left the countryside to work in industrial factories they no longer worked directly with animals or on the land (see below, chapter 4). The working day, month and year were no longer strictly governed by natural cycles as they had been, and in many places still are, in societies that are reliant on agricultural work. They now lived amongst larger numbers of people, initially in dirty, polluted conditions with poor sanitation, much disease and ill health. They returned to the countryside for their relaxation and leisure pursuits. The countryside therefore became associated with peaceful and pleasurable enjoyment rather than hard work and drudgery. The growing towns and cities provided better incomes, but in terms of the quality of life compared unfavourably to country living, which came to be widely seen as health-creating, authentic and even beautiful. More people began to be emotionally moved by the sight of mountains that had previously been thought of as hideous and barren outcrops unworthy of the attention of civilized people. Artists, and especially painters, began flocking to paint the barren scenery and wild environments which had now found a new audience which demanded them. In a parallel development, the humane treatment of animals emerged as an issue for many people and visible animal cruelty was no longer deemed acceptable. Traditional pastimes such as bear-baiting, dog-fighting and cock-fighting were banned. Fox-hunting continued – but that is another story, too long to be covered here (see Tester 1991).

Sociologically, Thomas is describing the psychological and emotional effects of a gradual alteration in people's orientation to the natural environment brought about by fundamental changes in social organization and the rise of a modern scientific worldview (see below, chapter 2). The sociologist, Norbert Elias, argues that over the long term:

> as humans have gradually come to understand natural forces more, fear them less and use them more effectively for human ends, this has gone hand in hand with specific changes in human relationships. More and more people have tended to become more and more interdependent with each other in longer chains and denser webs.
>
> (Cited in Mennell 1992: 169–70)

Social organization has become more complex, more internationally connected and effective. Applications of science in transportation and communication technologies have also made the world seem smaller and opened up new ways of understanding natural events and disasters that counter beliefs that these are punishments from God. As a result, people have also become less frightened of natural environments and more sympathetic attitudes towards nature have emerged. In time, most industrialized societies have also seen the emergence of many conservation and preservation organizations that campaign to protect and defend natural environments, birds and animals. Many of them, and more, continue to do so today (see chapter 6).

These transformations of attitudes and beliefs in relation to natural environments have spread widely. Everywhere that industrialization and urban development took place has witnessed some similar changes, though there are noteworthy differences across countries and regions of the world. In the UK, conservation and management of the natural environment was the typical response, whilst in America with its large areas of wilderness and history of pioneer settlement, a less managerial 'wilderness preservation' set the tone for a democratically inspired population. In parts of Southern Europe, the British sensitivity towards animal welfare was and still is seen as taking things rather too far. In many developing countries of the world, natural environments are seen in yet different ways as the traditional home of indigenous peoples who have rights to the land that should be protected from the multinational corporations and national governments seeking to develop it for profit. Urban living and industrial production have distanced people from their previously more immediate and lived reliance on the natural environment. Once freed from this immediately evident dependence, it became possible to look back with a romantic fondness and appreciation for the countryside and for nature.

Humans in Natural Environments

During much of human development, early hominid groups struggled to secure enough food and shelter from the natural environment for their groups to survive into the next generation. Knowledge of natural environments was relatively localized with little systematic contact amongst geographically disparate groups of people. The spread of useful knowledge was therefore a slow process. Small-scale societies often felt at the mercy of natural forces, sometimes worshipping nature in the form of the Sun, Moon or spirits in attempts to gain favour over the natural forces they believed controlled their destiny. Of course, such forces were not experienced as 'impersonal' and 'natural' in the same way that many people today perceive them to be. Over a prolonged period of many thousands of years, human beings learned how to exert more control over their interchange with the natural environment and were able to pass on this useful knowledge across space and time. That means, to other groups who lived geographically distant from them as well as to younger generations within their own groups.

One especially significant development in human history was the discovery of fire and the invention of techniques for making, managing and keeping it under control (Goudsblom 1992). These techniques were passed down through generations who had to learn the same methods as well as how to stay safe from the dangers of fire. From small domestic fires used for keeping warm and cooking food, all the way to modern central heating systems and large power plants, the gradual expansion of fire-making has enabled, and indeed necessitated, a more complex form of social organization. All human societies now use fire. In the process, more people came to rely more than ever before on the ready availability, control and use of fire. Goudsblom's developmental history of fire use illustrates, in a specific area, the way that human societies generally try to manipulate and manage the natural environment to their own advantage. In the process of managing their relationship with the natural environment, pressure is also exerted on societies to change their own forms of social organization. When early humans learned how to make and manage small fires, they had to organize themselves to keep fires going, to monitor them and, at the same time, to stay safe. Much later, with the introduction of domesticated forms of fire into people's homes, societies needed specialists in fire control, fire brigades and fire prevention advisers. With the advent of large power-generating stations, it becomes important that these are protected from attack by others and are militarily defended if necessary. The point here is that changes in the methods of manipulation of the natural environment always go hand in hand with changes in social organization.

But there is one further element to be considered, and this is the changing psyche of individuals. In order to be able to use fire, people had to overcome their previous fear of it, borne of witnessing naturally occurring bush fires, lightning strikes and volcanoes. This was not an easy task, as it meant controlling their immediate emotional responses long enough to be able to take advantage of the possible benefits of using fire. Such emotional control takes place within the individual's mental apparatus and, over time, comes to be experienced as 'second nature' to them. They hardly ever think about how long it has taken for people to arrive at the present level of emotional control over their own feelings and deep-seated fears. It may well be that people never entirely lose their fear of fire, which today is often described as a 'healthy fear', particularly for children who have yet to learn about fire management. This is because, even today, fires can still cause harm, destroying people's homes, families and livelihoods. Fire is always threatening to escape the control of human societies, however firmly established that control may seem. The lesson we can take from this example is that the relationship between human societies and the natural environment inevitably takes the form of a two-way process and it is a relationship that cannot be broken if human beings are to continue to survive and thrive.

The powers of humans and natural processes

For modern people, the natural environment is often perceived as both their beautiful home which has to be protected and, at the very same time, the source of death, destruction and misery from which people have themselves to be protected. Such an apparent contradiction stems from the fact that human beings, like all other animals, depend on the natural environment for their very existence and can never opt out of their relationship with it. Unlike other animals, however, human beings have intentionally tried to exert more and more control over the natural environment to make their social life together safer and more predictable, even if this has been at the expense of destroying some of the environments on which other animal species depend. Rather then seeing these attitudes as contradictory, it is more accurate to say that there exists a tension between the modern appreciation (and often defence) of nature and human society's attempts to control natural processes and events. This tension is in fact a fundamental feature of modern life with which, given a few moments reflection, we are all familiar, even if in apparently trivial ways.

When gardeners admire the natural beauty of their back gardens, but also take steps to remove natural things called weeds and poison animals called slugs, which threaten to spoil their carefully constructed plans, their admiration for natural beauty is closely connected to their attempts at nature control. People may well take great pleasure in seeing small rodents whilst out walking in the countryside, but also be prepared ruthlessly to kill those same animals should they find them out of place in their own homes. Pet owners will often describe themselves as 'animal lovers' (at least in Britain) and feel genuine affection and closeness to their pets, being grief-stricken and emotionally devastated when they die. At the same time, the same owners will clip the wings of their pet birds, castrate their cats and dogs and keep fish in small tanks of water which leave very little room for movement. They may well see nothing wrong with any of these practices. People both love and seek to control the natural creatures that live out their lives with them. Such behaviour is characteristic of that tension between appreciation and control attempts in relation to natural things.

Sociologists, anthropologists and historians have found that people's attitudes towards the natural environment are variable. Not all societies exhibit the same attitudes as those with which we are familiar today and recognize from the descriptions above. There is a connection between the real extent of society's control over the natural environment and people's attitudes towards it. It seems that the more successful societies are in exerting a measure of control over the natural environment on which they depend, the more they come to appreciate parts of it as beautiful and as sources of value. The more that people's knowledge of natural environments allows them to manipulate these for their own ends, the less frightened they are of natural processes and objects. The less frightened people are of natural forces and processes, the more they are able to appreciate them as sources of beauty. And the more they appreciate natural environments as beautiful, the closer they feel themselves to be to their own 'natural' selves. Even in the early twenty-first century, though, the natural processes underlying this beautiful environment continue to demonstrate just how fragile societies' achievements in exerting this measure of control can be.

The year of 2005 saw a series of natural disasters across the world that led to the deaths of more people than the invasion of Iraq and recent terrorist activity combined. Newspapers around the world reported that 2005 was the year that nature 'took revenge' on human beings, and you could be forgiven for thinking that these natural disasters were battles in a long-running war between human societies and the natural environment. In earlier times, natural disasters were often referred to as 'acts of God' because they were so clearly outside the control of human beings. Even today, most insurance companies use this same language to cover those risks such as floods, earthquakes, lightning strikes and so on, that are plainly not predictable or under control. The Bible tells us of 40 days of rain causing a great flood, brought about by a God angered at human wickedness and determined to cleanse the Earth and start again with Noah and his family. Archbishop James Ussher (1581–1656) dated the start of this event precisely, at 7 December 2349 BCE. Working to a different timescale, some modern scientists argue that 65 million years ago, a large meteorite some 10 kilometres in diameter, struck the Earth and, as a result, the climate was so rapidly altered that it brought about the mass extinction of life, including the large dinosaurs. Natural events and disasters have long been the subject of concern in human societies around the world.

China has suffered many disastrous earthquakes, none more destructive than the one that hit Shensi on 2 February 1556. Because of the high density of population and the pattern of living within cave homes carved in the sides of cliffs, a staggering 820,000 people are estimated to have died. On 16 December 1920 another earthquake in Kansu, China led to the deaths of around 200,000 people. And even as late as 28 July 1976, a night-time earthquake under the city of Tang-shan lasting just 23 seconds destroyed most of the city's buildings and killed between 242,000 (official estimates) and 750,000 (unofficial estimates) people. One outcome of such catastrophic events is that China is today one of the leading countries attempting to develop earthquake prediction methods.

Volcanic activity has long been seen as 'the fire of the Gods'. When Mount Vesuvius in southern Italy erupted in AD 79, the cities of Pompeii, Herculaneum and Stabiae were destroyed and hidden under several metres of molten lava and mud, killing between 16,000 and 20,000 people. On 27 August 1883 the small, uninhabited Indonesian volcanic island of Krakatoa exploded. The bang was so loud it is said to have been heard 4,800 kilometres away. Raining ash and rocks, molten

lava, fire and tidal waves killed at least 36,000 people in the neighbouring area. Indonesia is one of the worst affected regions in the world with
around 80 recorded volcanic eruptions. Little wonder that human
beings had a healthy respect for fire and tried to stave off disasters
through their religious practices.

Many other types of natural disasters have occurred, including
floods, electrical storms, fogs, hurricanes, droughts and famines,
plagues and disease as well as all-consuming fires. However, two of the
most deadly episodes in human history were diseases. The bubonic
plague epidemics of the sixth, fourteenth and seventeenth centuries
killed approximately 137 million people. The fourteenth-century
pandemic killed around 20 million Europeans, about one-third of the
population at that time. The second was the 1918 flu pandemic, a strain
of avian influenza similar to that which was observed in several countries in 2005. Between 25 and 50 million people around the world are
believed to have died as a result of the rapid spread of this viral infec-
tion in 1918–19. In modern times, societies have increasingly tried to
use scientific methods to predict when and where such natural events
might occur, and to prevent, treat and eliminate infectious diseases.
They do this to try and provide early warning systems and advice on
how to limit the loss of life and destruction of property. However, these
attempts have only been partially successful, and in 2005 the current
limitations of human knowledge and technological forecasting were
thrown into sharp relief in a series of natural disasters.

On Sunday 28 August 2005, the Mayor of New Orleans, USA ordered
residents to evacuate the city as fears grew about the growing strength
of Hurricane Katrina as it approached the Gulf Coast of the USA (see
illus. 1.1). New Orleans is particularly vulnerable to hurricanes as it is a
city built two metres below sea level, defended against incursion from
the sea by a system of defensive fortifications called 'levees'. On
Monday 29 August, the Mayor's worst fears were realized as Katrina's
force battered the city, breaching the levees and flooding around 80 per
cent of low-lying areas. Over the next few days it became clear that up
to 100,000 residents remained in the city and later estimates suggest
that more than 1,300 people had been killed with a further 1,300 missing, feared dead in New Orleans and the surrounding area. Many more
remain unaccounted for. American President, George Bush, declared it
one of the worst natural disasters ever in the USA and, amidst reports of
looting, violence and chaos, troops were sent in to restore order. More
than 60 billion dollars was requested for relief efforts and estimates
suggest that the disaster may have led to a 0.5 per cent drop in the USA's
gross domestic product (GDP). More than 400,000 people lost their jobs
and homes and it will take quite some time before New Orleans can
return to anything approaching its previous state of normality. In the
wake of this disaster, many criticized the failure of the American
government to act quickly enough on earlier warnings and for not
ensuring that the defensive system had been improved to a satisfactory

1.1 Hurricane Katrina seen from space on 28 August 2005.

Source: USA National Oceanic and Atmospheric Administration (NOAA)/ Department of Commerce (courtesy of NESDIS) 2005

standard much earlier. Society's control attempts had spectacularly failed and people's sense of security was shattered.

On Saturday morning, 8 October 2005, a large earthquake measuring 7.6 on the Richter Scale (a 'major' earthquake) hit the city of Muzaffarabad, the capital of Pakistan-administered Kashmir, causing widespread damage, followed by four smaller aftershocks. Neighbouring towns including Bagh, Rawalakot, Balakot and many others also suffered damage, as did Islamabad, the capital of Pakistan. In Indian-administered Kashmir some 1,400 people were reported to have died with another 5,000 suffering injuries. In India 1,300 were confirmed to have died, but the death toll in the whole affected region has been estimated at between 73,000 and 100,000 people, the vast majority of these in Pakistan itself. Roads were blocked by landslides, buildings collapsed and relief efforts were hampered by difficulties reaching the more rural sites of the disaster. The landscape resembled a war-torn environment and up to 4 million people have been affected. The Pakistan authorities raised concerns about the effects of a cold winter on those who survived, but who had nowhere to live and work. Once again, a natural disaster shows us the immense power of natural processes that are beyond the control of human societies, whether relatively rich or poor, to disrupt the normal life of societies (Blaikie et al. 2003).

However, the worst loss of life caused by natural forces came during and after the undersea earthquake and subsequent tsunami around the Indian Ocean coastline at the end of 2004 (see box 1.1), which caused an enormous loss of human life. Taken together, it is hard to avoid the

Box 1.1

On 26 December 2004 came the most catastrophic natural disaster of recent times. An undersea earthquake in the Indian Ocean measuring 9.3 on the Richter Scale – the second largest ever recorded – shook the earth for eight minutes, raising the seafloor by 20 metres. This seafloor movement produced a huge wave of water – called a tsunami – forced outwards from the centre of the quake. Just 30 minutes later, and before any official warning could be issued, the relentless wave reached the city of Banda Aceh, sweeping everything before it, killing tens of thousands of residents and tourists. The waves were still powerful enough to cause deaths, injuries and destruction in Sri Lanka, India and the surrounding regions. The final death toll from this natural disaster has been estimated to be around 300,000 people, with millions more made homeless and unemployed (see illus. 1.2).

Although much more is known today than in the past about what causes earthquakes, where they are likely to occur and how they can be monitored, forecasting when and where they will happen is much more difficult and monitoring systems are expensive. Human knowledge and social organization have not yet reached the point at which earthquakes pose no danger, though fewer people today see them as the divine punishment handed down by angry Gods. And though many local people did view this disaster in religious terms, the authorities consulted geologists and seismologists for information and advice on how to guard against a recurrence, rather than priests and religious authorities. Hence, the **secularization** of knowledge and the dominant position of science in relation to other ways of knowing about the natural world has not eliminated the religious means of orientation altogether.

Geologists tell us that earthquakes are the product of natural processes, of shifting tectonic plates carrying whole continents across the globe. Where they meet, tectonic earthquakes can occur, as one plate slides below another. Clearly, human societies, whether relatively poor or relatively wealthy, cannot afford to ignore these natural processes and continue to improve their knowledge and understanding of them.

1.2 A submerged village on the Sumatran coast after the 2004 tsunami.

Source: Photo by Philip A. McDaniel, USA Naval Media Centre, 2004

conclusion that even in the twenty-first century, and with all of the technological wizardry of modern life, humans do not control or dominate the natural environment. In many ways, they remain dependent on and are sometimes at the mercy of natural processes and events, struggling to manage their relationship with the natural environment.

Natural and Artificial Environments

Look around and note down those things that you think are 'natural' and those that are not. Ask yourself, why are some things just not 'natural'? Looking out of my own window I can see trees, flowers, birds, clouds and rain (it does occasionally rain in Scotland). All of this seems so obviously part of the natural environment, and I experience it as pleasant to look at. On the other hand, through the same window I can also see roads and cars, concrete walls, houses and streetlights. None of these appears to form part of that same natural environment and I don't particularly enjoy looking at walls or roads and could well do without the noise and pollution caused by cars, though I drive one myself. They are not alive and, more importantly, all of them have been created by human beings. Surely this makes them somehow 'artificial' rather than natural. You may well agree with me. But is this commonsense distinction between the natural and the artificial, the products of nature and the products of human activity really such a firm one? Is it solid enough to withstand examination?

On reflection, the trees I observe were planted by human beings some time ago and they are regularly trimmed and shaped by the local council. Last year, one was cut down altogether, as it leaned too far over the road and was unstable in high winds. These trees are certainly alive, but they also owe their very existence to the human beings who planted them. Does this make them natural or artificial? Exactly the same question can be asked of the flowers. But are birds different? Well, they are alive, they fly wherever they want to and are apparently unaffected by human beings who keep other birds in cages. However, it is estimated that there are around 5 million domestic cats in the UK, which kill many millions of sparrows, blackbirds and other garden birds every year. Many people also enjoy feeding these garden birds, especially in winter, thus ensuring that more of them survive the winter than might 'naturally' be the case. On the other hand, some other birds are not welcome in the coastal towns of Britain. Seagulls scavenge in human rubbish causing mess and littering towns, and local authorities sometimes cull them to reduce the problem. Human actions therefore make a significant contribution to bird populations in the UK, helping to determine how many of them there are and which ones are more likely to thrive. Indeed, one of the most influential environmentalist books ever written, Rachel Carson's *Silent Spring* (1962), takes its title from the destructive effects of an agricultural pesticide known as DDT, on wild bird populations. The book's title refers to the loss of birdsong as a result of the poisoning of bird populations. Does all of this make wild birds somehow artificial as well?

Conversely, think about the obviously 'artificial' things I noted above. Roads and cars are largely made from rocks, minerals and metals extracted from the ground. Strangely though, when they were actually in the ground, people probably saw them as part of the natural landscape and took pleasure in looking at them. It is only when quarries are established and rocks and minerals removed for use in the road-building process, eventually to be driven on by motorists in their polluting vehicles that we see them as somehow artificial. Something similar could be said about concrete walls, houses and streetlights, all of which again begin as 'natural' products before being turned into something 'artificial' and useful for people. And what of human beings? Are they not part of nature themselves? If they are, then can anything they do or anything they produce ever be described as artificial or unnatural anyway?

It is quite common in everyday conversation, and not a little socio-logical discourse, to think and talk about *natural* and *artificial* environments. The way I defined 'natural environment' above makes some concession to this commonsense way of thinking about the difference between, say, an ocean and a city. It surely makes little sense to see cities and oceans as similar in kind. One seems natural, the other – well, for want of a better word, artificial. It is quite common for environmental campaigners and some sociologists to describe cities and urban environments as 'artificial' in comparison to the 'reality' of nature (see Goldsmith 1988; Giddens 1990). But *why* are they 'artificial'? What makes them so?

Perhaps the answer is that people create cities, and if there had been no people, then the natural environment would not have sponta-neously evolved cities. Let's pursue this a little further. Are cities really 'artificial'? It is certainly true that people create cities, but does that fact alone mean they are not part of the natural environment? As we saw above, people are animals too. If badger setts, birds' nests and rabbit warrens are natural phenomena, then surely that makes cities natural too. Let's try another answer. Maybe cities are artificial not just because of their human creation, but because they contain little of the non-human natural environment within them. Cities are largely built from concrete, brick, tarmac roads and industrial estates, and this means that city-dwellers live, in the main, in an artificially constructed environment. And that is not to mention the pollution from cars and indus-try that affect the natural air quality we all have to breathe. Again though, just how artificial is this way of living? The material used in roads and buildings comes from quarrying 'natural' rock, and pollution from cars is a mixture of gases, most of them found elsewhere in the natural environment, albeit not in the same quantities or density. Of course, cities are not just 'concrete jungles' either. They have parks, lakes, gardens and lots of wildlife. Are these also somehow artificial, having been designed, created and maintained by people? It is perhaps not quite so obvious that cities are unnatural things compared to natural environments.

Now take that ocean we mentioned as so obviously natural by comparison. Is it too not affected by human activity? Ships sail across it, toxic waste is dumped into it, wars have been fought across it and oil rigs drill into the seafloor extracting the oil that literally fuels all of those cars that cause so much pollution and promote ever more road-building in cities. Can we say with any certainty that anything is purely artificial or purely natural when human activity now affects even the climate and weather systems? In their attempts to prosper, human beings have diverted rivers, created new lakes, drained swamps and brought some animal species to the brink of extinction whilst preserving others in carefully controlled environments called zoos and wildlife parks. So, although what people mean by 'the natural environment' seems like common sense, sociologically, things are not so simple.

The problem we have run into here is caused by our neatly separating out the 'natural environment' from 'society'. But increasingly, sociologists and social scientists have come to see this separation as unhelpful and misleading. Society and the natural environment are inevitably intertwined and perhaps we need a better way of thinking about their ongoing relationship that gives adequate weight both to natural environmental processes and human actions. But this is an issue for chapter 2 and beyond.

Conclusion

Today, when tourists travel the world looking for natural beauty (and 'better' weather), when environmentalists campaign against roads and industrial development and when some people genuinely believe that animals have the same rights as human beings, it is clear that natural environments and natural things have become much more highly valued than they were in the early modern period. The trend of modern psychic and emotional life is towards preferences for country life over towns and cities, untouched wilderness rather than development, conservation of nature over its conquest and a concern for the welfare and even rights of animals. But such a widespread transformation of social attitudes has taken many generations and is bound up with industrial and urban development. During the process, the dominant meaning attributed to nature has also been transformed in the ways described above.

So far, we have barely scratched the surface of some very complex and fascinating debates about the relationship between society and nature. There is much interesting research currently taking place in the natural and social sciences, including, somewhat belatedly, sociology. By the end of the book my hope is that we will better understand how these recent sociological and social-scientific studies of human-environment relationships are changing the way that we think about environmental issues. Consequently, they also ought to have some impact on what we might be able to do or indeed, may have to do to resolve at least some of the pressing environmental problems troubling societies across the world.

Readings

A good place to begin is with David Harvey's discussion of the meanings of 'environment' in his 'The Nature of Environment: The Dialectics of Social and Environmental Change' (1993). This is not an easy read, but it is worth the effort. From here, an exploration of Western ideas of nature and the natural can be had from Peter Coates's *Nature: Western Attitudes Since Ancient Times* (1998). Keith Thomas's *Man and the Natural World: Changing Attitudes in England 1500–1800* (1984) has been enormously influential and contains much fascinating historical material. I thoroughly recommend it. A parallel sociological account is Norbert Elias's *The Civilizing Process: Sociogenetic and Psychogenetic Investigations* (2000[1939]). However, readers will need to find their way through this book's main argument to lift out Elias's ideas on natural environments. A book of original source materials covering the transformation of attitudes and sensibilities referred to in this chapter is Alasdair Clayre's (ed.) *Nature and Industrialization: An Anthology* (1979). See also Derek Wall's (ed.), *Green History: A Reader in Environmental Literature, Philosophy and Politics* (1994).

The story of fire is wonderfully told in Johan Goudsblom's *Fire and Civilization* (1992). Piers Blaikie et al.'s *At Risk: Natural Hazards, People's Vulnerability and Disasters* (2003) is a good guide to the social aspects of natural disasters.

2 Knowing the Environment

We know from chapter 1 that people's understanding of the natural environment and what nature actually is have changed over time and are cross-culturally diverse. It has also proved to be difficult to locate the proper place of human beings in relation to animals and the natural environment with any certainty, as the way we understand human beings and nature are closely connected. Some sociologists have suggested that the development of large-scale, modern, industrialized societies has dislocated people from an immediate contact with nature so that their understanding is in large measure now mediated through a variety of representations. In this chapter we explore the way that modern science has come to claim a special knowledge of the natural environment and what the consequences of this scientific representation have been. We then move on to outline two of the dominant ways of approaching the environment and environmental issues from within sociology itself. What will become clear is that sociologists disagree about how environmental matters should be handled. We will also see that the role of science and its place within society has turned out to be just as contentious within sociological circles as it is in the wider society. Once we have a clearer sense of the ways in which knowledge of natural environments is produced and disseminated, we will then move on to look at people's experiences of the natural environment in chapter 3.

Involvement and Detachment

From where do people get their knowledge of the natural environment? They watch TV and read newspapers, where journalists report on environmental issues, natural disasters and the campaigns of environmentalists. If they watch TV they will also see some strange representations of natural things: for example, cartoons, in which animals with human personalities also wear human clothing, speak, walk and behave like human beings (Paddington Bear, Garfield, Mickey Mouse); and natural history documentaries, which show the fabulous social lives of insects and penguins and the life and death dramas of predator and prey confrontations. They can also watch films in which the animals are the heroes (*Lassie, Black Beauty, Finding Nemo*). Children are also taught biology and geography in schools using textbooks derived from scientific research, and the natural environment is represented in the corporate branding of big business (Shell, BP, Monsanto) as well as in advertising, soft furnishings, maps – and lots, lots more. And of course, people also experience the natural environment themselves much more directly (see chapter 3). Modern societies make use of natural imagery in seemingly limitless ways to entertain, inform and sell products, and this imagery doubtless has an influence on the way in which people perceive the environment. Not only do people live within the natural environment, they also live within social representations of the natural environment, and it is often difficult, if not impossible, to separate the two. Nevertheless, amidst this rich variety, one form of knowledge makes a claim to superiority. Modern science claims a special knowledge that is more realistic and useful than any other and science has enabled human societies to achieve an unparalleled manipulation of nature, unique in human development.

The scientific knowledge that modern societies produce underpins the specifically modern type of technological and material development. Scientific knowledge is a keystone of modernity, with its own methods, communities of scientists, publication outlets and productive applications. Nevertheless, modern science is not the only form of knowledge about the natural environment. For many centuries, religions have performed some of the same functions as science does today. Religious beliefs and the knowledge founded on them provide people with a *means of orientation* to the world. That means religions provide meaning, offering answers to some of the fundamental questions of life, such as what happens after death and why human suffering continues. But they also provide guidelines for living and explain what the 'proper' relationship between human beings and the natural environment *should* be.

Religions supply different views on the place of people in the world and how the environment should be treated. Pre-Christian pagan religions encouraged people to experience the natural world as full of spirits and essentially alive. These nature-worshipping religions made no firm distinction between human beings and the natural environment, with people seen as just one part of a much wider nature. Some Eastern religious traditions promote a retreat from the world rather than an aggressive engagement with it. Chinese Buddhism has been interpreted in this way as a religion that encourages self-knowledge as more significant than objective knowledge of the external material world. In this sense, some have seen the social practices rooted in Eastern traditions as less environmentally destructive than those based on Western religions. This destructive potential is explored by one American scholar, Lynn White Jr. (1967), who described Christianity as the most **anthropocentric** or human-centred religion the world has ever seen. This is because Christianity sees Man as created in the image of God and the Bible contains statements telling Man to multiply and fill the Earth. Christianity also describes God as granting to Man dominion over all the living things of the Earth to do with as he pleases. White saw that modern Western science had developed out of Christian beliefs and practices and that modern technologies had continually built on the agricultural tools developed in early Christian societies. White's judgement of Christianity's 'anti-environmentalism' may seem a little harsh with hindsight, as the Bible, like all religious texts, is open to different interpretations. It can be pointed out, for example, that 'dominion' may not be the same thing as 'domination'. Dominion also requires the wise management of natural environments rather than the simple provision of legitimations for untrammelled damage and degradation.

It is also worth remembering that the nominally non-religious, atheistic communist societies of East Central Europe can hardly be held up as paragons of environmental virtue either. In the brief period of communist domination between 1917 and 1989, the former Soviet Union, its allies and satellites treated the natural environment in very similar ways to the Judaeo-Christian countries of the capitalist West. Determined to demonstrate that communism was superior to free market capitalism, the Soviet Union pursued equally damaging large-scale projects to impose human designs onto the natural world, and prioritized economic growth over environmental protection. Levels of pollution and waste in these officially non-religious societies made them amongst the worst environmental offenders of any of the nation-states in the international system, which has left a difficult legacy of environmental problems for post-communist governments to rectify.

As forms of orientation to the world, religions continue to provide meaningful answers to the difficult and particularly unknown or unknowable questions that people still ask about life and the universe. This is especially so in the absence of widely accepted scientific answers to such questions. However, religious knowledge about the natural environment has been overshadowed by the enormous growth of scientific knowledge and the development of distinct scientific disciplines such as astronomy, physics, chemistry, biology and geology. The knowledge these disciplines produce is empirical, based on observation and the interpretation of evidence, and is always open to challenge and change should new evidence come to light. This is a quite different form of knowledge from that which is revealed in ancient (and some more recent) religious texts, which is not amenable to challenge and change in the same way.

A useful way of thinking about the difference between religious and scientific knowledge is to view *all* human knowledge as both emotionally or politically involved, but also as relatively detached from such involvements. The involvement–detachment balance in religious knowledge lies closer to the involvement end of the spectrum because religions demand faith-based commitment. Challenges to religious knowledge can then also be experienced as challenges to people's own selves and self-identities. This is because people have prior commitments to the guidelines and rules of their religion, which makes it difficult to reconcile these with contrary evidence. What is at stake for people when presented with religious knowledge is not just the information itself, but also their own 'worldview', sense of security and sense of self. A specific example will illustrate just how disorientating the experience of confrontations with new knowledge can be.

Until the sixteenth century, European peoples thought that the objects they saw in the sky – the Sun, Moon and stars – all revolved around the Earth, which was therefore at the centre of the universe. This was an obvious everyday fact, witnessed by anyone who cared to look and did not require any specialized equipment or knowledge. The evidence from people's own eyes was enough to prove that Sun, Moon and stars plainly did move around the Earth. This was a geocentric or 'earth-centred' perspective. However, by the early sixteenth century this self-evident explanation was being challenged and an alternative theory was developing. One Polish astronomer, Nicolaus Copernicus (1473–1543), worked out that existing beliefs about the planetary bodies' movements were wrong. Instead of 'heavenly bodies' moving around the Earth, in fact the Earth was itself a moving body that circled the Sun in a regular cycle. The Sun and not the Earth was at the centre of what turned out to be a 'solar system', and recognition of this effectively marked the shift away from the geocentric view. Copernicus's theory was published in the same year that he died, 1543, but took much longer to become accepted.

A significant supporter of the new heliocentric theory was Galileo Galilei (1564–1642), an Italian mathematician and astronomer who produced a reliable telescope with which to view the stars. Galileo used his astronomical observations to demonstrate and persuade others that Copernicus's theory was in fact correct. The Earth *did* move around the Sun, not the other way around. But the Catholic Church authorities could not accept such a theory. The problem was that Copernicus's ideas threatened to decentre the Earth within the universe and thereby made human beings appear less important than the Bible suggested. Galileo's vocal support for the Copernican system brought him before the Inquisition in 1633, where he was forced to recant his belief in a solar system and was kept under house arrest until his death. The new 'scientific' understanding clearly threatened the privileged status of religious beliefs and religious authorities in society. Even more than this, the new knowledge forced people everywhere to re-evaluate themselves and that of human beings in relation to the rest of nature. It was an emotional shock to be told that humans were not at the centre of the universe. The more detached, but less emotionally comforting knowledge of natural reality was hard to come to terms with.

Of course, these different forms of knowledge enable different practices, and it is inconceivable that twentieth-century societies could have made their journeys into space travel without the reorientation of perspective brought about by the Copernican system. The balance of involvement and detachment in the social fund of useable knowledge of the natural environment had started shifting towards more emotional detachment. And although this promised more realistic knowledge, it also reinforced feelings of detachment from nature that legitimized some aggressive interventions and economic practices, such as mining for fuel and minerals, which had severe consequences for the environment.

The Scientific Revolution

The development of modern science was a long social process over several centuries, but within this period the 150 years from the 1540s to around 1700 saw some of the central ideas and fundamental principles of modern science becoming established. This period has come to be described as the 'scientific revolution'. We have seen that scientific practices and understandings were already well in train by the sixteenth century. In the seventeenth century, Isaac Newton's radical ideas on the fundamental physical properties of matter and Francis Bacon's argument that scientific knowledge must be used to control and subdue the world of nature, whilst scientists should become society's elite, opened the way for later scientists. Bacon saw no contradiction between such ideas and his Christian beliefs. Science enabled a better understanding of the world of nature, but that world had been created and set in motion by God. Religion and science were not necessarily opposed and many scientists since Bacon have been content with this solution to the problem of religious belief and scientific practice.

Carolyn Merchant's (1982) influential survey of the scientific revolution brings to light some of the impact of the new scientific thinking on both the lives of women and the natural environment, which she sees as closely linked. Merchant shows that the emergence of modern science and scientific methods not only decentred human beings but also contributed to the 'death of nature'. What she means by this is that the natural environment came to be perceived as a lifeless world, at least until it was cultivated and shaped by human beings. In contrast to medieval views of the natural environment as being alive and full of spirits, modern science treated nature as inert, as something to be probed, investigated and manipulated to force it to yield up its secrets. In this way Merchant believes that science and scientific methods have led directly to the justification of environmental damage, because the natural environment has been devalued, becoming merely the backdrop to human activity, which is then seen as much more important. Instead of being a living thing that should be treated with care, nature came to be seen as rather more like a machine whose workings could, like all other machines, be understood and explained.

More than this, Merchant finds connections between the devaluation of nature and the devaluation of women in society. This happened because women and nature were seen as closely linked. The female role in human reproduction, carrying and giving birth to children and biological bodily cycles such as menstruation were seen as physical demonstrations and reminders of the special connection between women and nature. This was in contrast to the way men were viewed, as more cultured, civilized and rational creatures. Merchant sees previous ideas of the protective Mother Nature, which could also be wild and uncontrollable, as losing ground during the scientific revolution because of the intrusive examinations and methods of science. The wild, uncontrollable side of women was evidenced in the persecution of thousands of women as witches who, it was thought, could control animals and connect with evil nature-spirits and make contracts with the devil. Witch trials in Europe took place during the same period that modern science was beginning to emerge after the Protestant Reformation. Merchant says that, as Baconian ideas about science's domination of nature became established, they also fed into beliefs about the inferiority of women, precisely because of the supposed natural connection. In more modern times it is also possible to see such a linkage spreading to developing countries. As scientific knowledge, technologies and methods have spread to the agricultural systems of the developing world, many feminist writers and campaigners have pointed out that this is destroying the traditional knowledge base of indigenous women that has been passed down through many generations. Local knowledge of crop-growing techniques is once again being sacrificed in favour of an expanding male-dominated science that views such local knowledge as unscientific and largely irrelevant to the task of modernizing food production.

A particularly intensive phase in the modernization process occurred between the middle and the end of the eighteenth century in Europe, during a period known as the 'Enlightenment'. Enlightenment philosophers rejected the assumed authority of religion and tradition, seeking to bring human reason and rationality into all areas of life. If superstition and traditional knowledge could be replaced with science and reason, societies could be subject to planned construction and continuously improved to increase human happiness and well-being. In France, such Enlightenment ideals were motivating factors for the radicals behind the French Revolution of 1789, which marked the end of the old aristocratic *ancien régime*. The French philosophers were looking to expand reliable human knowledge, which could then be of use in reshaping societies. This period also saw the establishment of scientific disciplines that challenged traditional religious knowledge in many areas and sometimes brought out their differences in conflict and open disputes. One of the most famous disputes was between religious authorities and geologists over the question of the age of the Earth. In briefly reconstructing this dispute, we can learn something about the relationship between knowledge of the natural environment and the fragile achievements of scientific explanations.

In 1788, Scottish farmer and amateur geologist James Hutton (1726–97) sought out and located what he considered to be solid

Source: John
Clerk's 1787
illustration of an
unconformity
found in Jedburgh,
Scotland

2.1 James Hutton is rightly regarded as a founder of modern geology and was the first to realize that the Earth was 'immeasurably old'. The rock pattern he first observed at Siccar Point is now known as 'Hutton's unconformity'.

evidence for his controversial theory of the Earth's history. A central part of his theory was that Earth was much older than anyone had thought. His view contrasted sharply with the work of biblical scholars and the established churches in Britain. James Ussher (1581–1656), Archbishop of Armagh, had calculated that Earth could be no more than 6,000 years old, based on tracing the recorded lives and ages of people named in the Bible. His chronology reached a very wide audience, as it was used in the page margins of the King James Bible (Repcheck 2003) and became standard knowledge for generations of believers. Hutton, however, following his detailed observations and interpretation of rock formations in Scotland, disagreed.

Hutton's crucial evidence was found at Siccar Point on the east coast of Scotland, just south of Edinburgh. He showed his colleagues a rock formation consisting of strata or layers, formed by different types of rock. Instead of lying horizontally, the lower and oldest strata lay almost vertically upright, whilst the upper and younger strata made of red sandstone overlay these horizontally (see illus. 2.1). How had this come about? Hutton argued that the rocks had formed from sedimentary deposits on the sea-bed which had been laid down over very long periods of time. The lower rocks had also been laid down horizontally, but at some point had been raised to a vertical position by earth movements. The sedimentation process had continued, thus laying down the sandstone on top of the now vertical cliffs. This geological process could not have taken just 6,000 years to complete and Hutton suggested that by examining ongoing geological processes we could get an insight into the timescale involved. In fact, said Hutton, as far as he could see there was 'no vestige of a beginning and no prospect of an end' to these natural processes. The Earth was 'immeasurably old' and biblical scholars were simply wrong. By the mid-nineteenth century, scholars had come to see the plausibility of Hutton's theory and observations, and much later – in the 1950s – Hutton's theory was confirmed in its basic principles by radiocarbon dating, which put planet Earth at around 4.6 billion years old, the age which remains broadly accepted today.

Hutton's ideas were part of the Scottish Enlightenment, a period which saw the flowering of new ideas in economics, philosophy and the sciences. But it was left to Charles Darwin (1809–82) and Alfred Russell Wallace (1823–1917), with their theories of evolutionary development, to locate human beings themselves within such a long timeframe. Darwin's *On the Origin Of Species by Means of Natural Selection* (1859) was seen by some critics as blurring the boundary between human beings and animals, and, of course, it did. From this point on, more detached, rigorous and empirical scientific methods began to prevail over the more emotionally involved and traditional ways of knowing the natural environment. Gradually, science became the established form of environmental knowledge, with new disciplines claiming expertise in the study of environments. Geology, biology, ecology and environmental sciences are all now studied within universities, and the knowledge they produce is used to advise government policy at national and international levels. Religious and revealed knowledge of the natural environment has largely been overtaken.

However, even in 2007, such scientific theories and evidence do not go entirely uncontested. Some Christian groups for instance, still retain a belief in the 'young Earth' idea and promote their alternative perspective across forms of new media such as the Internet. Websites with names such as *Project Creation* aim to challenge and counter the Darwinian theory of natural evolution and the geological evidence of immense planetary age with their own ideas. And although now in the minority, this older view continues to find a place and remains meaningful for some people. In some states in the USA, creationist theories are also finding their way back into mainstream education classes as biblical creation stories are redesigned as theories of 'intelligent design', which are presented as alternatives to Darwin's and on the same plane as scientific knowledge.

Sociologically, what we can take from this potted history of a knowledge controversy and its consequences is that, even in the twenty-first century, there still exist different ways of knowing the natural environment, though some are clearly more widespread and evidence-based than others. It is also notable that Hutton, like Bacon, adhered to a form of deism rather than atheism, believing that the universe was created by God, but after creation, natural processes were set in motion that could be studied and understood by human beings. Nonetheless, such a view is only possible if there is a clear division of labour between religion and science. The new theorists of intelligent design and a young Earth simply do not accept this division, and it is interesting to see them making some headway at a time when global environmental problems seem most threatening. Are such escalating fears in the face of uncertain risks beginning to feed into desires for reassurance and certainty that modern science, which is constantly changing, is simply not equipped to provide? This is a question that is dealt with more systematically in chapter 5.

Social Constructions of Nature

Sociology was a late developer amongst academic disciplines, coming into existence only in the late nineteenth century. However, this is no real excuse for the relatively late arrival of sociologists to the study of contemporary environmental issues. It was not until the 1980s that a distinctive **sociology of the environment** began to emerge and the discipline started to include environmental problems among its concerns. Of course, many sociologists in the past have had things to say about nature and about human society's relationship with natural environments. But these have always been secondary to the main sociological issues of social class, inequalities, crime and deviance, health and illness and so on. Sociologists have been mainly interested in specifically social and very *human* problems rather than dealing with problems of the *natural* environment. The latter were thought to be outside both the interests and the competence of sociologists. However, what environmental campaigners and organizations made very clear was that *environmental* problems are always *social* problems too, because they involve the relationship between people and their environment. It follows that if solutions are to be found to environmental problems, then it is people and whole societies that will have to change their currently damaging practices. And if we are to understand those people and societies, then we will need the knowledge of the social sciences. Geologists, biologists, ecologists and environmental scientists can enlighten us on the naturally occurring processes underlying environmental problems, but they are not experts in social processes and the study of social change. The rest of this chapter explores the two most widely adopted sociological methods of studying environmental issues to have emerged since the 1980s: **social constructionism** and **critical realism**.

Social constructionism is an approach to studying social problems, including environmental problems, which takes ideas from an older 'social problems' perspective, the **sociology of knowledge** and sociological studies of science. Because of this combination, social constructionism has been especially influential in the study of environmental issues, as these require an understanding of both problem claims and scientific evidence. Social constructionists have investigated how some environmental issues come to be seen as urgent social problems, whilst other environmental issues fail to be taken seriously and are largely ignored. They have posed a series of important questions about environmental claims. What is the history of the claim and how has it developed? Who makes the claim? What do they say about it? How do they say it? How do the unequal power chances of social groups impact on the success and failure of problem claims? Who opposes the claim and on what grounds? Digging into environmental claims has allowed sociologists to carve out an original role for themselves and to add something original to the study of environmental issues and problems. Social constructionists argue that all environmental problems are partly socially created or 'constructed' and that the process of construction can be examined, understood and explained. In doing so it may become clearer whether an environmental problem really is as serious as the claims-makers say it is.

Strict and contextual constructionism

A helpful distinction can be made between *strict* and *contextual* approaches to social constructionism (Hannigan 1995). Strict constructionists (the minority) point out that the natural environment can never speak to us directly and always needs people to speak for it. Ideas, theories and concepts within society can therefore shape the way the natural environment is perceived, appreciated and thought about. As we saw in chapter 1, sensibilities and attitudes in Europe towards the natural environment did change considerably between 1500 and 1800. Some constructionists go further. They suggest that natural things can really only be said to exist if they are either amenable to investigation or useful in some way to human societies. One startling example of this comes from Keith Tester's book on the arguments for and practice of animal rights. Tester says: 'A fish is only a fish if it is socially classified as one, and that classification is only concerned with fish to the extent that scaly things living in the sea help society define itself' (1991: 46). This seems impossible. Surely, fish just are fish whatever we think about them and however we classify them. But are they? Well in one sense, no, they are not. Fish certainly are scaly creatures that swim in water, but for human societies they are much else besides. Fish can be eaten as food. Fishing is also a sport enjoyed by millions where the main aim is not to eat but to compete. People keep fish in decorative tanks in their living rooms as pets; others are kept in hospital waiting-rooms as ornaments that help patients to relax. Yet other people see fish as creatures with rights that have to be respected, and they want both fishing and pet-keeping banned. In short, strict constructionists might say that fish are not just fish: they are in fact social constructions *and* they are constructed in different ways. And if fish are socially constructed, then the rest of nature must be too. One major problem with this strict constructionist version is that it is really focused on human beings, not on fish. In fact, after reading accounts such as the one above, we are none the wiser about fish. All it really tells us is that people think about and use fish in a variety of ways in human societies. This is a useful finding that makes us reflect on how these uses came into being. However, if we apply the same approach to the natural environment then we might learn about how people have used and are using it, but we will not learn much about the natural environment itself or the impact of human activity on it. There seem to be clear limits to the utility of strict versions of constructionism, at least for studying environmental issues.

Contextual constructionists (the majority) start from the premise that environmental problems may well be very real. However, there are also many environmental problems, some of which are seen as serious, others less so. Environmental problems seem to be ranked in order of their perceived significance. Governments and environmentalists might agree that **global warming** is more serious than ozone depletion, which is more serious than river pollution, which is more serious than street litter, and so on. If we carried out a random survey, we might even find that the public share these priorities. It is this social ranking of problems that is of interest, because environmental problem claims exist within a changing *social context* and are influenced by prevailing scientific and political ideas, economic circumstances and cultural attitudes. Are environmental problems ranked in order of their real potential harm or has the ranking been created using some other criteria? Can powerful social groups keep some problems off the agenda or can relatively weak groups get their voices heard? How would they do that? Contextual constructionists argue that this is exactly the point at which sociology can perform a useful function by investigating *all* environmental problem claims, whoever makes or denies them.

John Hannigan's (1995) excellent account provides several case studies and a useful contextual constructionist way of approaching these. Hannigan argues that there are three stages in the construction of environmental problem claims: assembling, presenting and contesting the claim. We can trace two environmental problems – **biodiversity** loss and **acid rain** – through these three stages to see what constructionism can help us to understand and explain.

First, claims have to be *assembled*. This is where a *possible* environmental problem is turned into a *real* one – that is, one that people believe in. This stage requires evidence to be collected which helps to justify the claim. The 'biodiversity' loss claim rose to prominence in the 1980s when the human impact on flora and fauna and species extinctions came to be seen as a key environmental problem. Although the human impact on species extinctions was previously known about, these were localized problems in particular countries. A legal and organizational infrastructure within the United Nations had developed in the 1970s with some international agreements such as the World Cultural and Natural Heritage Convention (1972) and the Convention on International Trade in Endangered Species (known as CITES), which gave political credibility and legitimacy to the biodiversity claim. In the 1980s the evidence collected systematically by scientists put the amateur efforts of natural history clubs and individuals in the nineteenth and early twentieth centuries in the shade. A new sub-discipline, **Conservation Biology**, was formed, combining biological evidence with a desire for conservation. The Society for Conservation Biology was launched in 1985 and a new Centre for Conservation Biology was created in 1986 at Stanford University, USA. Conservation biologists identified endangered species and habitats across the world, thereby lending scientific credibility to the claim. Linking biodiversity to extinctions also gave it an urgency that other claims did not have.

The acid rain claim also involved scientific research and evidence, though in this case the science of chemistry was more complex for the general public to understand. Acid rain is caused when gases from coal-fired power plants and vehicle emissions merge with moisture in the air to fall back to earth in the form of rain or snow. This means the acidic gases pollute rivers and lakes, damage forests and thus kill off wildlife. Again, this process was known about much earlier. The term 'acid rain' was coined in 1852, and in the 1950s scientists in the UK and Canada had reported on the problem without it becoming a major environmental issue in society. What helped in assembling the claim was a forum for disseminating the issue at the UN's Stockholm Conference on the Human Environment in 1972. This led to more media interest in the effects of acid rain and kept the issue on the agenda. Naming a claim can also have an impact on its success or failure. 'Biodiversity loss' was a useful label because it tied the problem to something generally understood, namely the extinction of dinosaurs in popular science and children's educational programmes. Although less well understood, acid rain conveys a clear sense of threat and urgency, as the word 'acid' is popularly understood as a 'bad' thing for humans to come into contact with. As **symbolic interactionists** have argued, labelling can be a very powerful social process. When people are labelled as deviants and criminals, it can have severe effects on their self-identity if the new label can be made to stick. Similarly with environmental problems. If an environmental problem can be given a label, this is more likely to make it stand out from others and improves its chances of success in the ranking order. Assembling a claim also involves identifying the enemy – the person or people responsible for creating it. If we can blame a person, politicians, business leaders or even a country, then the rest of us who are not to blame become a large potential audience and support for the problem claim.

Secondly, the claim has to be *presented*. Presentation means doing things that grab people's attention or persuade them. In the last 30 years or so environmentalists have become specialists in grabbing the public's attention with set-piece demonstrations and direct actions geared to presentation in the visual mass media. You will not have missed some of the Greenpeace actions against whaling, GM crops and **nuclear power** or the anti-roads protests in the UK involving occupations of construction sites in tree-houses and tunnels. These ways of presenting a claim try to shake people into action by example, perhaps showing them things they did not know of and appealing to their emotions. Animal rights activists regularly do this, using graphic scenes of animal experimentation in drug-testing laboratories. If presentations can move people emotionally, then the claim may be morally as well as scientifically legitimized. The biodiversity loss claim was initially difficult because the main losses were felt in developing countries rather than industrialized ones. Why should the latter care about what happens in the former? One way of countering this was to argue that, say, tropical rainforests were planetary resources that hold unique reserves of biodiversity that may be used in the medicines of the industrialized countries. Western corporations therefore shared an interest in preserving them in order to further their own 'bioprospecting' efforts. This presentation of the issue brought the losses inferred by scientists into an understandable and relevant framework for the general public in both developing and industrialized countries. Presenting the acid rain claim also faced the problem of geographical distancing. Countries that suffer acid rain pollution are generally not the same ones that produce it, because acidic gases travel on weather systems to be deposited far away from their origin. The acid rain problem was therefore assisted by presenting it as one of national sovereignty and fairness. Why should some countries be allowed to produce material that pollutes others? The claim therefore tended to present evidence that national natural resources were under threat from foreign invaders and, unlike the globalizing claim of biodiversity loss, acid rain supported and required a national public consciousness. In the short term this was quite helpful, but over the long term it may have been detrimental in allowing acid rain to fall below the more global issues in the environmental problem hierarchy.

Thirdly, environmental problem claims are *contested*. Claims-makers always upset others. Governments may not find it easy to face the implications of environmental claims and try to limit them or deny them. Businesses may not want to hear that their activities are polluting the environment, and to avoid doing this will cost them a share of their profits. You and I might not like to hear that we are contributing to climate change just by driving our cars and using up enormous amounts of energy at home and work. Suddenly we seem like the enemy! We may then find the arguments of the claims-deniers more reasonable than those of the claims-makers. Environmental problems are also in competition with other *types* of problem. Which is more important? Preventing child abuse or cutting down on household waste? Reducing homelessness or doing more recycling? You may think we should and could do all of these things. However, with limited resources it is inevitable that some issues and problems will receive more attention (and funding) than others, and environmental problems are competing for attention with many other social problem claims.

Contestation of the biodiversity loss claim involved the relationship between the developing South and industrialized North. Western companies sought agreement on their right to patent genetic material from their bioprospecting efforts that would allow them to exploit natural resources for profit. Environmental activists and some national governments in developing countries rejected these arguments and opposed the legal rights of companies to 'own' genetic material. At the 1992 UN Earth Summit in Rio de Janeiro, the American delegation simply refused to sign the Biodiversity Convention against 153 other national representatives who signed, because this would have required American companies to pay royalties and share information with governments of developing countries. The contest in this case was not about the science and other evidence of loss. Rather, it was who owns biodiversity and what rights do people have over it. But the contest itself actually helped to popularize the claim in a relatively simple and easily understandable way, and in that sense, contestation often brings welcome publicity for the claims-makers.

In the case of acid rain, the initial 1980s claim was simply denied by energy generators, government ministries and mining companies. This was possible and plausible because acid rain effects are notoriously difficult to prove, as they depend on the local environmental context. Some natural environments are more easily damaged by acid rain than others. Scientific uncertainty played into the hands of the claims-deniers. Political arguments also worked against the claim because it was possible to interpret the claim as part of an attempt by some nations to force others to spend more on cleaning up their act and thus gain a competitive economic advantage. This was evident in the reaction of the United States to Canada's complaints of cross-national pollution. Here again, the process of contestation did not help the claim. Instead, traditional national rivalries prevented acid rain from becoming part of the longer-term environmental agenda. By the mid-1990s, acid rain had slipped out of public awareness and other global issues such as global warming and biodiversity loss had become the priorities.

Reflecting on these two examples, it seems they tell us very little about the main question you may be asking yourself at this point. Are acid rain and biodiversity loss genuinely serious environmental problems that require urgent remedial action, or are they not? Is biodiversity loss really a more urgent problem to solve than acid rain pollution or not? Social constructionism's analysis of claims-making and claims-denying activities tells us much we did not know before, but it cannot tell us what to do about biodiversity loss and acid rain. This is its frustrating aspect, especially for environmental activists who *are* convinced of the need for action.

But perhaps the task of sociology is not to offer solutions to such problems anyway. Social constructionism deepens our understanding and opens up scientific and political issues for wider discussion. But making decisions about which environmental problems to tackle and how they should be addressed is something for everyone in a democratic society to consider. These are properly political decisions, not simply matters of science or social science, and although they should not be left to sociologists, they should not be restricted to a small number of scientific experts either. The great virtue of constructionism is that it can facilitate just such a wider and better-informed public engagement with environmental issues. Academics, politicians and the general public will know much more about the claims and be better informed about their origins and history. In this way, there is much work for sociologists to do in producing knowledge about the natural environment, environmental issues and environmental problems. Nonetheless, if you do not think this is a satisfactory response, there is a clear alternative to constructionism in the form of critical realism.

Critical Realism

Critics of social constructionism have generally been unhappy with what they see as its failure to accept or acknowledge the reality of the natural environment, which always seems to be the 'elephant in the room' of constructionist debates. What may be needed are ways of bringing nature's reality into sociological research; the most widely advocated method is critical realism, sometimes referred to as 'environmental realism' in this field (Bell 2004). I will use both terms interchangeably in this section. Critical realism is a method of scientific inquiry that potentially brings together social and natural scientific evidence to better understand why environmental problems occur. Their starting point is that human societies are part of the natural environment and both should be studied together using the same method. They also say that this method has to be capable of getting below the surface of the visible evidence to uncover the underlying causes of events, things and problems. In contrast to the agnosticism of social constructionism towards the reality or otherwise of environmental problems, critical realism is prepared to accept and debate knowledge and evidence from the natural and environmental sciences within its studies.

The best way to understand critical realism is to look at some examples that demonstrate some of the key points and arguments. Modern agriculture is a good place to begin. Traditional farming methods continue in many developing countries, but in the industrialized world farming has become an industry which uses the latest technologies and machinery to produce more than ever before and make profits at the same time. Animals and crops alike are produced in huge quantities and crop yields have been massively increased. Commercial crop production now produces yields that are literally impossible using traditional methods, and the widespread application of pesticides and fertilizers have allowed societies to clear the natural obstacles to food production. Farmed animals are treated as commercial products, with

Source: Farm
Sanctuary, USA

2.2 Intensive or factory farming is particularly constraining for animal natures. Some sows spend their lives in these 'gestation crates' and similar 'farrowing' crates for giving birth, which clearly do not allow them even to turn around. Each sow can produce 20 piglets per year using such methods.

cattle selectively bred and scientifically interfered with so as to produce rapid muscle-growth in beef production and cows that are always pregnant in order that a continuous supply of milk is available for human consumption. For human beings, the industrialization of agriculture has been of immense significance. However, in the process we have also seen the natural capacities and abilities of plants and animals pushed to their natural limits and sometimes beyond. Evidence of this can be found in the suffering of cattle because of their size and weight which puts additional strain on their bones, and in the forced pregnancies of cows whose calves are now so large that the natural act of giving birth has become too risky to be allowed without human intervention. Similarly, chickens are densely packed in broiler houses that are so alien to their natural ways of existence that many die off. Even if they survive, their rapid growth leaves many unable to walk and those that can fail to develop a natural 'pecking order' and their beaks are trimmed to avoid cannibalism. Animal welfare organizations claim that chickens suffer constant pain from this treatment, as their beaks contain nerves, unlike human fingernails.

Pigs sometimes fare no better. Naturally intelligent animals needing stimulation and activity, they can become so bored in factory farms that they will bite off each other's tails and ears, whilst respiratory disease is widespread in such environments. Sows are also routinely kept in cages that do not permit movement (see illus. 2.2). Industrial crop production has led to quite staggering amounts of chemical pesticides and fertilizers being used on the land which leech into watercourses and pollute rives, seas and lakes. Crops also become overly standardized thereby reducing biodiversity and leading to the effective extinction of some species through loss of habitat.

For environmental realists, animal welfare and agricultural pollution tell us something sociologically significant. This is that animals and plants, indeed the natural environment as a whole, are much more than just the ways in which human societies use them. The natural environment is a reality that must be understood and natural things have capacities, abilities and powers that determine what can be done with them. In short, there are some limits to human interventions and if those limits are exceeded then the consequences may well be unpredictable, even disastrous for people and animals. Arguably, one of the most striking examples in recent years of this 'intransigence of nature' – the natural limitations of human manipulation of natural things – was the British epidemic of so-called, 'mad cow disease', technically called **Bovine Spongiform Encephalopathy**, or BSE for short.

BSE in cattle is a fatal neurodegenerative disease, similar in symptoms to that known as 'scrapie' in sheep and Creutzfeldt-Jacob Disease (CJD) in human beings. The symptoms include loss of coordination, nervousness, loss of memory and aggression (hence 'mad' cows). Scrapie has been known about since 1732, but has not interfered with sheep-farming and the consumption of meat from sheep because the disease does not appear to be capable of crossing the species barrier into the human population. CJD is a recognized but very rare disease in human beings, unrelated to BSE. However, in 1996 British government ministers eventually admitted the theoretical possibility that at least ten recent human deaths had been caused by a new variant of CJD in humans (vCJD) which may have developed as a result of people eating BSE-infected beef during the 1980s. This was a huge shock. How had it happened?

Although the UK BSE Inquiry (1998–2000) identified the cause of BSE in cattle as a gene mutation in a single cow (named Cow 133), the most widely accepted explanation for the spread of BSE is that cattle were being fed BSE-infected offal (Macnaghten and Urry 1998: 253–65). The Inquiry Report said that the problem was, 'the recycling of animal protein in ruminant feed'. This longstanding practice had apparently continued in spite of previous warnings of the possible dangers of feeding animal protein to cattle which are naturally herbivorous – non meat-eating – creatures. One theory suggests that prior to the 1980s, the scrapie agent had been destroyed by chemicals and high temperatures in the production of animal feed. But once temperatures were lowered in this process, the scrapie prion survived, leading to the spread of BSE in cattle which made its way into the food chain and led to the emergence of vCJD in humans who had eaten contaminated beef. The BSE Inquiry noted that the link between BSE and the human vCJD 'was now clearly established'. The possibility that the millions who had eaten beef in the 1980s could potentially be future victims caused widespread panic, and the industry suffered enormous commercial damage as people stopped eating British beef across the world. On 2 June 2006, the National Creutzfeldt-Jakob Disease Surveillance Unit in Edinburgh reported that 156 people had died from vCJD, though estimates of future deaths vary widely due to the long gestation period of the disease. Meat-rendering practices were changed and new rules brought in to prevent a recurrence, but public confidence in science, politics, regulatory bodies and the meat industry were thoroughly shaken by the episode.

What is the realist lesson from mad cow disease? On the face of it, this may seem like a naturally occurring problem of disease in animals which was identified by scientific methods and then handled and resolved through the political process. However, we now know that the transmission of BSE was the product of decisions within the animal feed production system. It has also been accepted that the previous assumption that such diseases could not cross the species barrier into humans is false. BSE-infected beef did lead to vCJD in humans, against all existing scientific knowledge. Treating cattle as products and denying their herbivorous nature by feeding dead cattle to other animals produced an unexpected outcome that no one had forecast.

In order to properly understand the BSE issue, we need to know what kind of creatures cows are: what are their natural capacities and powers? We also need a similar grasp of human beings so we can understand why the disease had such devastating effects on people. What happens when infected foodstuff finds its way into the human body? However, that is not enough. We also need to know how the animal food production system operates, how it came to allow animals to be fed back to animals, what political and economic decisions were made and, of course, why so many people eat so much beef in some countries. This means bringing together knowledge from the whole range of scientific disciplines, including both natural and social sciences. We need research findings from biology, zoology, history, sociology, political science and more. Only in this way can we properly explain how and why BSE and vCJD were such a problem in the 1980s and '90s. It was, after all, *people* who decided to turn natural herbivores into carnivores and it was *people* who ate contaminated beef.

Like social constructionists, realists would agree that cows are social as well as natural creatures. As Irwin says, 'The modern cow is the product of generations of human-controlled cattle-breeding, feeding and housing' (2001: 80). However, unlike constructionists, environmental realists point out that there is a reality to cattle that has to be considered, debated and understood if we are to arrive at a satisfactory explanation as to why BSE and vCJD developed. There really are natural limits to what humans can do with cows and, by extension, with the natural environment more generally. Of course, this does not mean that societies should not push farm animals to and beyond their limits; that depends on whether we think it is a legitimate risk to take. After all, although many thousands of cattle were slaughtered to stop the further spread of BSE, most of the other farming practices reported above continue with no evidence of ill effects on people, whilst restrictions on the export of British beef are being gradually eased as consumer confidence returns.

From this brief review, it is evident that environmental realists are prepared to explore and debate the natural science of environmental issues in ways that social constructionists would not. Environmental issues always involve both natural and social processes, and in order to understand them we need to be able to bring these together. What environmental realism shows is that taking into account the objective reality of natural objects and environments would mean some rethinking of sociological theories and concepts so that the discipline can accommodate natural processes. Nevertheless, what it also demonstrates is that environmental issues cannot be properly understood and explained by natural and environmental sciences alone. Knowledge from sociology and the social sciences are absolutely necessary components of an environmental realist perspective.

Conclusion

Science has a special place in the knowledge production of modern societies. Natural science disciplines have a special place in the study of environmental issues. Only in the natural sciences has reliable and systematic evidence of increasingly global environmental problems been collected, which shows that human activity is having detrimental effects on the **biosphere**. But the special place that science enjoys is dependent on people feeling that sense of security and freedom from being at the mercy of natural processes that scientific knowledge and its applications have produced. If perceptions of global environmental problems begin to erode that sense of what Anthony Giddens (1991) has called, 'ontological security', or trust that relations with the natural environment are under control, then scepticism towards science and its institutions is likely to grow as people look elsewhere for reassurance. Perhaps with this in mind lies an important motivation for natural and social scientists to work more closely together at better understanding environmental problems and their social creation.

Readings

Norbert Elias's *Involvement and Detachment* (1987) is a stimulating read and a good place to think through the differences between modern science and other forms of knowledge. Lynn White Jr.'s influential paper is also helpful: 'The Historical Roots of Our Ecological Crisis' (1967).

Alexander Wilson's *The Culture of Nature: North American Landscape from Disney to the Exxon Valdez* (1992) is a fascinating and critical account of the way natural imagery is used in American tourism, business and culture. Alison Anderson's *Media, Culture and the*

Environment (1997) is also a useful discussion of media presentations of environmental issues. Carolyn Merchant's excellent *The Death of Nature: Women, Ecology and the Scientific Revolution* (1982) connects Western scientific methods to changes in gender relations.

John Hannigan carefully outlines the contextual social constructionist position in his *Environmental Sociology: A Social Constructionist Perspective* (1995), while Alan Irwin's *Sociology and the Environment, A Critical Introduction to Society, Nature and Knowledge* (2001) explores the constructionist versus realist debate and provides a welcome discussion of the organization and regulation of science. Peter Dickens's *Society and Nature: Changing Our Environment, Changing Ourselves* (2004) is an excellent critical realist introduction to environmental sociology. Ted Benton's 'Biology and Social Science: Why the Return of the Repressed Should Be Given a Cautious Welcome' (1991) is a short but engaging discussion of why (some) biological ideas should be welcomed into sociology.

3 Experiencing the Environment

In the previous chapter, the professional and socially organized ways of knowing natural environments were strongly to the fore. The natural sciences and their highly specialized methodologies, together with the in-house debates and disagreements in sociology, were shown to be important sources of knowledge and orientation. Of course, in the industrialized high-technology societies which demand similarly high levels of knowledge, this is entirely understandable. However, a large number of people even within these societies would probably argue that they have gained quite a good understanding of the natural world without ever training to be a biologist, environmental scientist or sociologist, simply by living within their local urban and natural environments. Children are often fascinated by the natural world around them even before educational institutions begin to teach them formally to study it. Factory workers with an interest in their gardens and allotments often know more about how to grow food than many natural scientists and probably even more sociologists. It is not just cognitive knowledge and formal teaching that produce our understanding of natural environments; practical experience teaches us much as well. In this chapter, then, we turn our attention to the other side of the coin, as it were, by investigating our sensual, emotional and personal experience of the natural environment, which will allow us to gain a more fully rounded picture of the quite complex ways in which we make sense of the world around us.

An Environment of the Senses

Many people alive today have access to large amounts of information about the natural environment, which is unprecedented in human history. They can learn about biology, **ecology**, zoology, gardening, meteorology, geology and geography. And they can do all of this by studying at university or college, reading textbooks, watching television, videos and DVDs or by surfing the Internet. Of course, no single person could ever hope to learn all the facts, theories and methods presented in these various disciplines, but that information is out there and available should one want to try. Whichever form of knowledge people choose to learn about, it is likely that their education will leave them better informed than before and their knowledge of the natural environment will be improved. On the basis of what they have learned, they may even make some changes to their lifestyles in order to 'tread softly on the Earth' and thus protect the environment. They may have reached this conclusion because they are rationally convinced that the evidence collected in these disciplines shows that such action is required to prevent further environmental damage.

However, people do not just know about the natural environment by imbibing information collected by others and then rationally weighing up the consequences of their actions. We also *experience* the natural environment directly ourselves and, in doing so, all our senses may be engaged, not just our mental functions. The natural environment is a sensual experience which can be health-promoting or health-destroying, pleasurable, emotionally moving, frightening, disturbing or repulsive. This experience brings its own knowledge, and many people who have never formally studied it can legitimately claim much knowledge of the natural environment. Parents can amaze their children with knowledge of garden birds and their song patterns collected by watching and listening to them over many years. Grandparents enjoy teaching their grandchildren about the trees and flowers they climbed on, used and grew over a lifetime. They also like to remind junior members of society not to go out in the rain with wet hair or risk catching a cold.

Go outside on a bright sunny day and feel the warmth of the sun on your skin. Most people sense this as pleasurable and enjoy the experience. Traditionally, holidays from work have been taken during the summer months to take advantage of the extra sunshine hours available. People in cooler climates sometimes bathe in hot sunshine in order to achieve a 'healthy-looking' tan, though with our improved knowledge of the damage that ultraviolet radiation can do to human skin, fewer now actually do so. Many more take the precaution of applying sunscreen before venturing out on hot sunny days, thus combining their desire to experience the pleasures of sunshine and its warmth with the knowledge of how to minimize the risks of doing this safely. They combine pleasurable experience with their rational understanding of the risks involved. While you are enjoying the Sun's rays, your experience may be enhanced by the smell of the flowers and grass and the sound of birdsong. You might pick and eat a few berries straight from a bush or chew on a blade of grass. With a bit of luck you might even catch sight of some of the attractive birds themselves, maybe even of something quite rare for your area. Simple everyday experiences of this kind demonstrate something quite sociologically important. People do not just learn about the natural environment from scientific experts: they actually experience the environment themselves and in many ways are 'experience experts' who are able to pass on a certain kind of knowledge of the natural environment to others.

Not all sensual experiences of the natural environment are as pleasurable of course. Now imagine a cold day: it is dull and raining heavily. Your damp, cold clothes are sticking to your skin and you feel uncomfortable. All of those attractive birds have (sensibly) taken shelter and are no longer singing, while the overwhelming smell is an earthy one emanating mainly from the overworked drainage system. You make it home and tell your family that 'it's really miserable out there'. You turn on the TV and a weather forecaster confirms your description. You are told that it will be 'a horrible day' with rain and low temperatures, but 'should get better' tomorrow when there will be more sunny periods. Here is another important sociological point. Even sensual experience almost always involves an *evaluation*. In modern industrialized societies, rain is bad, sunshine is good; cold is bad, warm is good; dull is bad, light is good – and so on. When weather forecasters tell us that rainy days are horrible or sunny days are beautiful, they are making value judgements about an aspect of the natural environment, and we all do this too. But these evaluations differ across societies and are not just individual preferences. One reason that people in modern societies are prepared to accept that rainy days are miserable is because they no longer rely on rainfall to grow crops or fill rivers; they buy their food in supermarkets and work in factories and offices, not in agricultural settings. They experience the sunshine as pleasurable, in part because they work shorter hours than their grandparents had to do, and look forward to their expanded leisure time, which many of them now spend outdoors. It is easy to see how, in other societies which depend more directly on regular rainfall for their food and water, rain may be welcomed, rainfall on the skin would be pleasurable, while yet another day of relentless sunshine may be experienced as 'horrible', especially if people have to spend their daytime hours performing hard, physical agricultural labour in very high temperatures. Sun may be bad, rain good.

Although all human beings have the same basic senses – sight, hearing, smell, touch and taste – how these are used and the meaningfulness of the information they convey depends on the way that societies are organized. In some societies, viewing wild nature is experienced as tedious and boring; in others, people sit for hours 'taking in the view'. In modern, urbanized societies people like to escape the city on occasion and enjoy the (relative) silence of the countryside. In other societies the sounds and sights of the hustle and bustle of city life represent very welcome commerce and economic development. Similarly, Western environmentalists' exhortations to developing countries to protect their natural environment may fall on 'deaf ears' when polluted air and waterways are experienced as positive signs of progress, as indeed they were in Western societies in an earlier period. For some people, the sight and smell of dead animals hanging in butchers' shops is enough to make them feel physically nauseous, while others work amongst such sights and sounds daily and yet others buy the goods they sell and eat them (usually *after* cooking). The senses are clearly part of the natural or biological capacities of human beings, but the way they are engaged and the evaluations of the sensate information they convey differs across societies and historical periods (Jütte 2005).

Experiencing Environments

If individual experience of natural environments is closely related to the form of social organization in societies, then it is also true that societies value environments, regions and things differently too. Some environments may be valued and protected, while others are relatively neglected. Some animal species may be revered and defended, while others are hated and destroyed without a second thought or regret. An investigation into the evaluation of natural environments and phenomena can provide some useful insights into how societies are organized in relation to the environments on which they depend.

Phil Macnaghten and John Urry's (1998) research into the way that people experience the natural environment and their attitudes towards environmental issues is probably the most systematic sociology of sensual environmental experience yet produced. One of their interesting findings is that such experiences and attitudes are closely related to *social practices* – that is, the activities that people are involved in and which give structure to their lives: practices such as making a living, working on the land or in factories, engaging in tourism, hill-walking, taking part in sports and so on. These practices are differently organized across societies and involve a range of social factors. They involve talking about nature, the full range of human senses, the dimensions of space and time and ideas of human nature or what humans are naturally capable of. As this is rather too abstract a discussion, an example from Macnaghten and Urry will bring out the implications of this approach for our understanding of environmental issues.

Experiencing the English Lake District

Some areas of nature in the form of land, the countryside or wilderness are considered to be particularly beautiful and so highly valued as to warrant a special status. They are often protected by legislation or given a special designation, such as a national park or an area of special scientific interest. It is also not unusual for them to be seen as embodying the character of the nation, representing something of its heritage. Some especially favoured and valued sites today have been given the designation of World Heritage Site, a recognition that they are valued not just in their home nation but across the world, and should be protected. Australia's Great Barrier Reef, the Ajanta Caves in India and the Serengeti National Park in Tanzania are just a few of 180 such natural sites. Proposals have already been put forward to make a bid for World Heritage status for the English Lake District National Park in 2008 (see box 3.1).

One reason that the Lake District is seen as special is the social discourse, which portrays or, perhaps, constructs the Lakes as a source of unspoiled natural beauty. It is not the only such place of course, but the discourse of English natural beauty says that the Lakes are special.

Box 3.1

The Lake District National Park (LDNP) in Britain is widely seen as an outstanding area of natural beauty under the authority of the National Trust. The Trust's founders also had strong connections to the Lake District and saw it as a special place. Millions of people now visit every year, many of them international tourists.

'The Lakes', as they are widely known, have been the subject of social concern for the last 200 years. In 1883 the Lake District Defence Society was created to protect the region from damaging human development in an age of railways and the emergence of mass tourism. Attempts to make use of Lake District water to supply the industries and people of the expanding city of nearby Manchester were viewed with horror. But why are the Lakes viewed in such reverential ways as special to the nation?

3.1 Lake Windermere with the Lakeland fells in the distance. This is the kind of natural scenery that attracts millions of international tourists to the Cumbrian Lake District in England.

Source: Photo, Pat Sutton, 2005

Many British writers, poets and novelists have spoken of the Lakes in this way, including internationally famous writers and critics of the eighteenth and nineteenth centuries such as William Wordsworth and John Ruskin, both of whom lived in the Lakes for much of their lives. Wordsworth's romantic ideas of nature contrasted with the mainstream eighteenth-century idea represented by Daniel Defoe's view that the mountainous rocky character of the Lakes was, 'the wildest, most barren and frightful' he had ever seen (Macnaghten and Urry 1998: 114). At this time, Wordsworth was considered a radical thinker in debates on the value of natural environments, refusing to accept that economic development was preferable to natural wildness. His romantic poetry was written on the cusp of a changing discursive construction of the Lake District from that of unproductive, unattractive wasteland to valuable, beautiful scenery. In the nineteenth century, Ruskin railed against the industrial system and its despoiling of nature, beauty and craft-based work. Ruskin wanted all artistic work to stay close to nature and would certainly not have made a good weather forecaster. He once said that, 'Sunshine is delicious, rain is refreshing, wind braces us up, snow is exhilarating; there is really no such thing as bad weather, only different kinds of good weather.' Today, both Wordsworth and Ruskin are seen as representatives of an early form of conservationism, or perhaps **environmentalism**, which is closer to the mainstream of society today.

The discourse of the Lakes is not the only thing to have changed. So too has people's sensual experience of it. The lakes and fells of the region are now seen as pleasant to look at and emotionally satisfying, provoking affective responses in viewers. For city-dwellers, the Lakes are experienced as a tranquil, natural healing salve to their overworked and polluted daily lives, an oasis of peaceful relaxation and serenity that recharges their batteries at least for a couple of summer weeks. Such sentiments are explicit and clearly expressed from my own straw-poll of visitor's books in Lake District guest-houses over the last decade. Visitors report that for their short vacation period they enjoy listening to the sounds of rivers and waterfalls, smelling the woods and flowers, touching the bark of old trees and walking amongst farm animals. You may have written something similar. Of course such experiences are far removed from their everyday lives in urban areas. The combination of these sensual experiences is involved in reconfiguring the nature experience of people. The point is not that people did not hear, smell or touch natural things before this time; what Macnaghten and Urry's scheme shows us is that the *meaning* of these experiences is different for modern people, who now seek out natural experiences rather than trying to avoid them. Some people also experience themselves and other human beings as bound up with and part of the natural environment instead of feeling separated from it.

Space is also a significant aspect of Macnaghten and Urry's analysis. Many people take their dogs on holiday with them and engage in the typical tourist practice of walking with their dogs around the lakes and through forests and woods, which allows them to experience and perhaps discuss the natural sights and sounds of such environments. In the Lake District, the practice of hill- or fell-walking has also become popular with tourists. Fell-walking makes a statement about the capacities of humans and their connection to the rest of nature. Rather than seeing such activities as the exclusive preserve of experts and risk-takers, not only is fell-walking in the Lakes more common than ever today, but even climbing high mountains once thought only accessible to experienced mountaineers is now on the itinerary of some Western tourists. Such spatial practices help to shape the experiences of people in natural environments. One reason for this new-found appreciation is that people now see nature as eternal and continuous, comparing it favourably with the transient, continually changing environments of modern societies. To climb the Lake District fells is to commune with traditional and timeless natural forces. This means that *time* is part of people's experience of nature.

Exploring the Lake District in this way brings all of Macnaghten and Urry's elements together through studying the changing social practices of real people who represent and establish new meanings of nature, newly found sensual experiences and revaluations of time, space and human nature. This means that **environmental sociologists** need to find ways of examining sensual experience, as well as exploring what people say and do through questionnaires, interviews and other traditional sociological methods. Existing research methods, such as attitude surveys, will continue to play a part, but other methods may help to tap into the less well-developed experiential dimension. The benefit of focusing on social practices may be that it effectively bypasses both environmental realism and social constructionism as *separate* approaches to the study of environmental issues (chapter 2). We do not have to accept that nature speaks directly to society, but nor is it necessary to claim that nature has no causal powers of its own, apart from those that humans give to it. Rather, the natural and the social are closely bound together within the same embodied social practices. Though there are other sociological ways of dealing with these matters, Macnaghten and Urry have clearly opened up some important avenues for rethinking the sociology of environmental issues.

Ecological Identifications

Environmental campaigning in defence of natural environments and animal welfare is now a commonplace occurrence which takes many novel forms (chapters 7 and 8). Direct actions in defence of the environment and animals can be emotionally satisfying as well as exciting for individuals. In contrast to the mundane pleasures to be had from working life, with its fixed hours and set roles and tasks, not to say routine and boredom, political activism can feel energizing and liberating, enabling the creative, spontaneous side of human existence to rise to the fore. Certainly, those who engage in direct action often report feeling at the height of their powers during the action and can feel disappointed, sometimes disillusioned and even depressed, when a movement ends, even if it has successfully achieved its aims. Political direct action can be an end in itself with its own attractions as well as being goal-directed activity with clear objectives in mind. But what such an explanation does not explain is the substance of the action. Why become involved in environmental protest rather than, say, equal rights or workplace issues? What motivates people to become involved specifically in the defence of nature?

A starting point is to recognize that people can identify with, sympathize or empathize with others and become motivated to help them. Many nineteenth-century philanthropists sought to improve the unhealthy conditions of life for themselves and others in urban environments and industrial workplaces through the creation of public health policies (Ashton and Seymour 1988). This identification may not be confined to other human beings, but can also spread to animals and natural environments. When people identify with others, they connect themselves to others in ways that bind their own sense of self and who they are, to whatever it is that they identify with. People's sense of self will, of course, be partly as an individual in their own right, but no one is entirely an individual. We are all connected in many ways to other people, some of whom become our role models and we try to mould ourselves in their image, others of whom we respect and value. These people and our perceptions of them partly shape who we are. We *identify* with them. If they are at risk, harmed or in trouble, we feel it very personally and intimately because 'they' are part of 'us'. Harm to them is therefore also harm to our own self, which we experience deeply.

Many environmentalists simply expand these identifications a stage further because they value trees, animals, plants and oceans in such a way that damage to these natural things is as deeply felt as damage to themselves. Their political actions to defend and protect nature then become a kind of self-defence. This may sound a little strange and improbable, but it really is not. Think about your own sense of self and its sources. There is (some) evidence that individual selves are partly the product of biological inheritance. Psychologists have argued that certain personality traits such as extraversion, introversion and impulsivity have a physiological component, which makes up part of a person's self-identity. However, a larger part of people's sense of self comes from social sources of identity such as their family, friends, local community, town or country of origin, none of which they have freely chosen. People frequently get upset when their family is verbally abused or wronged, and in the past have often fought to defend 'the family name'. In much the same way, people become attached to, identify with, the place where they grew up. Children and young people can be drawn into community disputes between gangs which identify strongly with their own areas, seeking to defend and protect them against 'outsiders'. People who have never been involved or interested in national politics will suddenly feel offended and personally aggrieved when they find out that 'their' country has been challenged or criticized. When, in 1982, Argentina invaded the British Falkland Islands, 6,000 miles away from the UK, there was popular support for the government's decision to send a military task force to retake the islands. Clearly, people's identification with 'their' nation had been stirred when they realized 'it' was being challenged. They felt the offence personally because national identification is one element of their own social selves, even though very few of them have ever visited the Falklands or even knew they were part of the UK.

In all of these ways, it is clear that an individual's self is built from biological sources and multiple social identifications. What sociologists argue is that people have individual *and* social parts to their selves and that these cannot be neatly separated, though the self does change over a person's lifetime. What environmentalists add to this picture is a relatively new idea, that what applies in human relationships can also be applied in human to non-human relationships. If people can identify with families, communities and nations – all of which are extra-individual entities – then there is no reason in principle why they should not also identify with animals, trees, oceans or the whole Earth. If they do so, then individuals could be said to be developing or connecting with their **ecological self**. And if they do that, then, some environmentalists argue, this is the route most likely to 'save the planet' from degradation by human activity. In the words of environmental writer and activist Bill Devall, 'Before changing paradigms or political ideologies or social institutions, it seems to me, we must change the way we experience life' (1990: 37). And that means developing new self-identities that are individual, social *and* ecological.

Theorists of ecological selves are critical of the way that the organization of modern industrialized societies has separated many people from the natural environment and thus allowed environmentally destructive ideas and practices to emerge. They argue that once established, this separation leads to some human interests and needs being given priority, even if this is at the expense of animal welfare, the natural environment and relatively less-powerful groups of people. Although this may sound quite sensible, we have to remember that human societies are dependent on the maintenance of a functioning natural environment. Prioritizing human needs may be beneficial in the short and medium terms, but in the long run it could leave future generations in great difficulty. The fact that modern societies are based on **anthropocentrism** may be stating the obvious, but unless this view is challenged, environmental problems will not be solved. Instead, it is argued that societies need to move towards an **ecocentric**, or Earth-centred, approach, which puts nature first. If societies put the planetary **ecosystem** or **biosphere** at the centre of their activity, then ecological selves would be promoted instead of being seen as eccentric.

Of course, this is to trivialize the difficulties involved in moving from here to there. The problem is simple enough: how to find ways of living together that are sustainable over the long term. But the solution is much more difficult: how do we achieve it? Do we raise people's awareness of environmental problems through education? Work to transform the institutions of modern societies? Change government policies on environmental protection? Encourage private companies to change the way they produce and stop them polluting the environment? Ecocentric theorists have argued in favour of all of these. But they also believe that people themselves need to change. And encouraging the largest number of people to experience their ecological connectedness and feel themselves to be part of the natural environment is the best way to get them to safeguard it because they will experience 'it' as an essential part of 'them'.

Ecological selves

If ecocentric theorists are right, them most modern people are not fully aware of an essential aspect of themselves. They do not routinely experience themselves as natural creatures and in fact may well believe themselves to be something other than animals. If they hold religious beliefs, they may think of themselves as beings created in the image of God. Even if they are not religious, they may hold humanist beliefs which still put people, not nature, at centre-stage. Modern people have grown up with quite a strange idea that human beings are somehow 'exempt' from the laws that govern the rest of nature. But there is a good reason for this. **Human exemptionalism** (Catton and Dunlap 1978) has become widespread because industrialization has enabled people (born without wings or gills) to fly above the earth and to travel beneath the oceans and to flout all the limitations apparently imposed on them by their nature. For a long time it really did seem that human technological inventiveness meant that humans were becoming exempt from natural laws. However, many people are rather less certain about this in the age of climate change and ozone depletion, when inexorable natural processes are becoming the common currency of intergovernmental conferences and political movements. Catton and Dunlap (1978) made an early call for sociologists to recognize the 'exemptionalist' defect in their discipline's basic assumptions and adopt their own **New Ecological Paradigm** (NEP) instead.

Ecocentric theorists aim to challenge all ideas which suggest that human beings are somehow exempt from the natural processes and natural laws that all other animals have to live within. They see this notion as similar to Karl Marx's theory that capitalist societies generate *alienation*, the separation of essential elements of human life from humans themselves. Here is a simple example from Marx. When people work in capitalist manufacturing they collectively create fabulous, useful objects using their biologically given capacities and talents and their learned skills and crafts. But at the end of the process, the objects they have produced are taken from them by factory owners and turned into commodities for sale in competitive markets. The workers have no say in what happens and no right to lay claim to the products of their labour. Instead, they are paid a 'wage' for their labour-power, which still leaves room for the owner to make a profit from the products when sold. For Marx, the products of the workers' labour have become 'alienated' in this process – that is, they have been separated from their rightful owners and then sold back to them as 'things'. Workers experience little if any satisfaction from this process.

Now, ecocentric theorists see the separation of human beings from their ecological roots in a very similar way. If human beings are a part of nature, then they should experience their relationship to nature as satisfying and self-affirming rather than perceiving life as a battle between themselves and the natural environment on which they depend. The latter view is a form of ecological alienation that leads directly to environmental damage. Environmentalists want people to treat the natural environment with more care and have provided numerous ethical reasons why they should do this. Natural creatures are sentient beings and feel pain, so we should treat them with respect and keep their welfare in mind. The natural environment has a value over and above its worth for human beings – an *intrinsic value* – and like all valuable things it deserves to be protected from harm. But environmental ethics, though necessary, may not be a sufficient way of changing people's behaviour. What marks out the more radical forms of environmentalism such as **Deep Ecology** is their insistence on practical and realistic changes to people's lifestyles and ways of living. One of the most famous deep ecological thinkers, the Norwegian philosopher Arne Naess, has said that what is required are not yet more moral arguments but 'beautiful actions' (1985: 264) This is because most people have little interest in eco-philosophical questions about whether nature has intrinsic value or whether it is humans who attribute value to it. What they want instead are concrete ways in which they can contribute to lessening the 'ecological footprint' of societies. They want to know how to live ecologically and what social practices contribute to this. They do not want to wait for philosophers to decide on such questions before they take action, because many people are already convinced that action is required. They just want some practical guidance on what to do. Rational, logical arguments are not necessarily viewed as superior to experience, intuition and identification with nature, so standard philosophical arguments do not have any special status. An intuitive feeling of natural connectedness may offer the best hope for positive change. Of course, such an approach is not shared by all environmentalists, some of whom have seen it as too close to 'New Age' ideas to be successful. Nonetheless, ecological self-realization means expanding people's self-experience to take in not just other people, but also animals, bioregions and even the natural environment as whole.

Another deep ecological thinker, Warwick Fox (1995), describes this process of identification quite accurately as 'transpersonal ecology'. That is, encouraging different thinking and practice that moves beyond the separation of society and nature so that damage to nature is also experienced as damage to the self. This should lead to renewed caring for the environment in the same way that people care for humans and their own selves, so that respect for others is extended to the widest possible ecological community. Currently, we can say that this kind of expanded ecological identification is limited to environmental campaigners and those looking to feel more in touch with their natural selves. The task for ecocentric theorists is therefore to involve the non-committed public in much larger numbers if they are to be successful. Perhaps the best way to do this is to propose small lifestyle changes that, when added together, will transform social practice. But what would this involve?

Ecocentric practice can be developed in everyday activities as obvious and necessary as eating and drinking. How and where was your food produced? Have any animals been harmed or forced to suffer unnecessarily to produce it? Have chemicals and pesticides been used? What has been added purely to make it look more appealing or taste sweeter? Establishing the connection between the make-up of the human body and its sources in food production systems means that people will be less tolerant of pollution and environmental damage, which is not just happening to something outside themselves, but is, in fact, directly a part of themselves. In this way, nature has become part of their own experience of self. Modern city-dwellers have become used to systems which, in many instances, allow them to bypass natural seasons and cycles. For them, fresh fruit and vegetables are available throughout the year in supermarkets, water is literally 'on tap' in (apparently) limitless quantities whenever they want it and is not just for drinking. Ecocentrics want to remind us all of the hidden social processes underlying our comfortable lifestyles and the price paid in damage to the natural environment as a result.

Many deep ecologists want people to shift people away from their materialistic lifestyles, which use up enormous quantities of energy and natural resources. Some suggest that the Western world is suffering from 'affluenza', the 'disease' of over-consumption. Instead, they promote simple living and 'voluntary simplicity' that reduces the human impact on the environment, thus preserving nature. Simple living involves the conservation and recycling of resources and using products and eating foods made and grown locally to avoid transporting goods over large distances, which causes unnecessary pollution. It also means cutting down on the sheer levels of mass consumption. The focus should be on the *quality* not the *quantity* of life.

Needless to say, none of this will be achieved overnight, but will require consistent actions and persistent vigilance. It will also mean less conventional business activity and profit-seeking and more cooperation and mutual assistance to encourage people to be self-sufficient and to grow their own food wherever possible. The kind of approach being advocated by ecocentrics and deep ecologists is reminiscent of the small communes and experimental communities that have recurred at many other times in recent modern history. It also draws on the individual examples of people who went 'back-to-the-land' to learn and live from nature, such as Henry David Thoreau (1917–62) in the USA and Edward Carpenter (1844–1929) in the UK. However, today there is no suggestion that commune-building will be necessary or that small-scale experiments will be enough. Instead, it is mainstream society that is the target, because for ecocentrics, industrialism has failed and whole societies need to be changed.

Ecofeminism

Feminism is a political ideology based on the premise that society is male-dominated or *patriarchal* and a women's movement is necessary to challenge this and bring about gender equality. Feminist organizations and groups have found it necessary to attack all ideas that suggest women are closer to biology and nature while men are closer to culture and rationality; linking women to biology has allowed men to present them as emotional creatures not suited to rational thought and has justified, amongst other things, the exclusion of women from universities and high-level positions of power. Over the twentieth century, the feminist movement achieved much that improved women's position in society, such as equal rights legislation and the movement of women into the labour force and politics in large numbers. By the late 1970s and 1980s, however, a new type of feminism emerged that was influenced by environmental issues and arguments.

Ecofeminism raised again the question of women's relationship to biology and nature. But this time, instead of rejecting the connection, some ecofeminists were prepared to accept that there may be one. Needless to say, this was a controversial position to take. Ecofeminists then went a stage further, suggesting that a special connection between women and nature may actually be a uniquely positive feature of feminism in an age of increased environmental dangers and risks. Does this mean that women have a special interest in environmentalism? If it does, then does it also follow that environmentalists have a special interest in patriarchy? Perhaps, but the evidence is not yet clear. Women do seem to be involved in local or grassroots forms of environmentalism in larger numbers than they are in mainstream politics, but women do not appear to form a majority *within* the established environmental groups (Blocker and Eckberg 1997).

Ecofeminism comprises quite a diverse body of ideas and practices which include liberal, social, socialist, cultural and 'Third World' ecofeminism (Merchant 1992). However, one notable aspect of some ecofeminist politics is the sense that women have a special or 'essential' relationship to nature which may give them a unique knowledge of the natural environment. If true, then perhaps we should expect women to play a stronger role in environmentalism than they have in labour, liberal or conservative politics. In particular, it should be easier for women to develop their ecological selves. The strongly felt connection with nature was a theme of early ecofeminists such as Susan Griffin, who stated: 'We know ourselves to be made from this earth. We know this earth is made from our bodies. For we see ourselves, and we are nature. We are nature seeing nature. We are nature with a concept of nature. Nature weeping. Nature speaking to nature of nature' (1978: 40). Later ecofeminist writers have modified this strong essentialism, arguing instead: 'Women are not "closer to nature" than men in any absolute sense. Both women and men are "in/with/of nature", but attaining the prize of masculine identity depends on men distancing themselves from that fact' (Salleh 1997: 13). This repositioning of essentialist ecofeminism moves away from a simple identification between women and nature, but maintains that, because of their devaluation within patriarchal cultures, women still have a different, special interest in environmental politics.

Ecofeminists argue that modern societies have devalued *both* women and nature and this has to change, but it also means that environmentalists and ecofeminists share the same goal, namely reversing the negative cultural valuations attached to women and nature. The human domination of nature and the male domination of women may be linked. Some ecofeminists look back to the pre-Christian era in which the image of the Goddess supported forms of nature-celebration and worship, such as pagan rituals, ideas of 'Mother Earth' and the natural cycles of the female body, promoting positive experiences of connectedness to nature (Starhawk 1999). This has led some to believe that reinvigorating older religious traditions would help to raise the importance of both women and nature. One obvious problem with the ecofeminist perspective is that it seems to have little room for men. Unlike mainstream feminism, which promoted equal rights and could be promoted by men as well as women, ecofeminism presents women as having not a different but a superior experience of the natural environment.

Cultural ecofeminism perhaps offers a way out of this dilemma. Rather than seeing the difference between men and women as 'essential', cultural ecofeminism focuses on the way that associations connecting women to emotions and nature and men to reason and culture are socially constructed. This means exploring the norms of masculinity and femininity and the way that these become attached to men and women respectively. Val Plumwood (1993) argues that these must be challenged, as we need a general 'human ideal' for all people – one that rejects the traditional masculine attitude towards nature that has been so destructive and oppressive. On this view it is not men who are the real problem but, rather, the social norms of masculinity which shape how men are encouraged to behave and think. This form of ecofeminism perhaps offers the possibility of gaining a wider support base which also includes men, as it shifts the blame for environmental damage away from men onto the society that promotes traditional masculine ideals. And if cultural norms and learned social behaviour are the real problem, then there is no reason in principle why these cannot be changed.

To summarize the main issue in this section: for deep ecologists, transpersonal ecologists and essentialist ecofeminists, a human identification with nature is a vital prerequisite in the movement towards a more sustainable society that treats the natural environment with respect. The fact that ecological identification does not yet exist shows how difficult this might be to achieve and it also demonstrates how powerful social processes are in forming the identities of people from an early age. In addition, cultural ecofeminists recognize that it is possible for both women and men to benefit from transforming the environmentally damaging patriarchal, capitalist culture. Ecofeminism and ideas of ecological selves also show us that for many within the environmental movement, not just rational argument or philosophical reflection are the keys to an ecologically enlightened society. The missing element in all previous theories is their relative lack of attention to experience as a way of changing people's behaviour. The more people experience themselves as natural beings with strong connections to the natural environment, the more likely they will be to protect and defend it against over-development and damaging practices.

Ecological Citizenship

If people are able to identify themselves as inevitably bound up with the natural environment, then anthropocentric ideas of human superiority are significantly challenged. It may become possible to envisage an ecocentric society that puts nature first and shapes social organizations to fit into it rather than ignoring natural ecosystems. What such changes might intimate is the emergence of a new form of citizenship, something Mark J. Smith (1998) has called **ecological citizenship** and Dobson and Bell (2006) refer to as environmental citizenship. The concept of citizenship itself is not new and can be divided into different stages. *Civil citizenship* emerged with modern property ownership, as this imposed certain mutual obligations on people to respect each other's rights to property leading to a responsibility to maintain social order. *Political citizenship* emerged next, during which voting rights expanded, working-class groups and women were brought into the suffrage and rights of association (as in trades unions) and free speech developed. The third stage, *social citizenship*, saw rights to welfare and responsibilities for collective provision of social benefits. These included a responsibility to contribute to the social fund used for supporting the vulnerable and for the right to a share of the welfare safety net when needed. What Smith envisages is the creation of a fourth stage, in which ecological citizenship rights and responsibilities form the centrepiece.

Ecological citizenship would involve new obligations: to non-human animals, to future generations of human beings and to maintaining the integrity of the natural environment (Sandilands 1999). The new obligation to animals means reconsidering all human uses of animals that infringe their rights to leading a natural life and expressing their natures. Vivisection, hunting, farming methods, breeding and pet-keeping would all need to be assessed in light of the extension of rights to the non-human animal population. Ecological citizenship's new obligation to future generations of human beings involves working towards **sustain-**

able development over a long time period. Will current economic development plans threaten the ability of future generations to provide for their own needs? If they do, then other forms may have to be designed and planned. Political and economic planning must become future-oriented and take a long-term view rather than adopting a short-term, free-market or *laissez-faire* approach. Finally, all human activity should be considered with reference to its effects on the natural environment. A *precautionary principle* needs to be adopted that puts the onus on developers and those who would intervene in natural ecosystems to justify their actions in ecological terms. If development cannot be justified in these terms, then it should not be allowed to go ahead. In essence, ecological or environmental citizenship introduces a new demand for people to take account of the human 'ecological footprint' – the impact of human activity on the natural environment and natural processes.

Clearly, ecological citizenship would demand some pretty fundamental changes to modern societies and the way they impact on the natural environment. It would also change the way that politics is conducted, because some groups would be required to 'speak for nature' and bring the interests of animals and natural environments into political decision-making. But perhaps the most radical change would be to people themselves, as ecological citizenship presumes a transformed human experience of nature and a corresponding sense of the self as bound up with the natural environment. In the same way that people had to start to perceive themselves as citizens with rights in order for political citizenship to take hold, ecological citizenship is unlikely to develop fully unless people's identities also include the experience of having ecological selves.

Moreover, it is important to remember the point made by Macnaghten and Urry, that such changes are not likely to materialize unless they are embedded within transformed social practices. For this to happen, then not just more environmental education, information and scientific knowledge will be necessary, but also new ways of living and working that set attractive and realistic examples for others to follow. Given the expansion of capitalist industrialization across the world's societies and large-scale urbanization, this is an enormous task. Can the world produce enough food for the six billion humans on the planet by scaling down industrial food production and encouraging self-sufficiency? Will enough people really be prepared voluntarily to give up their high consumption, materialistic lifestyles to live more simply and frugally? If they are not, should they be forced to do so in the interests of ecological sustainability? Clearly, these are questions that cannot be answered here, but they are serious issues for the future.

Readings

The most systematic text dealing with the issues in the fist part of this chapter is Phil Macnaghten and John Urry's *Contested Natures* (1998).

This is a very engaging text covering the range of sensual experiences of natural environments. Robert Jütte's *A History of the Senses: from Antiquity to Cyberspace* (2005) is not an easy read, but is the best general account of the history of human senses.

Arne Naess's deep ecological ideas can be read in the original with his 'The Shallow and the Deep, Long-Range Ecology Movement, A Summary' (1973), and ideas of simple living can be found in Bill Devall's accessible *Simple in Means, Rich in Ends: Practising Deep Ecology* (1990). On the ecological self, see Lucy Sargisson's short, critical article 'What's Wrong with Ecofeminism?' (2001) and Andrew Light's 'What is an Ecological Identity?' (2000). These can be read together as a useful introduction to debates on ecological selves and social identities. Freya Mathews's *The Ecological Self* (1994) can be approached for a more philosophical treatment of the issue. Ecofeminist ideas are well presented in I. Diamond and G. F. Orenstein (eds), *Reweaving the World: The Emergence of Ecofeminism* (1990). Catriona Sandilands's *The Good-Natured Feminist: Ecofeminism and the Quest for Democracy* (1999) sets ecofeminism into a wider context.

Mark J. Smith's *Ecologism: Towards Ecological Citizenship* (1998) is a helpful introduction to issues of ecological citizenship while a multi-disciplinary text on the same issue is Andrew Dobson and Derek Bell's collection *Environmental Citizenship* (2006).

4 Transforming the Environment

So far we have seen that the natural environment is understood, known about and experienced in different ways by differently situated groups of people, both geographically and historically. Sociologically, we might say that the type of society and forms of social relationships have quite a direct bearing on how natural environments are understood, known about and experienced. This is because people do not exist as isolated individuals entirely separated from one another by impenetrable walls around their internal 'selves'. Rather, people exist, even before birth, within social relationships, which shape and mould them according to the norms, codes of manners and values pertaining to the society of which they are about to become members. This doesn't make them all uniform or identical of course; societies are not homogeneous 'things', but are riven with group-based conflicts, disagreements and social movements pursuing specific changes. Nevertheless, there have been some major transformations in human history, which have been so huge that the consequences have been fundamentally to alter the human relationship to the natural environment. In this chapter we explore some of these major transformations and begin to assess their long-term consequences for the natural environment. We have to keep in mind at the outset that such major transformations were not planned, designed and implemented in the manner of a government initiative. Rather, they emerged from the continuous intertwining of intentional human actions and, as such, cannot simply be reversed. What we can do as sociologists, though, is to understand them better so that the many proposals for (sometimes radical) change can be realistically evaluated.

Social Development and the Environment

All human societies change and transform the natural environment in the process of gaining the things they need for their continuing survival and reproduction. During this process they are themselves changed, at the level both of social organization and of the individual. The national and centralized production of energy, which is distributed via electricity cables and gas piping to domestic housing, demands a more complex form of social organization and an extended division of labour rather than a system that leaves individual households to produce their own energy through home fires and candles. Individuals who use modern technological systems such as central heating and electricity need to have some knowledge of safety systems and what to do should things go wrong. They are required to have enough foresight to have fire alarms installed and to have a plan for getting out should a fire break out in the home. Such increased knowledge and forward thinking are quite common in individuals today, though they have developed over a very long period of time.

Karl Marx described nature as 'Man's inorganic body' because, although individuals may appear to be physically separated from nature, in fact they cannot survive unless they remain in constant interchange with it. Not only this, but our bodies are physically constructed from the food, gases and water that we imbibe from the natural environment. And if these are polluted or contaminated, then people will be too. One striking and often-cited example is the consequence of radioactive fallout from nuclear weapons testing and use since 1945, and from **nuclear power** plant accidents. The radioactive isotope, strontium-90, is now widespread in the environment as a result of such fallout, and people all over the world have some of it in their bodies. In small quantities this poses no danger, but the human body does not easily distinguish between strontium-90 and calcium. Therefore, when the former is absorbed into the body it replaces calcium in the bones and in larger quantities can lead to bone disease, cancers and leukaemia. The example shows that the connection between people and their environment is really a very intimate one, and the type of agricultural production and industrial production methods deployed in societies are matters of the utmost importance for human health, well-being and development.

Archaeologists and anthropologists tell us that modern human beings emerged and developed in (what is now) Africa between 100,000 and 200,000 years ago, spreading outwards to establish significant populations on every continent of the planet. Hunter-gathering and nomadic groups subsisted on the animals and plants naturally available to them, but they did not settle and grow their own crops or breed animals. The human population was therefore constrained by the availability of the means of subsistence. Around 30,000 years ago, foraging and hunting were still the dominant ways of subsisting, but human populations grew as more effective tools and tool use were developed. In some areas of the world, evidence of early human settlement have been found, particularly where edible plants and fertile soils existed. The transformation from nomadic and hunter-gathering groups towards more settled and permanent agricultural societies has been labelled the 'Neolithic revolution' and in its consequences it certainly was a revolution in ways of living. Settled agriculture enabled the production of a food surplus that supported higher levels of population and the geographical expansion of human settlements. Agricultural societies also developed new types of social organization in which property relations became relatively more significant, particularly the ownership and control of land that had very different impacts on the natural environment from those of nomadic hunter-gathering societies. Forests and woods began to be cleared for use in cooking food, in house-building and often simply to make room for the increasing size of human settlements. Once crops were grown in large quantities, people started to cross-fertilize plants and selectively breed animals, thereby beginning the long-term process of modification or 'cultivation' of natural things. Agricultural societies have had a major and permanent impact on the natural environment, changing the relationship between people and nature quite dramatically. By 5,000 years ago, more settled populations existed in most parts of the world and the evidence suggests that the rate of population growth increased with the first cities and city-states created in Mesopotamia, Egypt, China and India (Cowen 2001). Recognizable large-scale human civilizations with complex social hierarchies, a division of labour and new agricultural techniques were emerging, and the relationship between human beings and the natural environment was altered forever.

However, we are still living with the consequences of a much more recent revolutionary period that many of us simply take for granted. Many sociologists and social scientists would probably agree that the extraordinarily rapid and revolutionary transformation of the relationship between humans and nature that came about as a result of the Industrial Revolution just 250 years ago has been just as dramatic as the transformation that was the consequence of the agricultural revolution. In fact, it may prove to have been the most ecologically disruptive social development ever seen. Industrialization not only produced new workplaces, increased pollution, new social classes, a vast increase in society's productive capacity and rising populations; it also totally reshaped agricultural production itself. And although industrial manufacturing did not simply replace agriculture, it did transform agricultural practices by mechanizing production methods, thus removing huge amounts of human and animal labour and providing the means for reducing human reliance on natural seasons and cycles in the production of food. Today, industrial production has enabled fabulous constructions and interventions into natural environments that previous generations of people would have considered impossible. A few examples demonstrate this.

In Canada, fewer than half of all rivers and waterways follow their natural routes; the rest have been diverted and rerouted according to human requirements for water and energy. Because human societies require so much water for household use, industrial processes and crop irrigation, the flow of the world's major rivers is at times so badly reduced that the Colorado River in North America, the Nile in Africa and even the Yellow River in China all fail to reach the seas. China's Yellow River has numerous dams along its route, which restrict its flow, and huge amounts of water are drained off to grow cotton. The river now falls short of making the sea on around 200 days of the year, with potentially damaging long-term consequences. In 2002, meteorologists recorded their concerns that China's planned Three Gorges Dam on the Yangtze River, which will cost $25 billion and involve the forced movement of more than one million people, will bring about significant changes to the local climate and even lead to the warming of parts of Japan. There is little doubt that human societies have enormous power at their disposal to shape the natural world according to their designs, though the consequences are still not fully understood. In order for us to understand and appreciate better the world-historical significance of this process of social change and human development, we need to investigate some of its key characteristics and impacts.

One of the major claims put forward by radical environmental campaigners and thinkers is that industrial civilization is the primary cause of the large-scale environmental destruction and species-extinctions which have led us to the brink of an ecological crisis of global proportions. What they suggest is that industrialized societies are simply not sustainable long into the future and that if nothing is done to reform them, these societies will eventually collapse. This is because industrial capitalist societies tend to destroy the very functioning natural environment on which all human and animal life depends. In this respect, industrial civilization is ultimately self-defeating. Such a perspective is briefly, but very well, described by Greenpeace in a campaigning leaflet, which tells us that, 'Planet Earth is 4,600 million years old'. It continues:

> If we condense this inconceivable time-span into an understandable concept, we can liken Earth to a person of 46 years of age. . . . Modern man has been around for 4 hours. During the last hour man discovered agriculture. The industrial revolution began a minute ago. During those sixty seconds of biological time, Modern man has made a rubbish tip of paradise.   (Greenpeace, *Against All Odds*, 1990)

What this statement points to is the fact that human beings have not been part of planet Earth for very long at all, but during this brief time they have had a catastrophic effect on the natural environment. Of course, as described above, human beings have been around for a couple of hundred thousand years, but this is quite recent when seen in geological perspective. Staying with that extraordinarily long-term view allows Greenpeace to show that the last 250 years of industrial culture have transformed the natural environment in more far-reaching ways than in the whole of recorded human history. Still, I suspect that many people who are aware of the use of atomic weapons in Hiroshima and Nagasaki in 1945, Pacific nuclear testing, climate change and ozone depletion, to mention just a few human 'achievements', would perhaps agree with Greenpeace about the destructive potential and reality of industrial civilization. Before you reach your own conclusions though, let's explore exactly what we mean by 'industrialization'.

Industrialization

Most people have an understanding of what industry involves. Ask your friends and relatives and they will probably paint you a picture that includes factories billowing out plumes of smoke and gases, huge work-forces trudging to workplaces where they remain for eight, nine, ten hours and longer to produce material goods and raw materials such as coal, iron, oil and plastics. As a result, immense amounts of products are produced for sale in consumer markets: cars, clothing, furniture, foodstuffs and today even computers and information-technological devices such as games consoles, mobile phones and iPods. Giddens says that industrialization can be defined as different from capitalism:

> [I]f capitalism means a competitive economic system, in which commodities are bought and sold on national and international markets, and in which wage labour also becomes a commodity, it is distinguishable from industrialism. By industrialism we can under-stand a certain type of production process, linked directly to specific modes of social organization. Industrialism presumes the applying of inanimate sources of power to production technology, and thus repre-sents a prime medium of the interaction between human beings and the material world.　　　(1990: 20)

Industrialization therefore leads to the increasing separation of human beings from a direct reliance on the natural environment. Industrial machinery mediates between people and nature, thereby taking the place of human labour and freeing people to create more interesting lives. Certainly, that is the way that labour-saving devices are often portrayed.

This is not an entirely inaccurate picture of industrialization, though in the relatively rich countries of the Western world it is becoming less and less accurate. This is because industrial production is moving around the world to places where labour is cheaper and state regula-tions are weaker and less strictly enforced so that capitalist companies can make and increase their profitability. It is truly remarkable that US-designed products can be manufactured in China and shipped to Europe for assembling before being exported back to North America, and that this pattern of production is cheaper than if the whole process took place in North America. This points to enormous social inequali-ties across the world's societies, which make it cheaper to produce in developing countries. However, it also shows why environmentalists are concerned. Imagine the many tons of pollution created during the transportation of these goods by air, sea and land and the massive expenditure on the infrastructure needed to facilitate it. The modern global production system may well be delivering profits and relatively cheap products for some groups of people, but many believe that it is just not sustainable in the long term. Because industrial manufacturing has shifted away from Western societies, the latter are now increasingly characterized by a newer 'post-industrial' pattern of employment and work. This has developed since 1945 and is much more centrally focused on the provision of services such as education, social welfare and the production of knowledge and information rather than on material goods. Industrialization continues, but increasingly it takes place in China, the Philippines, Taiwan and India rather than England, the USA and France. Remember, though, that even post-industrial societies cannot avoid the environmental consequences of the industrial pollution being generated elsewhere.

The meaning of the Industrial Revolution

There are three ways in which we might define what we mean by industrialization and the Industrial Revolution. First, it can describe a period in which a society or societies create and introduce new tools, technologies or methods of working which change the way that they work on and relate to the natural environment. This kind of industrialization has happened many times in human history and in many societies across the world. We could say that there was something of an 'industrial revolution' in the thirteenth century, the sixteenth century and the eighteenth century. It is useful to look at these examples of industrialization because they help us to avoid the inaccurate idea that the Industrial Revolution of the eighteenth century came out of the blue and no industry had ever existed before. It is much better to realize that human beings have constantly invented new tools and shaped new ways of working on nature.

Secondly, industrialization refers to one very specific period, namely from about 1750 to 1830, beginning in Britain and spreading rapidly elsewhere. This period saw revolutionary changes in technological inventions and the associated social, demographic and economic changes that led quite directly to mass movements of population away from rural life and agricultural work into expanding towns and cities and factory-based work. On this definition it becomes possible for the first time to speak of an industrial *society* and not simply industrial tools or technologies. The enormous pace of change and the radical transformation of social life during this period and beyond demonstrate that, for the first time in human history, manufacturing industry was taking precedence over agriculture: a genuine 'revolutionary' human event. A numerical majority of the working population began to be involved, either directly or indirectly, in producing material goods, while, at the same time, smaller numbers of people were needed to grow crops and produce food. For the first time, more people found themselves living in urban rather than rural situations and this had an impact on the way that they saw and appreciated the natural environment (see chapter 1).

Our final meaning of industrialization is the widest of all. Seen in the very long-term perspective of Greenpeace and world historians, industrialization is an 'evolutionary' social development of the human

4.1 Industrialization had many positive aspects but, as cities rapidly expanded, dense urban populations led to terrible conditions for the working poor. Cramped inner-city housing such as this Glasgow slum was commonplace. Friedrich Engels is credited with coining the term 'Industrial Revolution' and recorded the way that living conditions deteriorated in *The Condition of the Working Class in England in 1844* (1845).

Source: Photo, Thomas Annan, *Slum in Glasgow*, 1871

species as such. The closest parallel would therefore be with the Neolithic revolution, which brought about settled communities and agricultural production and which also transformed the way in which large numbers of people lived their everyday lives in all kinds of ways. On this definition, industrialization is the process by which human and animal labour is systematically and continuously replaced with that of machines. Seen in this way, we get the full force of industrialization and a sense of the huge significance of the process for the human relationship with the natural environment. As an evolutionary development now of global proportions, industrialization has in fact been a very long-term social process, dating back much earlier than the British Industrial Revolution. It is also almost irreversible, barring a major societal collapse, huge reductions in human populations or a correspondingly massive reduction in material production and material prosperity.

Because we have these three meanings of industrialization in play, things can get a little confusing. In particular, some sociologists have argued that because the majority of the populations of Western countries no longer work directly in industrial manufacturing, these countries can now be seen as 'post-industrial' societies. And in that simple sense, they are. However, this does not mean the end of industrialization, nor does it mean that 'post-industrial' societies can avoid the consequences of industrialization taking place elsewhere in the world. Pollution does not respect national political boundaries (see chapter 5). In terms of world-historical development we should not be too eager to dismiss the process and significance of industrialization. Historian William McNeill rightly reminds us of this in the following passage:

> It seems likely that the change in ordinary everyday experience and habit implied by wholesale flight from the fields will alter society as fundamentally as it was altered when men ceased to be simple predators and began to produce their food. If so, it is difficult to overemphasize the historical importance of the industrial revolution and impossible to believe that the social organization and styles of life that will eventually prove to be best attuned to industrialized economies have yet clearly emerged. (1979: 425)

So although we can say that industrialization is a process of evolutionary development, the Industrial Revolution of the eighteenth century intensified the spread of industrial processes, which led to the emergence of recognizably industrialized societies. Even today it remains the case that information systems, computers, electronic microcircuits, satellites and the Internet are all modern industrial technologies and do not actually take us beyond industrialization. Computers still have to be produced in industrial factories and they work using electricity generated in power stations. The Internet is a wonderful global means of communication, but it cannot be accessed without the relevant technological devices and a power source. Needless to say, all this production and use also leads to waste and pollution.

Many environmental campaigners assert that because societies and the natural environment are in continuous interchange, it is not just societies that are being industrialized; the **biosphere** – planet Earth – is undergoing industrialization too. In the process, people have become distanced from an authentic connection to the natural environment as they increasingly live within the human world of material goods, technological devices and, of course, other humans. The environmentalist Edward Goldsmith calls the latter, the 'surrogate world', arguing that it is in direct competition with the real world of nature (1988: 185). This has to be so, because the surrogate world can only expand by using up matter and resources taken from the natural environment and by pouring the waste products from societies into rivers, landfill sites and the atmosphere. This distinction between the 'real' and 'surrogate' worlds has been important because it has motivated many people to become involved in environmental politics. The 'real' world of nature is seen as a finite world with a limited amount of natural resources. If true, this means that there are some natural limits to the human exploitation of nature. There is only a certain amount of natural material available for human use, and when it is used up there is no more. For example, forecasters have been predicting the end of oil supplies at various times over the last 40 years or so, though so far their doom-laden predictions have not come true because they failed to take proper account of better technologies that allow oil previously considered out of reach to be extracted. They have also not been able to forecast the potential discovery of new supplies of oil or novel end-user developments enabling oil to be used more frugally, such as more economical and efficient vehicle engines or mixed-fuel systems. This example shows that the limits of natural resources cannot be assessed in isolation from the technological means for extracting them.

A second argument put forward by environmental thinkers like Goldsmith is that the artificial world of urban settlements cannot exist without the real world of nature, but the reverse is not true. Therefore, we should be prepared to privilege the real world over the artificial one and put the onus on those who want to expand the artificial human world at the expense of natural environments to explain and justify their actions. Development has to be more tightly controlled and regulated than it is at present. Goldsmith's perspective is clearly not a happy one for human societies or animals, because what he describes is a kind of inevitable war between modern societies and the environment. So although, as an environmentalist, he effectively puts himself 'on the side' of the planet in this struggle, in a strange way his argument is a mirror image of the nineteenth-century views we discussed in chapter 1. The latter also saw society–nature relationships as inevitably a battle, but for them nature had to be subdued and dominated. Goldsmith and other **ecocentric** thinkers have turned such arguments on their head, but the question remains, is he right about the real and artificial worlds?

As we saw in chapter 1, part of the problem with this view of industrialization is that it portrays human beings as somehow *not* a part of nature. The contrast between a natural and a surrogate world simply reinforces this idea. For example, if cities are genuinely 'artificial', then what would constitute a 'real' form of human society? Sociologically, urban environments are no more 'artificial' than rural villages, towns, communes or even tribal communities. They are just larger, more complex and denser forms of human association and organization, which generate different problems that need to be addressed. Because human beings, unlike birds and honeybees, do not rely on an instinctive behavioural pattern for their community-building, the forms of life they make together are constantly changing. Urban living is just the latest form of this. Perhaps it would be better to accept that all human societies have impacts on the natural environment, and that this is not necessarily a problem in itself. The real issue is that of managing society's relationship with the environment rather than trying to eliminate the problem altogether.

The eighteenth-century Industrial Revolution did transform human relations with the natural environment and, in the process, led to a parallel social process of urbanization, which dislocated people, very often forcibly, from their more immediate, everyday reliance on the non-human natural world. Nevertheless, the problems that industrialization brought with it usually require modern science and industrial technologies if they are to be solved. This means that unless human societies are to become much smaller, the global human population drastically reduced and many modern technological devices and scientific knowledge simply abandoned, then ways will have to be found to manage the human–nature relationship better in the long-term interests of both human and environmental sustainability.

Urbanization

Anthony Giddens (1990) argues that one of the most significant consequences of industrialization is the production of a 'created environment' for human beings. What he means by this is broadly similar to Goldsmith's concept of the 'surrogate world' described above, and we have seen how this view of a separation of human and natural environments is flawed. In fact, cities have existed in many historical periods. Ancient Rome in the first century BCE was a typical walled city of around 300,000 people; Egypt, China and other regions also had recognizable cities, though these tended to be much smaller then modern ones, some of which now have as many as 20 million inhabitants. The process of urbanization that accelerated in the eighteenth century – defined as the (often forced) movement of rural populations towards the expanding towns and cities – was more rapid than in earlier periods because it was linked to industrialization. Industrial production provided more raw materials for house-building, factories and infrastructure, thus speeding up the flight from rural ways of life. In 1800, less than one-fifth of the British population lived in urban locations. In the 1851 Census this had risen for the first time to 50 per cent, and by 1900, urban living had reached three-quarters of the British population. The Hungarian economic thinker Karl Polanyi observed that the spread of machine industry actually came as a surprise that no one had forecast, so that 'the industrial regions of that age resembled a new country, like another America, attracting immigrants by the thousands' (1957: 91). To many, such regions represented the emergence of a new world of impersonal social relations, elected local government, a range of modern inventions such as gas and electricity, and higher wages and yet at the same time they were beset by a raft of new social problems.

Negative views of this emerging 'new world' were not confined to the rural landowners and workers who saw their traditional ways of life disappearing, but were also held by many urban-dwellers, many of whom felt that the countryside promoted higher morals than towns and cities. Much Victorian art and literature was also highly critical of industrial machines and commercial morality as well as urban social problems. Of course, even in the nineteenth century there were still people alive who remembered what life used to be like and many still felt that the countryside rather than the city was really 'home'. Such views also found their way into early sociological work, which contrasted what was emerging with what was being lost.

The German sociologist Ferdinand Tönnies (1855–1936) described this as a changing balance between the social bonds of *Gemeinschaft* and *Gesellschaft* (1887). *Gemeinschaft* (community) bonds were traditional, natural, authentic and spontaneously generated, thus tending to be long-lasting, while, by contrast, *Gesellschaft* (associational) bonds were impersonal, transitory and relatively weak. Urbanization tended to shift the balance, promoting the latter at the expense of the former so that modern people were becoming more rationalistic, calculating and individualistic in more areas of life, rather than community-minded and dutiful. Like Giddens, Tönnies saw the move away from rural life as the loss of an important direct connection with the natural environment, with the consequence that new types of modern people emerged who were much more individualized and self-interested than their predecessors. Other sociologists worked with this type of contrast. Emile Durkheim (1858–1917) perceived the shift away from an unreflectively generated or 'mechanical' solidarity towards a new source of 'organic' social solidarity rooted in the extended division of labour. For Durkheim, occupational groups and voluntary associations could fill some of the roles and functions previously played by strong communities and he was much more optimistic that people would find new ways of preserving or recreating their necessary social bonds.

A similarly rapid process of urban social change occurred in the USA and everywhere else that industrialization took hold or was planned. By 2000, more than 75 per cent of the whole world's population of around six billion people lived in urban areas. City-living itself is often experienced as a mixture of positive and negative features. It can be stimulating, culturally diverse, enabling of individual talents and opening up new opportunities. It is also the source of many social movements for 'progressive' social change and is hardly ever dull or boring. But at the same time it can be experienced as isolating, lonely, risky and crime-ridden. These are two sides of the same urban coin and are not necessarily contradictory or opposed.

The German sociologist Georg Simmel (1858–1918) pointed out that the metropolis produced a particular type of mental life amongst its residents. To an outside observer, urbanites can appear to be aloof, blasé, even disdainful of others. You may have had similar conversations with your own friends about how 'nobody speaks to you' in cities, whilst people are 'much more friendly' in smaller rural villages. However, Simmel's point is that such typical characteristics develop precisely because of the demands that city life places on people. City-dwellers are not born naturally inhospitable and rural people are not inherently born the salt of the earth. An exaggerated representation of this argument is to be found in the popular film *Crocodile Dundee* (1986), in which an Australian backwoodsman, played by Paul Hogan, makes the journey to stay in New York. On leaving his city-centre hotel, he attempts to

Box 4.1

Seen from above, probably the most striking feature of human activity is the enormous expansion of population centres – cities – and the suburban growth surrounding them. Combining the inner city with its suburbs, many modern *megacities* have populations of more than 10 million. Tokyo and surrounds is the largest with more than 30 million people. Amongst the 24 others are Mexico City (22 million), Seoul, South Korea (22 million) and Jakarta, Indonesia (17 million). The modern city offers employment opportunities, excitement, multiculturalism and a multitude of facilities. However, cities have a tremendous impact on the natural environment. Their population density makes cities voracious users of energy and natural resources that deplete natural reserves elsewhere. Consequently they also produce large amounts of waste material and pollution that finds its way into watercourses and landfill sites. Traffic fumes lead to air pollution, **smog** and rising levels of respiratory diseases such as asthma, while inner-city areas are blighted by high levels of crime. Many environmentalists see cities as unsustainable forms of social organization that have to be radically transformed if the human impact on the natural environment is to be minimized. Even planned cities such as Brasilia in Brazil have not been particularly successful in mitigating the environmental problems of urban living.

4.2 The familiar skyline of a modern city: Buenos Aires, Argentina as seen from an ecological reserve on the banks of the River Plate.

Source: Photo by Luis Rock, 2004

exchange polite greetings with everyone he meets, with predictably hilarious results. Of course, urban populations are so high and densely packed that the simple passing of friendly 'hellos' which are everyday occurrences in smaller rural towns and villages is just not perceived as possible or realistic any more. People's expectations of an acceptable level of sociability change along with new environments, though of course this does not stop them from being critically aware of this.

Urbanization has clearly become a fundamental and dominant social process for the contemporary pattern of global human settlement. But for those interested in protecting and preserving the natural environment, cities look much more like huge concrete monsters devouring unsustainable amounts of energy while generating similarly staggering amounts of human waste (literally) and waste products that end up in landfill sites, rivers, seas and even the air that we all have to breathe. Seen from the air, they are also connected by a network of roads and motorways that cut a swathe through the natural environment. Murray Bookchin (1986), the radical ecological writer and activist, sees cities this way. His own version of 'social ecology' advocates a return to smaller-scale, more self-reliant communities as solutions to the damaging 'bigness' of modern life. For Bookchin, the 'environmental crisis' is in reality a crisis of modernity, that optimistic Enlightenment-inspired project in which human beings are charged with the task of shaping nature to their own ends while also dealing with all the negative consequences. For environmentalists, the sprawling urban centres of the modern world now seem to be out of control, calling into question the most elevated ideals of modern life. Nonetheless, environmental problems are not just caused by industrialization and urbanization. Some believe that the constant quest for profit is a fundamental driving force that also has to be tackled. Capitalist economic systems have not factored in the environmental costs of business activity, making this appear environmentally cost-free. But the real environmental costs have mounted up behind our backs and are now threatening to reduce and ultimately eliminate the profit margins that capitalism demands. How has it come to this?

The Treadmill of Production and Consumption

Alan Schnaiberg (1980) has argued that environmental damage is not just the product of industrialization but is also an inevitable problem of competitive capitalist market economies in which profit-making is the driving force. This is because such economies create an economic structure which demands that firms compete for markets and profits, pushing them to constantly expand and grow just to keep up with their competitors. Schnaiberg refers to this compulsion for expansion and growth as the **treadmill of production**. Competitive pressures lead to a constant motivation for more and cheaper production of goods and inevitably, perhaps, a lack of concern for environmental protection, which would be more costly and prevent companies from being able to compete effectively. That means a lack of incentives within the economic system for environmental protection and a green light for pollution, waste and environmental damage, as long as this enhances profitability. One further consequence is that competitive corporate struggles force some businesses off the treadmill altogether and those that are left get bigger and more powerful. In time, some entire product industries become dominated by one or two multinational

corporations with annual turnovers larger than those of some developing countries. Such monopolistic tendencies, apart from ironically
reducing competition within the capitalistic free market, also increase
the power chances of those companies that survive, so they can
continue to ignore their environmental responsibilities.

If industrial capitalistic production sets societies on a treadmill to
environmental damage, then modern consumerism helps to keep that
treadmill running fast in this direction (Bell 2004). Consumption is
something that human beings have to engage in to survive, but modern
mass consumption is very different from all earlier forms. Clearly, if
there is mass production, it follows that there must be mass consumption. The products that industry produces have to be bought and
consumed by people, though producing and consuming may well be
acted out in very different geographical locations as products tend to be
produced wherever it is cheapest to do so, but consumed wherever the
best price can be gained. In the last 60 years or so, this has meant in
practice moving industrial production to developing countries where
wage rates and taxes are lower and environmental regulation is weaker
than in the industrialized countries. The rapid transformation of the
newly industrializing countries (NICs) such as Hong Kong, South
Korea, Singapore and Taiwan in the 1970s and industrial development
in India, China, Malaysia and many others is testimony to this process,
which is partly responsible for the globalization (see chapter 9) of
human activity. China is now the third largest industrial producer in the
world, though much of its production is aimed at the export markets of
the relatively wealthy countries of the West. The movement of industrial manufacturing around the globe has led to a de-industrializing of
many industrialized countries. And of course, if these newly industrialized countries become wealthier and wage rates creep up, the push for
tighter regulations and environmental protection may become an issue
and the itchy feet of capitalist companies are likely to take them on yet
another global quest for cheaper places in which to produce.

Consumerism can also be seen as a way of thinking, a mentality or
even an ideology. We can understand this aspect better if we ask
ourselves why people continually consume and want to consume. One
reason may be that they find the products of industry useful. Washing
machines, cars, TVs and mobile phones have a certain 'use-value' for
people that makes life seem that bit easier, saving them time and effort.
But such labour-saving devices also bring with them new standards
and needs, which then serve to encourage people to meet them,
making the initial gains much less clear-cut. Additionally, what about
those luxury items whose use-value is much less clear? Ornaments,
expensive home furnishings, sports cars and fashionable clothes are
less easy to characterize as simply useful. They also show us another
side to consumerism, namely its value within the social status competition in society. Social status refers to the way that people are perceived
and evaluated by others, and mass consumption allows for highly

complex and fine-grained distinctions to be made according to the styles and fashions that people adopt. Status competition can lead to the exchange-value of some products being much higher than their use-value or production costs would command. People may be prepared to pay a premium for the latest fashion or for those items that are in short supply. This is because these products allow people to say something about themselves, to communicate their status or their status aspirations in highly visible ways to others. Even products with a clear use-value, such as shoes, are also fashionable items which are often discarded and replaced before that value has expired.

Another element of modern consumer behaviour is its pleasurable aspect. Shopping can be enjoyable – or so people tell me. But *why* is it pleasurable? Some sociologists have argued that the pleasure of consumerism does not lie in the *use* of products but in the *anticipation* of purchasing them. You want a pair of shoes. You spend time searching shoe shops until you find a pair that you really like (perhaps famous celebrities with high social status wear a more expensive but essentially similar-looking pair). You go home and from time to time you continue to think about and talk to others about the shoes you really want. Every time you walk down the high street you can't resist glancing at them in the window. Eventually you go in, try them on and buy them, probably using a credit card. You get them home and wear them, showing them off to friends next time you go out. But soon the novelty wears off: they are just another pair of shoes and you start looking around for another new pair. You start searching the shoe shops again and find a different pair and the whole process begins anew. Colin Campbell (1992) says that we do this because the most pleasurable part of modern consumerism is the wanting, the longing after, the seeking out and desiring of products, not the use of them. It is a 'romantic ethic' of consumption based on desire and longing and one that advertisers know all too well. The marketing of products and services plays on this anticipatory consumerism, framing its hard sell in seductive ways that create and intensify people's desires. That is why we keep going back for more and are never truly satisfied. From the perspective of the natural environment, this 'romantic ethic' of consumerism is disastrous. It means that we constantly demand new products and more of them, and that means more production, so the cycle of mass production and mass consumption continues to churn out pollution and wastes natural resources. At the input side of production, natural resources are used up in enormous quantities; at the output end of consumption, people throw away useful things not because they are use-less, but because they are no longer in fashion or fail to represent their status aspirations.

What we can see from studying the treadmill of production and consumption is that the combination of industrialization, capitalist economics and mass consumerism has transformed the way that societies exist within the natural environment. Many environmentalists and more than a few social and natural scientists have come to the conclusion that the environmental damage caused by the continual expansion of economies and the continuing promotion of economic growth cannot carry on indefinitely. The pollution that results from the dash for growth may have been ecologically insignificant if it had been restricted to a small part of the global human population. But when industrial production spreads across the whole globe, a majority of people live in huge urban conglomerations, capitalist profit-seeking companies become multinational and mass consumerism seduces and is demanded by people in all countries, then the natural environment's capacity for recovery and resilience becomes weakened.

The previously 'eccentric' doomsayers within the environmental movement who forecast environmental collapse suddenly begin to look foresighted. The problem with modern treadmills, as the metaphor suggests, is that once on one, it is almost impossible to get off without switching it off. David Brower (1912–2000), first executive director of the USA's Sierra Club and founder of Friends of the Earth and Earth Island Institute, saw the problem clearly by directly comparing the 4,600 million years of Earth history to the six-day creation of the biblical Book of Genesis. On the foreshortened timescale of the biblical account, at one-fortieth of a second before midnight on the sixth day of creation, the Industrial Revolution began. Brower argues that 'we are surrounded by people who think that what we have been doing for one-fortieth of a second can go on indefinitely. They are considered normal. But they are stark, raving mad'. We will see exactly why they might be considered so in the next chapter.

This chapter has tried to do two things. First, to place current concerns about the transforming potential of human societies in to a longer-term context. This is important because we do not want to be misled into thinking that previous human societies were environmentally impact-neutral. The idea that people in previous types of society lived bucolic lives in happy harmony with their natural environment is patently false and bears more than a passing resemblance to the biblical story of the human species' fall from grace. Such a view leads to the equally misleading idea that modern industrial societies are artificial constructions by comparison. The danger with this line of thinking is that it might lead us to believe that a return to some previous type of social organization would solve all of our environmental problems. Just how unrealistic this idea is can be understood by asking whether current populations could ever be supported without industrial-scale food production. Ernest Gellner put this succinctly, saying that, 'Mankind is irreversibly committed to industrial society and therefore based on cumulative science and technology. Only this can sustain present and anticipated population levels. No return to agrarian society is possible, without mass starvation and poverty' (1986: 39). For those who hate the environmental and human consequences of industrial culture, this realization remains a bitter pill to swallow.

Secondly, the chapter has tried to demonstrate the world-historical significance of industrialization. It is important to grasp this because without appreciating the wide-ranging ramifications of the process, we can never understand current environmental issues and problems or the response of radical environmentalists to them. A sense of the quite unique situation we moderns find ourselves in is a useful thing to carry around, which helps to keep alive both the wonderment at such fantastic human achievements but also an awareness of the global environmental experiment being conducted with the Earth's **ecosystems**. Simply by standing on a city street and observing can easily achieve this sense of originality. Many thousands of people are walking around, most of them trying hard not to catch anyone else's eye; cars are hurtling past at 30 miles per hour and more, less than a metre from your face; aircraft are flying above your head travelling at more than 400 miles per hour to locations all over the world and trains are traversing the country at 125 miles per hour (on a good day). Modern societies are miraculous places to live in, but what effect is all of this having on the natural environment? The next chapter explores this question.

Readings

An excellent, brief global history of human development can be found in Noel Cowen's *Global History: A Short Overview* (2001), which is written in an accessible style. A very engaging and still unsurpassed account of the world-significance of European industrialization is David Landes's *The Unbound Prometheus: Technological Change and Industrial Development in Western Europe from 1750 to the Present* (1969). These two can then be followed with Brian Clapp's *An Environmental History of Britain Since the Industrial Revolution* (1994), which tells the story of industrialization from the standpoint of its impact on the natural environment. A short article by J. Frijns et al., 'Ecological Modernisation Theory and Industrializing Economies: The Case of Viet Nam' (2000), explores the prospects for industrialization in developing countries in more ecologically benign ways.

Edward Goldsmith's *The Great U-Turn: De-Industrializing Society* (1988) makes the Green case for a planned de-industrialization of societies, whatever your own view of the likelihood of this project. And although not focused on the natural environment, Anthony Giddens's *The Consequences of Modernity* (1990) moves along at a lively pace, showing the transformative power of modernity.

David Brower's environmentalist views are expressed in an HBO film, *Earth and the American Dream* (1992) directed by Bill Couturié. The thesis of the treadmill of production is best approached in Allan Schnaiberg's *The Environment: From Surplus to Scarcity* (1980), or the more recent A. Schnaiberg and K. Gould, *Environment and Society: The Enduring Conflict* (1994). There is also a helpful, shorter version of these arguments in Michael Bell's *An Invitation to Environmental Sociology, Second Edition* (2004), which is a very good introductory text.

5 Polluting the Environment

Chapter 4 showed us that human development has involved increasingly complex forms of social organization, the coordination of which has spread over ever-larger areas of planet Earth. Large, densely populated urban areas, immensely long road and transport networks, the industrialization of raw material extraction and food production and the twentieth-century mass consumption of goods have reshaped society's relationship to the natural environment. As we saw in chapter 1, for much of the modern period, such development was seen as entirely positive, progressive and much to be encouraged. However, the regular trickle of doubters who saw much more clearly the dark side of industrial development became something closer to a flood by the start of the twenty-first century, as issues of pollution, risk and the human cost of development are never far from our TV screens. In chapters 2 and 3, we traced the way that people's knowledge and experience of the natural environment also changed over this period. In this chapter we begin to investigate the dark side of modernity. We will spend some time considering pollution and contamination, asking just how serious this has become.

Alongside this, we also need to think about the issue of risk and the apparent precariousness of modern life. This is necessary because since the late twentieth century, some sociologists have argued that we are entering a period characterized by 'risk societies', which have to spend a good deal of their time and energy dealing with the hazards and risks generated simply by the continuing way of life that has also given the industrialized world its material wealth and relatively comfortable lifestyles. In this sense, we can ask whether the environmental 'bads' have started to overtake the material 'goods' we all took for granted.

Types of Pollution

Pollution can be simply defined as the release of potentially harmful contaminants into the environment. However, such contaminants usually have to be released by human activity to be considered as 'pollution'. Gases and materials released during volcanic eruptions may well cause harm to humans and other animals, but although technically they do pollute, they are not generally described as such. Carbon dioxide emitted from the burning of fossil fuels in power plants is considered polluting even though this gas does occur naturally anyway.

This being the case, pollution is probably best seen as an inevitable aspect of the emergence of human societies. It represents the potential 'dark side' of human societies, population expansion and technological development. Pollution therefore cannot be avoided, though the extent of pollution and the types of pollution produced in societies do differ widely.

We can narrow the different types of pollution down to those that affect the air, those that affect the water and those that affect the land. However, beyond these three main types, almost anything can be considered as polluting to human societies. Householders will go to court to stop their neighbours' noise from polluting their living-room environment with loud music, and the International Dark-Sky Association campaigns 'to protect and preserve the night-time environment and our heritage of dark skies through quality outdoor lighting'. You may be sympathetic to the latter cause should you ever want to see the stars the way your grandparents could, but find your view obscured by the hazy orange glow of badly designed street lighting that releases as much light pollution upwards to the sky as downwards onto pavements. There are obviously many more possible 'pollutants', but in this chapter we will concentrate on the three main types noted above.

Air pollution can be produced from car and other vehicle emissions, factory smoke and gases or from the infamous '**smog**' (a combination of smoke and fog) of UK and US cities in earlier decades and of India and China today. Water pollution can be produced from oceanic oil spills, chemical discharges from factories, untreated human waste making its way into watercourses and seas or the marine dumping of toxic and nuclear waste. Land pollution is evident in the huge landfill sites containing the garbage of everyday living. In Scotland for instance, some 90 per cent of household waste still ends up in landfill sites and household waste is growing at 2 per cent per annum (Scottish Environment Protection Agency 2006). Land can also be contaminated from overuse of pesticides in farming or increased radioactivity from **nuclear power** production. In all these ways, pollution restricts the human use of the natural environment and creates difficult, sometimes impossible conditions for other animals and plants.

The issue of pollution has become much more significant since the emergence of industrial societies, which have the potential to generate more and new types of pollution and to spread these across larger areas of the planet (and beyond in the form of orbiting detritus from space missions). Environmental campaigners have argued that human pollution of the natural environment is one of the most significant problems of modern life and one of the most urgent environmental issues needing to be tackled. But just how serious is pollution? In what ways is it affecting our lives and the lives of other animals and degrading the natural environment? This chapter outlines some examples and places these within the context of a rising awareness of the risks and riskiness of modern living. First, a brief historical sketch.

Awareness and Significance of Pollution

An awareness of pollution and its consequences can be traced back a very long way indeed. As early as 1273 a smoke abatement law was passed for London which banned the burning of coal with its attendant smoke, and in 1661 a Treatise by John Evelyn reported on the same problem, noting that on the approach to London one could smell the city in advance of actually seeing it, and that smoke was destroying buildings as well as human health. However, it was not until industrialization dramatically transformed the relationship between humans and the natural environment that awareness and worries about the effects of pollution became widespread. Once again, nineteenth-century Londoners faced the same issue of smoke pollution from domestic fires, but these were now compounded by industrial applications that massively increased the amount of sulphur dioxide, carbon dioxide and smoke in the atmosphere. In 1898 some environmental campaigners formed their own voluntary association, the Coal Smoke Abatement Society, to raise the profile of the problem and bring about action from government to solve it. The infamous London smogs that continue to give period crime dramas their distinctive air of menace were the source of heightened concerns. In 1952 a particularly bad London smog led directly to the deaths of some 4,000 people and brought about government action via the Clean Air Act of 1956.

Staying in London, the pollution of the River Thames caused by discharges from industrial processes and water-based transportation was once thought to have irretrievably killed off all life, though in recent years things have changed quite dramatically. The Thames has now seen the return of fish stocks and is generally accepted to have recovered from its earlier poor state. Indeed, the British Environment Agency reported in 2001 that waterways in England and Wales were 'probably cleaner than they were before the Industrial Revolution', with 94 per cent of rivers and estuaries having 'good' or 'fair' chemical quality and the return of wildlife. Cleaner and fewer industrial discharges into rivers together with tighter regulation and new investment by water companies seem to have made the difference. Similarly, in Scotland's 51,000 kilometres of waterways, 97 per cent are classified as 'unpolluted', with just 0.1 per cent 'grossly polluted'. Nature's powers of recovery and renewal are very often underestimated, though many other waterways, lakes and seas have not been quite so lucky. In recent years it has been reported that the Black Sea is suffering badly from eutrophication, an excess of nutrients that fosters the growth of algal blooms, which choke the **ecosystem**. The causes include nutrients from farming, industrial effluent, insufficiently treated sewage and oil pollution. These are carried by the River Danube, which passes through several countries, and deposited into the Black Sea. Many other lakes and reservoirs around the world had similar problems during the twentieth century.

Box 5.1

Since the break-up of the Soviet Union and the collapse of the communist regimes in Eastern Europe, the environmental problems left behind have been brought into sharper focus. During the Cold War period between 1945 and 1991, the Soviet Union and its allies competed for dominance with the USA and its allies. The competition spawned a nuclear arms race based on the assumption of 'mutually assured destruction' (MAD) should either side actually decide to use their nuclear arsenal. The Cold War also meant that the priority for both sides was rapid and continuing industrial production to support military expansion and demonstrations of ideological and economic superiority. For the planned 'command and control' economic systems of the communist countries, this was disastrous. On both sides, the pursuit of economic growth and crude measures of this led to a lack of concern for environmental quality and protection, but not much was known about the environment in Eastern Europe until after 1991. By the 1980s environmental pollution was becoming severe as the system allowed very little feedback through pricing mechanisms, local government or public information (Turnock 2001).

Opencast high-sulphur coal mining in Czechoslovakia caused regular smogs in Prague. In Poland's industrial Upper Silesian region, heavy industries polluted the air and rivers and some 700 tons of lead, zinc and iron were discharged annually into the River Tarnave in Romania. This untrammelled industrialization also resulted in reduced farming production as land became polluted and soils degraded. In rural Hungary, because of severe water pollution, some 700 villages had their water supplied in bottles, tanks and plastic bags. It was the 1986 Chernobyl nuclear disaster that provided final proof that the Soviet system had lost the Cold War. Since 1991, the newly independent nations have made some progress in tackling their environmental problems. One sign of this is that the Czech Republic, Hungary, Poland and Slovakia all ratified the Kyoto Treaty, committing to reduce their greenhouse gases by 2012, though of course, there is still much more to be done.

5.1 The first Soviet nuclear test in Kazakhstan, 1949.

Pollution today is a very obvious environmental problem that has to be addressed. However, for some politicians in developing countries, problems of pollution have been seen as the clearest sign of economic development and therefore of progress. Although this sounds counterintuitive, who would really want to see pollution? In fact, it merely repeats the assessment of many influential people during the earlier industrializing processes in Europe and North America. After the revolutions of 1917 in Russia, communist leaders embarked on a programme of rapid industrialization using slogans such as, 'the smoke of chimneys is the breath of Soviet Russia'. In this case, air pollution was perceived literally as breathing life into the emerging regime, which needed to be able to feed its people again after the disastrous experience of war. Only in countries that have reached a certain level of material well-being can pollution be considered a major problem that needs to be solved. When people are working hard to survive and earn a living, then pollution is a secondary consideration, as indeed it was when early industrialization processes occurred in the now relatively rich countries. So although awareness of pollution is now widespread, its evaluation as a social problem has changed considerably. This raises a key problem for the contemporary world. Western societies went through industrialization much earlier than elsewhere and experienced environmental degradation and pollution at a time when there was no general awareness of the attendant problems and no effective environmental movement to protest. But the developing countries are industrializing in a very different global context in which the pollution they generate is seen by Western environmentalists and governments as immediately harmful. Should developing countries be allowed to pollute the environment with impunity even though this increases greenhouse gases and depletes the **ozone layer**? Can global problems really be tackled if the very large populations of India and China can effectively opt out of the regulatory system? Would it be unfair or morally wrong for politicians and environmentalists in the industrialized world to try to prevent the industrialization and development of the poor countries of the world just because they were restricted from industrializing in an earlier time period? Should the industrialized countries share their technology with poorer ones to minimize the pollution associated with industrialization? The problem of equity in international relations is clearly a thorny one, and is central to any joint action to tackle global environmental problems.

The best way to grasp the extent and possible seriousness of modern pollution is to illustrate current debates with specific examples and this is what the rest of this chapter does in relation to oil spills, ozone depletion and nuclear power.

Oil spills

Geologists tell us that petroleum or crude oil is produced over very long timescales. Ancient vegetation and prehistoric marine animals mix with mud and sediments. The compression of this material causes heat, which in turn causes the compressed material to change in form from a solid into a liquid. The liquid, oil, is then trapped underground in pockets or 'oil fields' until human societies organize to drill down and pump it up from the ground. So although it is naturally produced, within a human timeframe at least, oil is considered to be a *non-renewable* source of energy just like natural gas. Once it has been pumped out and used, it is gone forever. The idea of non-renewable resources is at least partly based on the sheer speed with which modern societies use up natural reserves, which is infinitely more rapid than the geological processes that produced them. Some people have been forecasting the end of oil-based economies for at least 40 years, but so far, at least, oil remains a key part of modern energy production. Of course, there will be oil reserves that are not yet known about and others which are known of but which are just too expensive to explore and extract. This may mean that, should new technologies emerge that make exploration of such reserves cost-effective, a future 'oil crisis' could be averted. Environmentalists have long argued that dependence on oil and other fossil fuels is dangerous in itself, because the burning of all such fossil fuels releases carbon dioxide, which is a greenhouse gas and at the root of the human impact on climate change and **global warming**. They would like to wean us off fossil fuels and move towards *renewable energy* production instead. Renewables such as wind power, solar and tidal energy are not based on material which, when used, is lost forever, but take advantage of ongoing natural process to produce useable power. The major benefit of renewables is that they do not produce greenhouse gases or other forms of global pollution and, as such, are considered to offer long-term, sustainable sources of energy for human use (Smil 2005). The major problem, though, is that renewables have not been shown to be able to produce enough energy to supply the high production and consumption societies of today with the power they need to continue. If renewables really are the future of energy production, then it is very likely they will need to be combined with large reductions in energy consumption. It is probable that for the foreseeable future, non-renewable fossil fuels will continue to be the main sources of energy production systems across the world.

Oil has been a fundamental part of the economic development of modern societies. Oil is used not only to produce fuels that power the millions of vehicles, aircraft and ships, domestic and commercial heating systems, and lubrication for machinery, but also to make plastics for a multitude of everyday uses. Such mundane uses of oil probably pass most people by without much thought as to how it is extracted, refined and transported around the world. Once in a while, though, we are all reminded of our dependence on oil when an oil pipe ruptures or one of the many huge oil-tankers that sail the oceans runs aground. Such incidents are referred to as 'oil spills', although the word 'spill' actually fails

Table 5.1 *Oil spills*

Date	Oil-tanker	Oil lost (tons)
1967	The *Torrey Canyon*: UK	119,000
1978	The *Amoco Cadiz*: Brittany, France	223,000
1979	The *Atlantic Empress*: Tobago	160,000
1989	The *Exxon Valdez*: Alaska	38,800
1993	The *Braer*: Shetland, UK	85,000
1996	The *Sea Empress*: Milford Haven, UK	72,000
1999	The *Erika*: Brittany, France	13,000

to capture the large amounts of oil lost. Just a few of the worst examples demonstrate this (see table 5.1).

These spills (and the ones listed in table 5.1 are just a few of the most well known) represent the waste of millions of barrels of oil and, perhaps more importantly, create major pollution scares and potentially disastrous effects on local and regional ecosystems. One contributory factor has been the transportation of huge quantities of oil under so-called 'flags of convenience'. Ship-owners may register vessels more cheaply in a foreign country which also imposes lower taxes and has fewer regulations and restrictions. A typical example of this was the *Prestige*, an oil-tanker that sank off the coast of Spain in 2002 with 70,000 tons of heavy fuel oil on board. The ship was registered in the Bahamas, Greek-operated and Liberian-owned, but it had been chartered by a Swiss-based Russian oil company. Once registered, tanker-owners insure against pollution, but only to a maximum amount, with any compensation payments over that amount coming from International Oil Pollution Compensation Funds, paid for by the oil companies. Flags of convenience have allowed older, single-hulled ships to continue transporting oil, but once ruptured on rocks or grounded, they allow their cargo to be released and become unstable. Single-hulled ships should be phased out by 2015 under an international agreement designed to facilitate the move to a double-hulled design which is less likely to release the huge quantities of oil seen in recent spills. As in the case of the *Braer* in 1993, the sinking of the *Prestige* hit the national Spanish seafood industry badly. In the *Braer* spill, the lobster and mussel industries were closed for seven years and after the *Prestige* spill, despite a beach clean-up and government assurances, marine scientists warned that shellfish may be poisonous for up to ten years. Oil spills can have very serious and long-term effects on fishing and tourism.

The ecological impact of oil spills depends in large measure on the type of oil spilled. Lighter and more volatile oil can evaporate, while heavier oils can be much more difficult to clean up. Other factors include the weather conditions at the time, which affect whether the oil makes land or remains in the sea, and the local environment into which

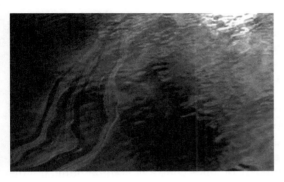

Source: USA National Oceanic and Atmospheric Administration, 2004

5.2 Several days after the *Exxon Valdez* released its cargo, the sea took on a visible sheen of heavy oil. Although by no means the worst oil spill in terms of quantity, the fact that Prince William Sound was an ecologically sensitive area brought home the potential for environmental damage in the USA.

the oil is spilled, which may be highly sensitive to disruption or more robust and resilient. The *Erika* spill of just 13,000 tons may not seem of the same order as that of the *Amoco Cadiz* with 223,000 tons, but the *Erika*'s cargo was heavy diesel oil which does not evaporate in the same way as the lighter crude oils, and therefore could have been more difficult to remove and damaging to wildlife. Environmental impacts also depend on the organized clean-up efforts. When some nine million barrels of oil were released into the Arabian Gulf by Iraqi forces in Kuwait in 1991, clean-up work was seriously hampered by the ongoing conflict, while in the case of oil transportation disasters, *where* they occur is often the most important aspect. If clean-up teams cannot gain easy access to the site, then the pollution may spread. However, even when clean-up efforts are relatively weak, there is some evidence that natural processes may do the job without human interference, given sufficient time.

On 24 March 1989 the tanker *Exxon Valdez* was grounded on Bligh Reef, Alaska and spilled almost 11 million gallons of oil into Prince William Sound, an ecologically diverse area. Many environmentalists feared this would create an ecological disaster from which Prince William Sound might never recover (see illus. 5.2). In the early days and weeks afterwards, their predictions seemed to be borne out. A quarter of a million seabirds, 300 seals, 250 bald eagles and large fish stocks died following the spill, and the clean-up operation cost more than two billion US dollars. However, there is considerable debate regarding the outcome. Some studies of the initial impact and recovery strongly suggest that although the spill was damaging in the short term, even one year later the natural ecosystem showed clear signs of recovery to normal and expected levels. Other studies have found that some species have yet to return to normal levels and that there is evidence of continuing harm. Certainly, the more extreme predictions of total ecosystem collapse have not been borne out and it is therefore reasonable to conclude that although such a large spill, in such a sensitive area, may have seemed disastrous to environmentalists, in hindsight the recuperative powers of the natural environment were underestimated.

The *Amoco Cadiz* spill off Brittany, France in 1978 was, by sheer quantity, one of the worst five oil spills in history, caused directly by failure of the ship's steering mechanism. Some 220,000 tons of oil, or 1,619,048 barrels – the entire cargo – was lost at sea. The oil slick from this disaster was measured at 18 miles wide and 80 miles long, polluting around 200 miles of the Brittany coastline. Some of the 76 affected beaches had oil penetrating up to 20 inches deep. However, in the places where wave action was high and persistent, the oil only lasted a few weeks before being washed away, and the type of oil, medium weight oil, was not the most difficult to deal with. In other areas a hard asphalt crust formed that lasted for several years before being removed. This illustrates that, in spite of the enormous quantities involved in such spills, many environmental activists, whose catastrophic predictions have not been borne out in the majority of cases, have underestimated the recuperative and restorative powers of natural processes. Nature is not a passive recipient of human activity but has to be viewed as an active participant in environmental issues and needs to be understood in the way that critical realists argued in chapter 2.

It has even been suggested that more oil is routinely wasted in marine environments every year through the normal operation and maintenance of vessels at sea than in the spectacular, media-reported oil spills. Of course, the one aspect of such events that cannot be denied is the wastefulness of natural resources and human effort that brought them into use. Perhaps it is this symbolic message of modern industry's indifference towards the natural environment that strikes a chord with environmentalists and the wider public. Following the *Exxon Valdez* spill, the USA brought in a new Oil Pollution Act (1990), which may have had some effect in reducing oil spills in US waters. Nevertheless, it probably has to be accepted that as long as oil is transported in huge quantities across the world's oceans to serve the energy needs of populations that can afford it, then some spills are unavoidable and ways will have to be found to mitigate their most damaging aspects.

Sensitivity to Risks

As we know, industrial societies produce enormous quantities of material goods, and this chapter has explored some of the polluting consequences of this process. Taking a long-term view, we can say that over time the spread of industrialization generates increasingly more serious environmental risks or side effects, which have to be dealt with. The escalating costs and wider scope of such problems have raised important questions about industrial societies and consumer culture and some sociologists perceive that the industrialized world seems to expend just as much time, effort and finance trying to prevent and avert risks as it does on the actual production of manufactured goods. The German sociologist Ulrich Beck (1944–) has been the foremost theorist of the idea that what we may be witnessing is the emergence of a new type of society in which risk-consciousness and risk-avoidance are becoming the central features. Beck (1992; 1999) argues that we are, in effect, moving into a 'world risk society'. Let's explore this theory a bit further.

Throughout the nineteenth and twentieth centuries, the political systems of industrial capitalist societies were dominated by a major conflict of interest between workers and employers or, in Marx's terms, between the non-owning working class and the property-owning capitalist class. This broad social conflict shaped party politics with the emergence of labour parties seeking to represent the new social force of labour against conservative parties that represented business. The conflict came to be centred on issues of wealth distribution, as trade unions and labour parties sought a more equal distribution of the socially produced wealth. Such struggles still continue of course. Nevertheless, Beck argues that this distributional conflict is slowly losing some of its significance as a result of the growing environmental issue of pollution. As he says, more people are beginning to realize that although they have fought vigorously for a share of the 'wealth cake', the cake itself may, in fact, be poisoned (Beck 2002: 128). Industrial societies are slowly dissolving in the wake of the piling up of side effects, an unintended consequence of the rush for economic growth and material prosperity. Because this process was not planned or foreseen in advance, environmental problems have crept up and taken us unawares. The emerging risk society will remain dependent on science and high technology because it is only through scientific monitoring and technological solutions that industrial processes can be more safely and effectively managed.

No matter where industrial production takes place around the world, its side effects can be felt in distant locations. None of the post-industrial societies of the northern hemisphere is immune from industrial pollution and global environmental damage. National political boundaries cannot prevent pollution. As industrial capitalism spreads across the globe, human beings become more dependent on larger numbers of people, while global trading patterns make the human world appear smaller than it once seemed (chapter 9). Industrialization has always produced pollution, of course, and in that sense, risk societies are no different. However, the major change in recent times is the fact that today many risks are 'higher-consequence risks', which have the potential to affect people far away from the site of their production.

Anthony Giddens (1999) sees the production of such high-consequence risks as evidence of a 'runaway world', where no one seems to be in control and people are becoming uncertain and fearful about the future. The runaway world is like a huge juggernaut careering down a motorway at breakneck speed. Potentially, it could leave the road and take us down an unknown route, but, even worse, the driver is not really in control of it but is at the mercy of external events. Giddens and, especially, Beck want to show us that the environmental issue is moving from the margins of political concern towards the centre. One more point needs to be made about the risk society. Most of the risks faced are the products of human activity: they are not like the natural disasters discussed in chapter 1. This means that the natural environment becomes an issue for political debate and decision-making and we can see the creation of Green political parties in the 1970s as the first step in the inclusion of environmental issues into mainstream political systems (chapter 7).

The possibility of accidents and mistakes is ever present in the risk society and can produce alarming results. Nuclear power provides the typical example (Perrow 1984). Accidents within nuclear power plants show up the potentially serious character of such high-consequence risks, leaving people with a deep suspicion of nuclear technology that has been very hard to shake. They have also undermined public confidence in the reassurances of scientists. Once society's class of experts is undermined, this acts to reinforce people's feelings of uncertainty and insecurity. Following the Chernobyl nuclear accident in 1986, concerns were raised in Britain about the possibility of radioactive fallout being carried across to affect sheep farming in Cumbria. Sheep farmers, who could legitimately claim to have a better knowledge of local conditions and farming practices, were challenging the expertise and advice of scientists as to how to deal with the problem (Wynne 1996). Similarly, the outbreak in the UK of **Bovine Spongiform Encephalopathy** (BSE) in cattle and the rapid spread of foot and mouth disease in sheep were notable for the way that people's confidence in politicians and scientists quickly drained away.

Across Europe, people seem to display divided attitudes towards the control of environmental risks. Many seem to believe that social changes will help to halt the deterioration of the natural environment, but they are much less convinced that such changes will happen in time to stop further damage. For example, in a 2002 Eurobarometer survey, 44 per cent of Europeans agreed that, 'human activity has led to *irretrievable* damage to the environment' (European Opinion Research Group 2002: 7; my emphasis). Because South European countries industrialized later than those in the north and the experience is closer to collective memory, people in the south tend to report higher levels of concern about the environment. In the north, the experiences of air and water pollution are not so close to the experience of current generations, as they industrialized much earlier. The Eurobarometer survey also found that, 'without exception, women are more worried than men' (ibid.: 21). Does this support the views of **ecofeminists** that we

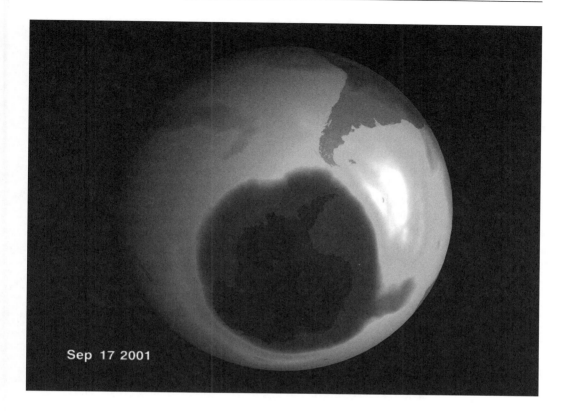

Sep 17 2001

explored in chapter 3, that women's experience of the natural environment is different from that of men, or are there other explanations for this difference?

Let us now look at two specific examples of high-consequence risks.

The risks from ozone depletion

Many people alive today will now know that the Earth has a protective layer consisting mainly of ozone, which blocks ultraviolet radiation from the Sun, thus preventing it from reaching the Earth's surface where it could cause skin cancers and other damage to people and animals. The stratospheric ozone layer is therefore instrumental in helping to maintain safe levels for the continuation of life. Just one or two generations ago only a small number of scientific experts and academics knew about the functions of the ozone layer and its importance. The vast majority of human populations across the world not only were unaware of ozone's protective function; in all likelihood they did not know such a thing as an 'ozone layer' even existed. What changed this situation were the cumulative observations of chemists, climate scientists and meteorologists and the widespread reporting of their findings through the mass media.

5.3 A striking image of the extent of ozone depletion in the stratosphere (bottom, centre) from 2001. Even though CFCs are being gradually phased out in industrial production, the ozone layer will take many years to be replenished.

Source: Greg Shirah, *Visible Earth*, North American Space Agency (NASA), 2001

Ozone was first discovered in the stratosphere back in 1879, though it was not until the early 1970s that the potential for human activity to cause damage to the ozone layer became a real cause for concern. Plans for supersonic aircraft that would fly within the stratosphere were announced in the former Soviet Union, America and in the British-French collaborative venture called Concorde, raising fears that more than a thousand planes could cause a significant destruction of stratospheric ozone. In the event, by 1975 only the Concorde project remained and even this had been scaled back dramatically (Rowlands 1995). The potential problem had been averted for largely economic, not environmental, reasons. At the same time, US scientists were reporting the potential damage that certain aerosol propellants might cause to the ozone layer, and in 1978 **chlorfluorocarbons** (CFCs) were banned in the USA. CFCs, human-made gases, were superbly effective for the purposes to which they were put, but the side effects of using them were potentially disastrous.

When CFCs are released, they rise into the stratosphere, which contains the ozone layer. Once there, radiation from the Sun causes them to decompose and release chlorine compounds, which then destroys ozone, thus depleting ozone levels (Yearley 1991). In 1987, scientists conducting an Airborne Antarctic Ozone Experiment definitively identified CFCs as the main cause of ozone depletion. The solution was therefore plain to see and relatively simple: stop using CFCs in aerosols, refrigerators and freezers and replace them with less damaging alternative propellants. Indeed, within a few short years, international agreement was reached on the control and phasing out of CFCs as outlined in the Montreal Protocol, which came into force in 1989. Since then, some amendments have also been worked out to assist developing countries in phasing out their use of CFCs. Many governments and local councils have also introduced measures to collect existing refrigerators and freezers containing CFCs so they can be disposed of without releasing the damaging gases. Of course, it will take some time for the ozone layer to be replenished even with the measures described above, and developing countries may well still find CFCs an attractive option if they remain cheaper than the alternatives. Current estimates suggest that it will be 2050, at the earliest, before the ozone layer will recover from the damage caused. Nevertheless, the polluting effects of CFCs are now widely known and monitoring systems are in place for the future.

What can we learn from the case of ozone depletion? First, industrial societies allow risks to be taken that most people are not even aware of. Who would have guessed that everyday consumer products such as aerosol cans could have produced such devastating effects on the global natural environment and, potentially, on human health? Other environmental problems have similarly mundane causes but may prove much more difficult to solve. For instance, people may well know and accept that their car-driving activity is contributing to potentially damaging climate effects and yet they continue to drive their children to school, to the shops and to and from work (chapter 9). Some habits are very hard to break.

Secondly, scientific knowledge was necessary for the manufacture of aerosols, freezers and refrigerators, and science therefore contributed to producing the ozone layer problem in the first place. However, it was also scientific research that discovered the existence of the ozone layer and scientists who confirmed the causal link to CFCs, thereby paving the way for a solution. In short, ignoring scientific research and knowledge is no longer an option in modern societies. They may not be the 'new priesthood' that Francis Bacon once wrote of (chapter 2), but scientists continue to perform essential functions that no other group within society can. The sociological study of science, scientific knowledge and the regulation of the institution of science will in all likelihood continue to be similarly essential.

Thirdly, the ozone layer issue shows that damage to the natural environment is relatively easy to do but can take much longer time periods to undo. For some environmental campaigners, this is an excellent example of why we need to move towards a 'precautionary principle' that restricts industrial and technological development until the evidence of their benign effects is clearly demonstrated. Such a principle is not entirely new, as many regulatory bodies in medicine and the pharmaceutical industry work on the basis of restricting the marketing of new drugs until clinical trials demonstrate both their effectiveness and safety. But anyone who has ever read the list of *possible* side effects on even the most widely used medications (I recommend that you do look at these) knows that risks cannot be completely avoided and will always have to be weighed against the potential benefits.

The risks from nuclear power

Attitudes towards nuclear technology have swung, pendulum-like, since the 1960s. From an optimistic engagement with the 'white heat of technology' and its potential for cheap and plentiful energy in the 1960s and '70s, to a pessimistic concern with accidents, nuclear weapons and waste in the 1980s and then again today, we are witnessing the first signs of a renewed optimism about the potential of nuclear power.

Nuclear technology is relatively recent, with most nuclear power stations being built in the 1960s and '70s. Of course, nuclear weapons had been used against Japanese cities in 1945 by the USA, and many countries have carried out nuclear weapons testing both at sea and over and below ground. The connection between the peaceful civil use and military deployment of nuclear weapons is one key reason why people have not taken up the nuclear option for energy production more enthusiastically. Nuclear power offers some unique advantages over many other energy sources. Nuclear power stations are costly to build but relatively cheap to run once in use. They also produce no carbon dioxide, the main greenhouse gas that contributes to global warming of the planet, thus making them potentially attractive to environmentalists as well as governments looking to maintain power supplies as fossil fuels run out. But nuclear power also has some unique disadvantages. It produces radioactive waste that remains harmful for thousands of years and, as yet, cannot be disposed of completely safely. Nuclear plants are potentially key targets for terrorist attacks and if more are built, they would need to be defended, militarily if necessary, on a much larger scale. Some people are concerned that this would probably mean some additional restrictions on people's civil liberties. Nuclear power generation also produces material for use in making nuclear weapons and loosening international agreements on nuclear power production may lead to a proliferation of nuclear weapons, something that has been resisted until now. Finally, although accidents in coal mines and other energy production sites have in the past had some devastating consequences and losses of life, accidents inside nuclear power stations carry the potential to affect people at large distances from the source if radioactive material is released. Politicians therefore face a difficult assessment of the pros and cons of nuclear power that is only made more difficult with the advent of increased terrorist activity.

More than 60 'incidents' have been recorded in nuclear power plants since 1945, the vast majority in the USA and the former Soviet Union. Some of the more widely publicized accidents have led to nuclear power being closely associated with risks and riskiness. The three worst accidents were at Windscale (now renamed Sellafield) in the UK (1957), Three Mile Island in Pennsylvania, USA (1979) and, most serious of all, Chernobyl in the Ukraine (1986). A fire at the Windscale plant led to a release of radioactivity which forced the authorities to destroy the agricultural produce from farms in the surrounding area. The partial meltdown of a reactor core in the episode at Three Mile Island has a place in common folklore even though only small amounts of radioactivity were externally released and there were no deaths or injuries from it. It was the *potential* for disaster and the exposure of poor safety standards in the nuclear industry that brought home the risks of nuclear energy generation. The plant never did produce any useable energy.

The Chernobyl accident, however, was a different matter. It became a key reference point in debates on the future of civil nuclear power and was a significant symbolic factor influencing the break-up of East European communism. An unexpected power increase caused an explosion at the Chernobyl plant on 26 April 1986. The reactor was destroyed, releasing large quantities of radioactivity which spread over a very large area. Although direct fatalities from the accident numbered just 31, birth deformities and early deaths are thought to have significantly raised the numbers of people affected. Many neighbouring towns were badly affected and some, such as Pripyat (see illus. 5.4), had to be evacuated and effectively abandoned because of the risks of radioactive pollution.

5.4 In the far distance, the stricken nuclear power plant of Chernobyl can be seen. The image is taken from the town of Pripyat, which was evacuated just days after the accident. Radioactivity from the explosion of 1986 spread widely, but towns close to the plant were most badly affected, with many rendered unsafe and uninhabitable. A 30 kilometre exclusion zone was imposed around the plant.

Source: Photo, Jason Minshull, 2005

Given the length of time it takes for radioactive material to degrade, there is no prospect of nearby towns becoming inhabited again in the foreseeable future. It would not be an exaggeration to say that the Chernobyl accident has had the biggest impact of any single pollution event. It reinforced an existing negative image of nuclear power and, in effect, negated the arguments of nuclear advocates for almost two decades. It also led to a growing awareness of environmental issues which boosted support for environmental organizations.

No nuclear reactors have been built in the USA since the Three Mile Island incident and nuclear power was abandoned in the UK 20 years ago. However, the World Nuclear Association reports that, as of 31 May 2006, there were some 441 active commercial nuclear reactors, with 27 more under construction (one in the USA) and a further 38 planned. In 2001 the American administration announced plans to expand its nuclear capacity and in 2005 British government ministers began to revisit the arguments for the benefits of nuclear power. Interestingly, their arguments centre on the contribution that nuclear power could make towards the reduction of carbon dioxide emissions which would thereby help the government to meet its commitments under the Kyoto Protocol to reduce CO_2 emissions below 1990 levels (chapter 9). This development shows how difficult some of the choices will be, not just for governments but also for environmentalists and everyone else in the future. Can an expanded nuclear power programme be justified if it helps to tackle global warming in the twenty-first century? If so, should all countries be encouraged to pursue one? Should Iran, which wants to start its own nuclear power programme, be allowed to do so? Is an expansion of nuclear power with its military by-products, waste and increased security concerns really a price worth paying to tackle global warming? These are the kinds of issue that will face us all in the next stage of the nuclear story and the outcome will have far-reaching consequences for energy production around the world.

Conclusion

Issues and examples of pollution may seem to be obvious and clear, but in reality they are not. Pollution is closely linked to questions of risk, and risks are not immediately obvious either. In the media-saturated societies of the modern world, people can be made aware of pollution issues that they would never have been aware of otherwise. Sometimes risk-awareness runs ahead of the reality of risks, so that people's fears and worries are unfounded, however real they seem to them. At other times the risks may be real enough but are not taken seriously because they are not widely reported or represented as problems. The role of science and scientific research in issues of pollution and risk is central. Scientists are still the experts whose knowledge we rely on, but at the same time, every accident and contamination episode calls the competence of scientists and their knowledge base into question. Without science, global environmental issues would never be known about and solutions would be impossible to formulate. The issue of ozone layer depletion reminds us of Marx's optimistic statement:

> [M]ankind always sets itself only such problems as it can solve; since, on closer examination, it will always be found that the problem itself arises only when the material conditions necessary for its solution already exist or are at least in the process of formation.
>
> (Cited in Bottomore and Rubel 1990: 68)

What Marx is suggesting here is that the same knowledge and technology that produces problems in the first place are usually capable of producing solutions to those problems. At least in principle. But this does not mean we should be complacent about the environmental problem of pollution. As the ozone layer example also shows, even if scientists identify a problem and suggest a solution and even if that solution is implemented relatively quickly, natural processes have their own reality and cycles that cannot be guaranteed to act as quickly as human scientists. The issue of divergent timeframes really does bring home the genuine novelty of modern industrialized societies which are capable of depleting natural resources on a scale previously unimagined. Such rapacious exploitation and use means that, in human terms, natural processes are unimaginably slow and gradual and the disjunction between the human and the natural timescale lies at the heart of some of the most crucial environmental questions for the twenty-first century.

It is also the case that at times the solution to the environmental problems of the industrialized world has been simply to export them to the developing world. In the global transportation systems of today, waste can be transported around the globe for treatment, recycling and dumping rather than being dealt with in the countries of origin. This may be politically advantageous and perhaps even cheaper. A very contemporary example can be found in so-called 'e-waste', that is, waste from electronic and electrical goods. Of course, much of this type of waste (though by no means all of it) comes from the burgeoning reliance of the modern world on computers, peripherals and other electronic information technologies. The rapid development of this technology produces a similarly rapid turnover of machines and products. Bigger hard drives, faster processors, better monitors and continually upgraded software lead to a desire and perhaps even a perceived necessity for businesses and individuals to have the latest versions. Fashion trends also operate within the high-technology world of information production and exchange. But what happens to the discarded machinery? Quite a lot of the USA and Europe's e-waste travels all the way to China, Vietnam, the Philippines, India, Pakistan and other developing countries. Ostensibly sent for 'recycling', this is where e-waste is broken up into its component parts and the metals separated out. In some villages of the Guangdong province of China, men, women and children perform this work for around $1.50 a day. The problem of recycling and dealing with e-waste has certainly found a solution, but it is one that takes full advantage of the wage disparities and inequalities within the global economic system.

Clearly then, pollution and risk can be exported in much the same way as useful products and even the most technologically advanced information technologies produce waste and pollution which impact on the natural environment and human well-being. This final example brings us back to a point made at the outset. Pollution is an inevitable part of modern life and how societies handle and try to reduce the extent of it, and which types of pollution take priority, are the crucial matters. It also shows that in a socially unequal world, one society's pollution might well be another's economic opportunity.

Readings

An excellent starting point is Steven Yearley's *The Green Case: A Sociology of Environmental Issues, Arguments and Politics* (1991), which is showing its age, but still explains why sociologists should be interested in issues of pollution and environmental damage. David Turnock's short piece on pollution problems in East-Central Europe, 'Environmental Problems and Policies in East Central Europe: A Changing Agenda' (2001), is a good summary of the changing region. Ian Rowlands has produced a very informative account of global atmospheric issues, *The Politics of Global Atmospheric Change* (1995), which is to be recommended. A more recent guide is Dessler and Parson's *The Science and Politics of Global Climate Change: A Guide to the Debate* (2006), which looks at the way that scientific research is used in political debate. Also, see chapter 9 below for a discussion of global warming.

A fascinating account of how people working in the nuclear industry manage to work with risk is available in Francoise Zonabend's *The Nuclear Peninsula* (1993). Vaclav Smil's *Energy at the Crossroads: Global Perspectives and Uncertainties* (2005) is a clear and accessible discussion of energy generation and alternatives to fossil fuels. David Elliott's *Energy, Society and Environment* (2003) provides a critique of technology-driven solutions reminding us that political and economic change will also be required to solve environmental problems.

Pollution and risk debates have been dominated by the work of Ulrich Beck. For this reason his original book, *Risk Society: Towards a New Modernity* (1992), is a good place to start. If this appeals, then his *World Risk Society* (1999) or *Ecological Politics in an Age of Risk* (2002) will take the argument further. Anthony Giddens's *Runaway World* (1999) also makes the argument in a very accessible way. For a more general introduction to the idea of risk in sociology, see Deborah Lupton's well-crafted *Risk* (1999).

6 Defending the Environment

Chapter 5 gave us a sense of the potentially serious environmental consequences of industrialization, increasing pollution and mass consumption, so it seems logical to follow this with a chapter on all those attempts to protect, conserve, preserve or otherwise defend the environment from despoliation and degradation. However, there is a somewhat ironic but important point to make at the outset, which should be borne in mind throughout this and the next chapter. This is that, however counterintuitive it seems, environmental protest and environmental political campaigns do not inevitably follow from a heightened awareness of environmental damage. If they did, then we would expect the most fervent and widespread environmental campaigns to take place during the initial stages of the industrialization process, when previous ways of life are being severely disrupted and the lack of regulation, management and infrastructure are most keenly felt. But the evidence does not support such a contention. In fact, some have suggested that during this initial period, people are so bound up with making livings and surviving the rapid transformation that they do not have the time or motivation to be too concerned about the natural environment. Instead, it may be that it is only when people's basic needs for food, clothing and shelter are met that their attention turns to issues of the *quality* of life rather than increasing the *material quantity* of it. This chapter therefore traces the emergence of modern environmental awareness and looks at some of the more and less organized attempts to defend the natural environment, both past and present.

Changing Attitudes

In chapter 1 we saw how the attitudes and sensitivities of many people in the industrializing countries slowly changed over the long period between the sixteenth and nineteenth centuries. People became more aware of issues to do with animal welfare and began to appreciate the wildness of untouched natural scenery when compared to the emerging 'concrete jungles' of over-populated and growing cities and towns. Some of the nature-centred poetry, writing and occasionally practices of nineteenth-century artists sound remarkably contemporary for this reason. For instance, here is the American 'transcendental' philosopher, Henry David Thoreau (1817–62), exhorting the virtues of nature: 'The earth I tread on is not a dead, inert mass, it is a body, has a spirit, is organic, and fluid to the influence of its spirit, and to whatever particle of that spirit is in me' (cited in Worster 1985: 79). And here is the Norwegian deep ecologist Arne Naess a century later:

> Every living being is connected intimately, and from this intimacy follows the capacity of identification and its natural consequences . . . Now is the time to share with all life on our maltreated earth through the deepening identification with life forms and the greater units, the ecosystems, and Gaia, the fabulous, old planet of ours.   (1986: 37)

In both statements, the Earth is alive and human beings should be encouraged to recognize their essential connection with the rest of nature.

One significant difference, though, lies in Naess's use of the concept of 'ecosystems', which did not exist in the same form for Thoreau. The term '**ecology**' was invented by the German biologist Ernst Haeckel in 1866 as the study of nature's 'household', compared with the management of that household implied in the term 'eco-*nomics*'. Ecological science, then, explores the interactions between organisms and their environment and how these interactions affect and exert influence on populations. Ecological thinking has also been an influential part of the environmental movement and Green political parties because it appears to lend scientific support to some of their central arguments. In particular, ecological science lends some support to environmentalist arguments in favour of preserving **biodiversity** and of taking the whole Earth as the environment for the human organism. A second major difference between Thoreau and Naess is that Thoreau's ideas did not immediately find mass appeal in the mid-nineteenth century, while Naess's deep ecological philosophy found a wider audience in the 'new' **environmentalism** of the 1970s and influenced the ideology of the emerging Green political parties (chapter 7).

What such attitudinal changes gradually produced was a resource of goodwill and potential support for the conservation and preservation of natural environments. Nevertheless, this was a necessary but not sufficient condition for specific conservation measures to be introduced. People had to take action as well as empathize with the cause. Similarly, real environmental issues and problems do not automatically lead to defensive measures to protect natural environments. As we have seen, pollution from early industrial factories could be viewed as evidence of economic progress and therefore as a welcome sign of progressive social change. Within the range of possible social problems that people want to see dealt with, the creation of jobs for the unemployed very often outweighs cutting back on industrial pollution. Because societies do not possess the resources to tackle every possible social problem, there has to be some prioritization, which necessarily means that some issues are not addressed.

Historically, unless directly tied to modernization or social improvements, protection of the natural environment has always fallen behind other social problems such as crime, taxation levels, unemployment, ill health and a lack of social welfare provision. Why has this been so? One fundamental reason lies in the character of environmental issues themselves. Unlike victims of crime, the unemployed and those with health problems, the natural environment does not have a voice and cannot speak for itself. Some groups of human beings have to be prepared to speak for it. In this regard, Ulrich Beck (2002: 159) reminds us that: 'Dying forests and songbirds do not metamorphose, in accordance with the laws of reincarnation, into protesting humans.' Quite so. And in order for protesting humans to emerge, three things are necessary. First, environmental issues must begin to be seen as just as significant and important, or even more so, than the range of other potentially noteworthy social problems in society. This becomes a possibility once sympathetic attitudes and sensibilities towards nature spread across many social groups. Secondly, a case on behalf of defending natural environments must be put together – by environmental claims-makers – whose aim must be to persuade both politicians who make laws and commit finance to solving social problems as well as the non-committed public whose support is vital if pressure is to be put on politicians for change. As we saw in chapter 2, one complicating factor may well be other groups of claims-deniers, who feel their interests are being threatened and who organize to resist or undermine the claim. Finally, people have to join together to make their case; very often, they create new organizations, clubs and societies to make sure that their initial optimism and enthusiasm are not lost. Collective action is more effective than individuals acting alone, though there will usually be disagreements and conflicts within and between movements, groups and organizations as well. The rest of this chapter, alongside chapter 7, briefly tells the story of how the defence of natural environments moved from being a marginal concern into the centre of modern political systems, and how environmental movements have now spread across the world.

An initially helpful way of thinking about the diversity within the environmental movement is to make a basic distinction between a gradualist, reform-oriented environmentalism and a more radical ecology or **Green politics** that wants to transform human societies, by deindustrializing them if necessary, to save the Earth's ecosystems. Environmentalists look to work with business, governments and the public to encourage them to take environmental issues seriously, and have been prepared to look to science and technology to help solve environmental problems. Although focused on environmental issues, most reform environmentalists see that cooperation with these bodies is necessary for human well-being. Many radical ecologists and Greens want to go a step further. They believe that the natural environment has intrinsic value and therefore should be defended and protected regardless of its beneficial effect for people. Many activists and campaigners against roads and industrial development that are ostensibly aimed at benefiting people fit the radical ecological or Green tag because they argue that the detrimental impact on wildlife, trees and nature is not acceptable, regardless of any benefits that might accrue to human beings. Radical ecological thinking tries to encourage people to live more natural lives, closer to nature, rather than continuing with the unnatural urban living that alienates them from it.

Unsurprisingly, environmentalists do not necessarily agree that this strategy will work and some argue that exactly the opposite is required. A good example here is Martin Lewis (1994: 8), who says that encouraging people to get closer to nature is a self-defeating strategy that, ironically, would result in more, not less, environmental damage. He argues: 'If all Americans were to flee from metropolitan areas, rural populations would soar and wildlife habitat would necessarily diminish.' Instead, Lewis's environmentalist solutions are based on 'decoupling' human societies from the natural environment, not moving them closer to it. Decoupling means using science and technology creatively and turning market forces towards working for environmental protection rather than against it. In fact, Lewis's ideas are not too far removed from the perspective of '**ecological modernization**', which will be discussed in chapter 9. Some of these ideas are already in evidence with the creation of carbon trading systems to tackle **global warming** and technological developments such as catalytic converters on vehicles and power plant filters that allow industrial processes and polluting machinery to continue, but aim to stop pollution at the point of emission.

This basic divide between reformists and radicals is not exclusive to the environmental movement, though in reality social movements usually involve a wide spectrum of views rather than just these two alternatives. For example, Marxist revolutionaries take a different view from socialist reformers, and radical feminists disagree with liberal feminists on the best way to achieve gender equality. Similarly, disagreement as much as agreement characterizes environmental activism. It is also the case that the environmental issues facing younger generations will, in all likelihood, be different from those of earlier ones. Nineteenth-century conservation attempts could not have known about anthropogenic greenhouse gases and the damage they threaten to do to the global environment. This partly explains why new organizations are continually being created to deal with newly identified issues and problems. It is not the only reason though. Over time, formerly radical groups become established and factional splits occur, very often leading to the creation of new groups claiming to be more radical or ideologically pure. This process has been repeated many times in the history of the wider environmental movement. Nevertheless, the movement expanded considerably over the twentieth century and continues to attract widespread support. We now need to explore where the movement came from by going back to its modern origins.

The Modern Origins of Nature Conservation

As urbanization and industrialization gradually removed large sections of national populations from everyday working contact with the natural environment, modern attitudes and sensibilities were transformed. More attentive attitudes to the environment emerged, providing a pool of potential support for the organized defence of natural things and environments. As democratic participation expanded to more social groups, including the working classes and women, the activities of networks of citizens and their creation of active, campaigning groups and organizations ensured that the non-committed public were alerted to the environmental damage caused by population growth, consumerism and waste, industrial pollution and urban development. The sum total of such groups in the field of nature defence is known as the environmental movement. It is very diverse and now includes Green political parties as well as organizations such as Greenpeace and Friends of the Earth. More accurately, we should say that there exist environmental movement*s*, as there are some national differences amongst the range of organizations and groups despite their more or less frequent collaborations in international campaigns. Sometimes these internationally diverse groups come together in a large environmental campaign or protest, and there are many links between organizations and groups across the world which facilitate such events.

You may already be familiar with the environmental movement. Indeed, you may even be a part of it. Anyone who has heard of, or contributed to, Greenpeace, Friends of the Earth, Earth First! or Reclaim the Streets and seen their activists campaigning against **nuclear power**, trying to stop commercial whaling and the dumping of nuclear waste at sea or pulling up and destroying genetically modified crop trials has seen environmentalism in action. What is perhaps less well appreciated is that the environmental movement has a much longer history of activity, stretching back into the middle of the nineteenth century. In that period, something genuinely new had arrived at about the same time that influential individuals were challenging mainstream beliefs in the right of human beings to dominate and subdue nature to human ends. This mid-nineteenth-century origin makes the environmental movement quite an old social movement.

The early environmentalism sprang from a variety of sources and concerns. Large cities were centres of industry and commerce with all the attendant environmental problems: factory smoke and city **smog**, polluted rivers and poor air quality, dirty streets and little effective sanitation. Many of these problems affected the wealthy as well as the poor and many early environmental organizations were created with financial resources and political commitment from society's elites, whose social networks and influence stretched into political parties and government circles. Middle-class philanthropic work brought reformers into contact with the poverty of the urban poor and their health problems were seen, in part, as the product of lives lived away from the health-promoting natural environment. The London-based Commons Preservation Society (CPS) wanted to save common land because they saw it as the rightful property of the whole nation, but also because the 'natural' commons along with public parks and gardens acted as the 'lungs' of urban life, oases of nature which were absolutely necessary for a healthy human life. The natural environment was beginning to be seen as a potential healer rather than an obstacle to be overcome.

Scientific findings were also building the case for better conservation of the natural environment. By 1880, some 100,000 people in the UK belonged to natural history field clubs, which allowed them to experience and enjoy the countryside while recording and providing hard evidence of increasing damage. At this stage, environmentalism was the preserve of small groups of enthusiastic, respectable people from society's social elites, who were part of the established order of society, capable of exerting an influence on legislation. Many practical achievements resulted. In Britain, much common land was saved from urban development, to become accessible to later generations for recreation and leisure pursuits. The development of the world's first national parks began in earnest in 1872 with the establishment of Yellowstone National Park, USA, and in 1879 the Royal National Park was created in Australia. Others followed in Canada, New Zealand and Sweden. Awareness of the need to preserve the natural environment and wilderness began to spread. In France, the Society for the Protection of Nature was founded in 1854 and it can reasonably lay claim to being the first 'environmental' group. A decade later, the British Commons Preservation Society was formed (1865) and in the USA the Sierra Club was founded in 1892. The Sierra Club embodied all the main strands of reform environmentalism. It produced a public access argument for conservation in its call to make the mountain regions accessible for the public to enjoy. It also sought to preserve the natural environment of the Sierra Nevada mountain range as part of the natural beauty of the region's heritage, and advanced the argument for creating a system of national parks. Lastly, it promoted the scientific understanding of the natural area, which would inform and educate the public. These three basic grounds for nature conservation – public access, aesthetic appreciation and scientific understanding – have been the main motivating factors in bringing more people into the wider environmental movement (Gilig 1981). A single example is the Australian Wildlife Preservation Society, which was formed in 1909 (now The Wildlife Preservation Society of Australia Inc.). The Society's remit was to protect the 'unique' indigenous wildlife of the country, thereby linking the appreciation of wildlife to the national identity of Australians. Many other local and national organizations were created in other parts of the world along similar lines (see table 6.1). Environmental movements also took on different characteristics according to national context.

Table 6.1 *The origins of organized environmentalism*

Organization	Date of formation
Society for the Protection of Nature (France)	1854
Commons Preservation Society (UK)	1865
Lake District Defence Society (UK)	1883
Natal Game Protection Association (South Africa)	1883
National Footpaths Preservation Society (UK)	1884
The Selbourne League (UK)	1885
The Audubon Society (USA)	1886
Society for the Protection of Birds (UK)	1889
Sierra Club (USA)	1892
The National Trust for Places of Historic Interest or Natural Beauty (UK)	1895
Coal Smoke Abatement Society (UK)	1898
Smoke Prevention Association of America	1907
Wildlife Preservation Society (Australia)	1909
Swedish Society for the Protection of Nature	1909
Swiss League for the Protection of Nature	1909

For example, the American idea of wilderness preservation contrasted with the very English focus on conservation and rational nature management.

The reformist character of the early conservation organizations is well represented by the National Trust for Places of Historic Interest or Natural Beauty, formed in England in 1895 (the Scottish National Trust was formed later, in 1935). The English Trust was the product of a desire to preserve and protect the nation's heritage in both the built and natural environments in an age when industrialization and urban development were transforming older ideals and relationships. The Trust's mode of operation has been to take stewardship of historic properties passed on to it but also to buy up land, including coastal sites, to preserve them for the future. That is, it holds property and land 'in trust for the nation'. More than this, its stewardship is 'inalienable': it cannot be taken away or bought out for development (though this has happened once, in the 1960s for road-building). In these ways the Trust symbolizes something of the wider early movement. It was not interested in creating a mass political movement to put pressure on governments. Instead, it sought to use its founders' and members' social connections to persuade legislators. Its solution to environmental damage was to take ownership of land and natural environments which made them easier to defend, but property ownership betrayed the essential political conservatism of the organization. Nevertheless, what the Trust achieved can be seen as socially progressive: the defence of the environment against capitalist commercial development and the uncontrolled sprawl of urbanization. Arguably, much of the early conservationism was of this kind – 'naturally' conservative, but at the same time 'socially' radical. On its own terms, the Trust has been very successful and is now one of the largest landowners in the country.

After the end of the nineteenth century, many more environmental organizations were created and national governments became involved in the conservation of resources for their rational or 'wise' use. However, the latter is associated with government, business and industry's justification for the continuing human-instrumental or anthropocentric approach to decision-making on uses of the natural environment. Environmental awareness and concerns expanded to new areas and regions and slowly an international character began to emerge. An example that demonstrates the emergence of an international orientation, but also shows its limitations at this particular time, is the International Council for Bird Preservation (ICBP) (now Birdlife International). In 1922 the ICBP looked to achieve a measure of agreement amongst national governments in order to protect migrating birds as they flew across national borders. The shooting of migrating birds took place in many countries and trying to stop the practice quite obviously required international cooperation. The Council's efforts failed though, largely because in 1922 there were no international political institutions for them to lobby. There was also no international body that could enforce any agreement that might have been reached. After the Second World War (1939–45) the International Union for the Protection of Nature (IUPN), a combination of governmental and non-governmental bodies, was created in 1948 as part of the emerging United Nations interest in resource conservation for human needs. In 1956, the IUPN's founders changed the Union's name and orientation towards nature defence ('Conservation' replacing 'Protection'; see McCormick 1992: 35–7), and in 1990 the network became the World Conservation Union. This gradual redefining of nature in international terms progressed slowly during the early to mid-twentieth century and then moved to a more global orientation during the 1970s (see table 6.2; also chapter 9).

After the early establishment of a respectable conservationism, the twentieth century was punctuated by two international wars, which involved many of the world's nation-states and populations and re-configured international politics. Many millions of people died as a result of the conflicts and the wartime economies produced munitions in previously unthinkable quantities. This transformation of warfare has been described as the industrialization of war. Yet in spite of, or perhaps in part because of, such human-made destruction, the environmental movement, though often disrupted, continued to build on its early successes. Over the century, more environmental organizations were formed and memberships grew steadily until the 1970s, when highly visible campaigns and increasing support for environmentalist organizations from the non-committed public rapidly transformed environmentalism into a mass social movement.

Table 6.2 *Twentieth-century environmentalism*

Organization	Date of formation
Society for the Promotion of Nature Reserves (UK)	1912
International Council for Bird Preservation	1922
The Izaac Walton League (USA)	1922
Council for the Preservation of Rural England	1926
Association for the Preservation of Rural Scotland	1931
Ramblers Association (UK)	1935
The Wilderness Society (USA)	1935
Ulster Society for the Preservation of the Countryside	1937
International Union for the Protection of Nature	1948
The Nature Conservancy Council (UK)	1948
The Council for Nature	1958
World Wildlife Fund (now Worldwide Fund for Nature)	1961
The Conservation Society (UK)	1966
Australian Conservation Foundation	1966
Committee for Environmental Conservation (CoEnCo)	1969

The Development of Environmentalism

By the early 1970s, what appeared to be a different type of environmentalism became visible and the 1980s saw a rapid period of membership growth and the formation of many new groups. We can say that at this time a genuine mass environmental movement was, for the first time, emerging. This period has been seen as ushering in a 'new environmentalism' as part of a series of what sociologists have called 'new social movements'. These included anti-Vietnam war campaigns, student movements in Europe and the USA, movements of disabled people and more. The new social movements seemed to differ in important respects from their historical predecessors. For new environmentalism, one major difference was the promise to include both the industrialized countries of the Northern hemisphere and the developing countries of the South. This was a genuinely novel development. Most of the international organizations with high media profiles and mass memberships stem from this time, including Greenpeace and Friends of the Earth in the 1970s and the loose networks of campaigners making up Earth First!, Reclaim the Streets and Critical Mass in the 1990s. The latter groups were forerunners of the anti-globalization and anti-capitalist protest networks which rose to prominence in the 1990s (see Wall 2005 for a discussion of the diverse positions within anti-globalization/anti-capitalism). So, what are the main features of this new environmentalism?

We can identify four main points of difference between the old and the new: their aims and objectives, their organizational forms, the type of campaigns they engage in and the social backgrounds of the people who become involved in them. We will take these four aspects in turn.

Aims and objectives

The new environmentalism has many similarities with the old. It remains focused on defending and protecting the natural environment and, in doing so, it also claims to be acting on behalf of people, for instance in the safeguarding of human health from excessive pollution. However, there are also some differences. New environmentalism is increasingly concerned with the global environment or planet Earth rather than with exclusively local or even national issues. Greenpeace activists operate internationally, while the group has nationally based organizations and memberships right across the world. This means that some of the main issues of concern are similarly international or global in scope. Greenpeace has opposed the continuation of the Japanese whaling industry, campaigned against genetic modification of crops in Scotland and England, opposed governmental plans for nuclear power in Brazil and campaigned for renewable energy use in India. Of course, Greenpeace may not always achieve its objectives, but the main aims are clearly much wider and more far-reaching than those early local and national forms of conservationism and preservationism. For that reason, they are also much more difficult to achieve and sustain.

We might say that for the new environmentalism, the natural environment is the entire planet, the **biosphere**, rather than a national territory or a national state. In summary, the key difference in aims between the old and new environmentalism is that:

> In the past, local solutions were sought. It was (or at least it seemed) possible to geographically restrict the impact of environmental hazards. . . . Obviously such local strategies are insufficient today. . . . The fundamental goal of the movement today is not particularistic. It serves the very survival of the human species.
>
> (Dalton and Kuechler 1990: 284)

Clearly, this is very far removed from the early environmental actions, at least in ambition and scale.

Organizational forms

The older conservation groups such as the National Trust were dominated by small numbers of individuals of high social status and did not represent the population as a whole. The organizations they created were similarly hierarchical and geared to exerting influence in the formal political system where legislative change can be made. Of course, these methods were very successful in many cases. However, concerns about the natural environment are not restricted to such small numbers of people and over the twentieth century they spread to many more social groups. Younger generations produced their own organizations, and by the 1970s these started to look and behave very differently from the earlier ones. In fact, many were little more than loose networks of people rather than formal organizations with membership lists and fees. Greenpeace began in Vancouver, Canada with a small group of peace activists, the 'Don't Make a Wave Committee', who planned to disrupt American nuclear testing in the Pacific Ocean. Since then, Greenpeace has become much more organized, bureaucratic and internationalized, partly to coordinate more elaborate direct actions. The organization has also adopted a more systematic use of scientific evidence and arguments in its campaigns. Some groups within the more recently created groups such as Earth First! have become increasingly anarchistic in avoiding formal organization, which they see as stultifying and not conducive to continuing with direct action. If we look at the environmental movement overall, then, it is very diverse in organizational terms but there does seem to be a cycle to its development. Many groups begin as loose networks; they attract supporters and grow, becoming more formal and organized in the process. This upsets and angers activists and splits occur, with the more radical groups breaking away, before the whole process begins again. In this way there does appear to be a cyclical, or perhaps more accurately a spiral-like, development to modern environmentalism (see Carmin 1999; Rootes 2003).

Campaigning methods

Since the 1980s in Australia, the radical environmentalists, the Nomadic Action Group (NAG), have been involved in a series of symbolic direct actions, a main feature of which is non-violence. Symbolic actions are those whose very design and intent are meant to convey a message to the rest of society. Greenpeace actions against whaling have been visually created as 'David versus Goliath' films in order to generate public interest and sympathy for the cause. The organization's small inflatables pitched against gigantic Soviet or Japanese whaling ships have been amongst the most vivid footage of environmental protest. The resonant symbolic imagery is of the plucky underdog battling against a heartless, commercially interested state machine.

Some of these actions have been very successful in terms of outcomes as well as in garnering sympathy and airtime. In 1983 a blockade campaign involving, amongst others, NAG, to stop a dam-building project on the Franklin River in southwest Tasmania raised awareness of the issue and ultimately led to abandonment of the

6.1 Greenpeace activists staging a symbolic direct action against Brazil's nuclear power programme in the capital, Brasilia, in 2004. Greenpeace now has offices and members across the world organized through Greenpeace International, based in Geneva. The organization continues to use symbolic direct action to raise awareness and build public support.

Source: Photo by Bruno Spada/ABr, Agencia Brasil, December 2004

project (Doyle 2000: 45–60). The group's blockades, including activists burying themselves up to the neck in mud or occupying trees on sites, are typical examples of radical environmental protest in the present period. Such tactics have also been seen in the UK (Doherty 2002). The new environmentalism emerged in the 1970s and '80s with small groups of activists campaigning against road-building, city traffic pollution and new motorways, leading to the formation of movement networks such as Reclaim the Streets and Critical Mass, again using blockades of streets, street parties and militant cyclist actions (Wall 1999). Although such activities attract public attention and make good copy for newspapers and television, the main work of environmental action (as in other social movements) is carried out in the relatively invisible network-building that goes on underneath these highly visible direct actions and makes them possible.

People

In the early years of the twenty-first century, many people now consider themselves to be part of the global environmental movement. Formal membership of environmental organizations runs to several millions across the world and supporters number many more than this. By 1990 the UK alone had an estimated 4.5 million formal members of environmental groups (8 per cent of the total population) and in the late 1980s, around 17 million people belonged to an environmental group in the USA (McCormick 1992: 137). We need to be careful about the numbers,

Table 6.3 *The 'new' environmentalism*

Organization	Date of formation
Friends of the Earth (USA)	1969
Greenpeace (USA/Canada)	1971
Chipko Andalan Movement (India)	1973
European Environmental Bureau	1974
Tasmanian Wilderness Society	1974
Green Belt Movement (Kenya)	1977
Earth First! (USA)	1980
Reclaim the Streets (UK)	1980s
Nomadic Action Group (Australia)	1980s
Citizens' Clearinghouse for Hazardous Wastes (USA)	1980s
Black Environmental Network (UK)	1988
Critical Mass (UK)	1992
Earth Liberation Front (UK)	1992

though, as there will be much overlapping membership amongst groups which is not picked up in these raw figures. The striking aspect of this enormous growth is that a large proportion of it is attributed to the support and membership amongst the middle classes rather than the working class. In particular, the new environmentalists seem to be closely linked to the new welfare and creative occupations that expanded after 1945 and this may account for some of the expansionary period of environmental activity. This is a conclusion drawn from numerous studies covering a range of environmental organizations and groups. Of course, large public demonstrations and formally 'environmental' protests do attract a diverse range of support from outside environmental groups. These larger demonstrations involve anti-nuclear, peace and anti-capitalist campaigners as well as many anarchists, socialists and feminists.

One other change you may already have noted is simply the language used in naming the groups, which has gradually moved away from words like 'national', or specific areas such as 'Lake District' and so on, towards the increasing use of 'international', 'World' and 'Earth'. The global reach of environmentalism is also worth pointing out.

Environmental politics is now not just a normal part of the post-industrial economies of the West, but is becoming important in developing countries too, where environmental protection is often linked to the land rights of indigenous people. Such a change is representative of the transformation of environmentalism into a global social movement that is helping to generate a wider global consciousness (chapter 9).

Although there is a clear contrast between old and new environmentalism, we should bear in mind that the movement as a whole has developed over quite a long period of more than 150 years. Contrasting the old and new allows us to collapse this timeframe in order to take some snapshots and see just how far the movement has travelled, but it does not mean that the old and new are entirely disconnected and disparate. The new forms have only been made possible by building on the gains already made and because new generations have reacted to problems left to them by their predecessors. The old and the new are both part of the long-term process of social change and development and we must take this long-term change seriously if we are properly to understand how environmental activity has been transformed.

An example that demonstrates the linkage between the old and the new can be found by examining what happened to the older groups once new environmentalism emerged in the UK in the 1970s. Not all the rising interest in defending the natural environment was attributable to the recently formed organizations and groups. Many of the much older established organizations have also seen their memberships continue to rise since the 1970s. Probably the most traditional and established UK environmental organization, the National Trust, witnessed a steady growth in membership over the entire twentieth century. By 1970 the Trust already had 226,000 members. But since then, during the period that the new environmentalism was developing, the Trust's membership has mushroomed, reaching some 3.4 million by 2005. Many other older, established or just less radically inclined environmental groups, including the Worldwide Fund for Nature and Royal Society for the Protection of Birds (RSPB), have also seen a period of rapid growth during the wave of 1970s new environmentalism. The RSPB alone had more than one million members in 2005. In fact, in terms of sheer numbers, the majority of people drawn into the wider environmental movement joined those organizations that pre-date the new environmentalism. The National Trust itself currently accounts for more than half of all environmental movement organization members in Britain.

What does all of this tell us about the new environmentalism? Well, perhaps it shows that the movement as a whole has benefited from the 1970s surge of support, and that the more recent organizations have moved off in new directions that the older ones simply were not capable of or inclined to pursue. But overall, the distinction between old and new organizations is not fixed. It is highly likely that people join, support and are active in more than one group. There is no reason why people should not join, say, the National Trust, but still send money to support the activities of Greenpeace and become active in Friends of the Earth's local campaigns. In other words, their commitment to the environmentalist cause may find numerous outlets. It is precisely because the environmental movement does have a long history that the resurgence of the 1970s was channelled just as much through existing organizations as through the newly formed ones.

In 1992 a different type of environmental group was being formed in the UK, calling itself the Earth Liberation Front (ELF). Disillusioned

Earth First! activists, who perceived EF! as becoming a home for 'campfire philosophers' and those more interested in self-realization than defending the natural environment, effectively broke away: a very typical instance of the factional splits that have regularly punctuated the movement. Using criminal acts to move the environmental agenda forward instead of relying on purely legal actions, the switch to guerrilla tactics emerged. An American version of the group emerged in 1996 (Leader and Probst 2003) and alongside the UK's Animal Liberation Front (ALF), such activism is estimated to have led to more than 600 acts of criminal damage. Adopting the anarchist principle of 'leaderless resistance', ELF has been involved in damage and arson attacks on construction sites, companies and research facilities that damage the environment or engage in animal experimentation. Though this type of environmental protest remains a very small minority on the outer fringes of the more reform-oriented mass environmental movement, it does show the lengths to which some committed activists, who see little real progress towards the defence of nature, may be prepared to go to defend it.

Environmental justice

One further development may prove to be important for the future of environmental politics, namely the emergence in the USA of grassroots 'environmental justice' networks (Szasz 1994; Bell 2004: esp. ch. 1; Faber 1998; Visgilio and Whitelaw 2003). This strand of citizens' environmental activity can be traced to Lois Gibbs's formative campaign in Niagara Falls, New York in 1978, seeking to relocate the Love Canal community, which she discovered had been built on a 20,000-ton toxic chemical dump. The community campaign was ultimately successful when 900 working-class families were relocated from the leaking dump in 1980 (Gibbs 2002). Environmental justice groups have focused on campaigning against the siting of toxic waste sites and incinerators in urban areas with high working-class and ethnic minority populations. Linking environmental quality to class inequalities shows that there may be more common interests than was previously believed between the mainstream environmental agenda and social class-based local activism. If so, then assumptions of the inevitable middle-class base of environmental organizations and protests may have to be revised. The concept of environmental justice shows that environmental issues and problems can be linked to working-class interests and has spread to other parts of the world. This is a different direction for environmentalism that begins to take account of social inequalities and real-world 'risk position'. In the USA, toxic waste sites have tended to be situated in black and Hispanic communities where citizen action groups are relatively less powerful, but Gibbs's campaign showed that they are not powerless. In the UK, the Black Environmental Network was founded at a 1988 Friends of the Earth and London Wildlife Trust conference.

Its focus is on persuading environmental organizations to include the environmental justice concerns of ethnic minority groups within their remit.

Environmental justice groups are potentially very significant. Their emergence has the potential to broaden the support base of environmental politics to currently underrepresented groups into the wider environmental movement, enabling it to throw off the charge that environmentalism is the preserve of the well-heeled middle classes. Friends of the Earth International (amongst others) has expanded its agenda, recognizing the need to tackle social problems if pressures on the natural environment are to be relieved (Rootes 2005). Environmental justice is concerned with some of the 'old' socialist issues of the material conditions of life and processes of social exclusion based on class, gender and ethnicity. Environmental justice movements also widen the existing definition of 'environment' from the one I have used in this book and which has motivated all previous environmentalists, namely the natural environment. Environmental justice takes us into the urban and inner-city environments, where most of the waste products of modern life end up, and this opens up environmental politics to people who may not have thought about their problems in such 'environmental' terms before. At the same time, environmental justice remains an issue about the relationship between human societies and the natural environment and in that sense it should become part of the mainstream of environmental concerns.

Probably the most significant consequence of environmental justice groups is that they offer the possibility of linking, in very direct ways, environmentalism in the relatively wealthy North with the environmentalism practised in the relatively poorer developing South. A recent example of Southern environmental justice activism was the protest against the operations of the multinational oil company, Shell, in Nigeria and its impact on the environment of the indigenous Ogoni people. The resistance campaign of the Movement for the Survival of the Ogoni People (formed in 1990) and the international support it garnered comprise just one example of the potentially unifying concept of environmental justice. Attempts by the Nigerian government to put down the resistance movement involved torture, ransacking of villages and, in 1995, the eventual execution of nine members of the movement's leadership, including the writer Ken Saro-Wiwa, in the face of international protest (Watts 1997). Such events reinforce the argument that the relatively powerless are made to bear the brunt of environmental pollution. Environmental justice campaigns demonstrate the potential for linking social inequalities and poverty to environmental issues, promising to make environmentalism more than just a nature-defence movement. Although many see this as a progressive development, the more difficult problems perhaps lie ahead when the defence of natural environments comes into conflict with the rights-claims of social groups to develop 'their' own land however they see fit. But that is something for the future.

Conclusion

The environmental movement has existed in one form or another since the middle of the nineteenth century. Many environmental groups and organizations have been created since then, and these are extremely diverse. Some are small networks of activists, others are large multinational formal organizations with huge budgets. Some campaign almost exclusively using direct action that targets polluters and other 'environmental offenders', bypassing conventional political lobbying channels. Others look to become more established and try to make their case using rational scientific arguments. What they all have in common, though, and therefore what allows us to talk about an 'environmental movement' in the first place, is a desire to defend and protect the natural environment against threats from socio-economic development, industrialization and urbanization.

It is important to remember that the uncommitted general public may only become aware of social movements when they are highly active, campaigning on key issues in very visible ways and attracting the attention of the mass media, which raises their profile still further. At other times there may well be little knowledge of particular groups and organizations. However, when an active phase of campaigning comes to an end and movement activists no longer make the news, it may then be widely perceived that the movement has ended or just lost its way. The social movements scholar Alberto Melucci (1989) tells us that these visible periods are usually not representative of the reality of social movement activity. What keeps movements alive beyond the spectacular set-piece demonstrations are the mundane, normal associations and communications that go on in the largely invisible world of everyday life. To understand environmental movements means that sociologists have to analyse this world as well as the protest actions. Just because the environmental movement fails to make the TV news for a time does not mean it has gone away. And if we consider the long history of the movement with its periodic 'booms' and 'slumps' in visibility and popularity, then there is ample evidence that Melucci is probably right.

One significant and relatively recent aspect of the environmental movement is the creation of distinctive Green political parties based on making the fate of the Earth central to political systems. Many of these parties see themselves and are perceived by others as part of the wider environmental movement, even though, as political parties, they have been forced to do more than cover issues emerging from within environmental organizations. Green parties have had to create foreign policies, employment policies, education policies and so on, that are all informed by their understanding of fundamental problems with the nature–society relationship. After all, the latter is what makes them Green. Whether they can be successful as Greens in all these other policy areas is taken up in the next chapter.

Readings

The literature on environmental movements is impossibly huge and my selections here are merely the tip of a very large iceberg. A good place to begin is with a global and general account such as John McCormick's *The Global Environmental Movement: Reclaiming Paradise* (1992), Brian Doherty's *Ideas and Action in the Green Movement* (2002) or Timothy Doyle's *Environmental Movements in Majority and Minority Worlds: A Global Perspective* (2004). These give overviews of the global development of environmentalism and Green political organizations. A useful collection of essays can also be found in Chris Rootes's (ed.) *Environmental Movements: Local, National and Global* (1999).

National case histories can be explored in Roger Gottleib's updated edition of *Forcing the Spring: The Transformation of the American Environmental Movement* (2005), Timothy Doyle's *Green Power: The Environment Movement in Australia* (2000) and my own *Explaining Environmentalism: In Search of a New Social Movement* (2000) for the British case.

For environmental justice groups, see D. Faber (ed.), *The Struggle for Ecological Democracy: Environmental Justice Movements in the United States* (1998). For an overview of environmental justice in developing countries see Carolyn Merchant's *Radical Ecology: The Search for a Liveable World* (1992). For recent campaigns against genetic modification, see D. A. Purdue, *Anti-genetiX: The Emergence of the Anti-GM Movement* (2000). And for anti-roads protests, see Derek Wall's *Earth First! and the Anti-Roads Movement: Radical Environmentalism and Comparative Social Movements* (1999). For a theoretical argument that environmentalism is at the centre of the New Social Movements, see Klaus Eder's 'The Rise of Counter-Culture Movements Against Modernity: Nature as a New Field of Class Struggle' (1990).

7 Politicizing the Environment

As we saw in the previous chapter, activity in defence of the natural environment is very varied and also has quite a long history, at least in some parts of the world. Organized conservation and preservation groups have undoubtedly had a measure of success in regulating the impact of modern societies on the natural environment, whilst environmental justice movements in developing countries have campaigned for the rights of indigenous people to the land. Since the 1970s what appears to many to be a new type of politics, a 'Green' politics, has also developed, which takes the nature–society relationship as its central concern. Green politics has a very broad scope; it involves a new political ideology and has led to the formation of Green political parties. Green politics is different from the mainstream of formal politics because it takes society's treatment of the natural environment as a key political issue rather than seeing nature as just a backdrop to the hard-nosed politics of competing social groups and classes. Once the natural environment becomes a political matter, other parties are then forced to come to terms with the Green agenda and to devise their own environmental policies. In short, the promise of Green politics is to introduce the condition of the natural environment into all areas of political decision-making in order to create societies that will be sustainable over the long-term. Nevertheless, as we will see in this chapter, this is no easy task, as the Greens are, like all political parties and movements, internally divided and sometimes fractious as they grapple with the difficult task of organizing to be able to compete for power.

A Politics of Nature

Today, every major political party's election manifesto contains a range of policies on the environment, while governments around the world have departments and ministers of the environment. A basic knowledge of key environmental problems such as climate change, nuclear waste disposal and the impact of house- and road-building programmes is a requirement for contemporary political debate. Many serious newspapers also have weekly environment sections and routinely report on environmental problems. But for long periods of time in the nineteenth and twentieth centuries, the political systems and parties of the industrialized world did not really seem to care too much about what happened to the natural environment. Instead, like most of their populations, they saw it as an obstacle to be overcome, controlled, dominated and managed in the interests of human beings (chapter 1). The formation of modern political ideologies in the wake of the eighteenth-century Enlightenment period and the French Revolution of 1789 produced the recognizably modern political spectrum stretching from left to right wing. Although the labels 'left' and 'right' have changed their meaning over time, the political left is conventionally associated with the representation of working-class interests, while the right is associated with the interests of business and commerce. This structuring of politics around the main class divide of industrial capitalist societies dominated the political decision-making process. In large measure, it still does. Matters of finance, wealth creation, economic growth, wealth distribution and employment are still central to contemporary political life.

Since the 1960s, though, inroads have been made into this basic structure by a range of 'new' social movements that have brought fresh issues, ideas and ideals into political life (chapter 6). Women's movements, civil rights movements, disabled people's movements and lesbian and gay movements have all had some successes in bringing their concerns and interests into the mainstream. Environmental movements have also brought issues of nature and environmental quality into political systems around the world. However, there are some differences between environmental politics and the other movements noted above.

First, the environment does not speak directly for itself, but needs humans to do so for it. Other social movements, being human-centred, can express their own interests. Secondly, most of the new social movements have challenged the view that their existing subordinate position in society is an inevitable consequence of their essential nature and thus cannot be altered. They argue, for example, that women are not essentially submissive, overly emotional and fit only for domestic life; that disabled people are not essentially incapable of working or playing a full part in society. These movements see essentialist arguments as supporting an unequal society and preventing change, when, in reality, the real problem lies not within the biological make-up of individuals but in the way that societies are structured. However, environmental politics is different. It actually makes recourse to the essential reality of the natural environment to inform its political strategy and gather support. Environmental politics looks to bring nature back into political discussions, not to rule it out. This is understandably worrying for other social movements that have spent so much time and energy trying to remove it!

From the standpoint of the politics of nature, all other social movements are engaged in promoting their own collective or group interests and all are **anthropocentric** or human-centred. But environmental politics potentially affects all social groups and therefore should involve a whole range of people. Since the 1970s, the creation of Green political parties has brought **ecocentric** ideas into contact with the anthropocentric mainstream and, although Green parties around the world have had some success, it is still difficult to gauge whether they will become permanent features of party political systems or fade away if existing parties are able to take Green ideas fully into their own programmes.

Some extravagant claims have been made for the significance of the politics of nature. In the mid-1980s when the new environmentalism seemed genuinely novel, the election manifesto of the UK Ecology Party (1983: 4) claimed that, 'Green politics is the single most significant international movement since the birth of socialism at the end of the 19th century'. Given the role that socialism, communism and labour parties have played in structuring political systems and societies across the world, this is quite a grand statement. The UK Green Party adopted the 'Blueprint for Survival' (1972) drawn up by the editors of the *Ecologist* magazine. This document stated: 'our Blueprint for survival heralds the formation of the movement for survival and, it is hoped, the dawn of a new age in which Man will learn to live with the rest of nature rather than against it' (Goldsmith et al. 1972: 10). This idea of the dawning of a new age has been common amongst some of the more spiritually inclined Greens. But is **Green politics** quite as significant as this interpretation suggests?

It has been argued by many Greens that their radical political position really is striking out in new directions and moving further away from the conventional, old, 'grey' political structure. One reason for this is that many Greens reject the left–right spectrum as an irrelevance to the politics of nature. Jonathan Porritt expresses the idea clearly in the following passage:

> The politics of the Industrial Age, left, right, and centre, is like a three-lane motorway, with different vehicles in different lanes, but all heading in the same direction. . . . It is our perception that the motorway of industrialism inevitably leads to the abyss – hence our decision to get off it, and seek an entirely different direction.   (1984: 43–4)

Note the assumption again here that the Industrial Age is drawing to a close and a 'new age' of **ecology** is dawning. If this is correct, then the left–right spectrum may well be losing its purchase on reality. For many Greens, nature politics is neither left nor right nor even centre, for that matter, but, as the slogan goes, 'out in front'.

One way of thinking this through is to take seriously the claim that since the 1970s a new political ideology has been born that has links to the mass reform environmental movement but is much more radical in its prescriptions for social change. This ideology is usually referred to as **ecologism**, which sounds a little strange but is really no different from social*ism* or femin*ism*. Political ideologies always present a diagnosis of society's current problems, a set of solutions to those problems and a strategy for getting from here to there. Ecologism does exactly this in relation to the society–nature relationship and the solving of environmental problems. So, ecologism says that there is a looming environmental crisis that needs to be solved and that doing so will need some quite radical changes to the social structuring of life. Greens of course have ideas on how this restructuring could be achieved. The emergence of such a 'political ecology' reflects the fact that the natural environment has become politicized to a much greater degree than in previous decades.

Ulrich Beck has made the point that environmental issues have become increasingly significant because nature has emerged as a political issue as awareness has grown that the hard and firm distinction between nature and society is being eroded. It is not that there is no real nature any more, but just that those things we previously thought of as 'natural' and therefore outside of human society are now coming to be seen as part of society itself. Take the **genetic modification** (GM) of crops. Scientists are now able to manipulate the genetic structure of natural species to make them more productive or resistant to disease. After being manipulated by people, are such crops and foods still a part of nature, or not? Certainly, environmental campaigns in Europe have targeted and destroyed GM crops as being 'unnatural' things that threaten to interfere with nearby 'natural' organic crops. But perhaps the right answer is that they are a bit of both. GM crops are part natural and part social. Anthony Giddens puts this a different way. He argues: 'Nature has become socialized. Today, among all the other endings, we may speak in a real sense of the end of nature – a way of referring to its thoroughgoing socialization' (1994: 77). The dividing line between the 'natural' and the 'social' has become increasingly blurred. The environmentalist writer Bill McKibben makes a similar point. He says that the effects of industrial production are now so strong that '[a] child born now will never know a natural summer, a natural autumn, winter or spring. Summer is going extinct, replaced by something else that will be called "summer"' (1990: 55). What he means by this is that the timing of the seasons is changing, as are the weather patterns that characterize them. Human societies are changing the cycles and processes of nature but, and this is an important point, they are not exerting *control* over them. These changes are unplanned, uncontrolled and for many people actually quite unsettling. Environmental issues are therefore one important source of that emerging 'risk society' that Beck identified in the late 1980s (chapter 5).

Risks, which might previously have been seen as 'natural', are now produced through human activities, and these are rapidly becoming political concerns. This has given environmentalism and Green politics a special place on the agenda, but at the same time it is beginning to displace labour movements and trade unions from the centre of politics. Workers who are tied to industrial production and rely on it for their livelihoods are not in a strong position to criticize the polluting consequences on the natural environment when their jobs are at stake. The more that the nature–society boundary is eroded and GM crops, animal cloning, human reproductive technologies and climate change become matters of social concern and political debate, the more likely it is that Green politics, or the 'politics of life', will move to the centre of modern politics. In this sense, Green politics is one sign of the emergence of a new concern with the dark side of industrialization and modernity, rather than its progressive, public face.

Ecologism: A New Political Ideology

Clearly, an ecocentric form of politics must, to some extent, break with the older humanistic basis of modern political ideologies. Some have even described ecocentric politics as 'anti-human' because of its focus on the natural environment rather than people. However, this does not necessarily follow if humans themselves are seen as part of nature anyway. It is also true that Green politics does not exist in a vacuum and has to make common cause with other parties and ideologies on shared issues of concern. For example, some have worked for an 'eco-socialism' or 'left-biocentrism' that connects environmental issues with a socialist analysis of the damage wrought by capitalist economic systems. Debates amongst the different parties always involve sharing policies and contesting the ground that others stand on, as it were. Luke Martell (1994) agrees that Green politics has introduced novel ideas and arguments, but that, in order to propose different ways of living, Greens are forced to draw on existing theories of social change and organization. In short, it is possible to envisage an ecocentric form of politics, but not quite so easy to see what an ecological society would look like.

Arguably, the most thorough argument in favour of ecologism as a new political ideology is in the work of Andrew Dobson (2000). This study is an important reference point for students of Green politics. Dobson begins with a simple observation: ecologism, a Green political ideology, is, like all ideologies, historically situated. It could not have existed in previous times. This is because the levels of scientific evidence which support the Green case have only become available since the 1970s. Without this evidence, Green ideas just would not be taken seriously, as not so long ago, of course, they weren't. In fact, in many previous periods, ideas of ecological catastrophe were seen as the province of eccentric scaremongers. To be taken seriously, Green ideas needed the legitimacy conferred by science, which holds a special place in modern life (chapter 2). For instance, scientific research into **global warming** has helped to legitimize the arguments of Greens and created a supportive cultural climate for the spread of an ecocentric ideology. Had this kind of evidence been unavailable, not only would Green politics still be seen as eccentric, but also much of it would have been literally unintelligible to a wider audience.

Dobson sees Rachel Carson's influential book, *Silent Spring* (1962), with its warning about the consequences of modern chemical pesticides on wildlife, as an important precursor to the emergence of ecologism, along with reports of the dangers of nuclear weapons testing, rising population levels and worries about the depletion of natural resources. But ecologism made greater inroads following the publication of a scientific report outlining the 'natural limits' to economic growth in 1974. This report forecast major social, economic and environmental problems in the twenty-first century if existing patterns of resource-use continued to waste fossil fuels and pollute the environment (chapter 8). Publication of the *Limits to Growth* report and the controversy it caused brought home to many more people the environmental damage being caused simply by the ordinary ways of life in modern societies. This was an important moment in the longstanding debate on whether there are absolute natural limits to economic expansion, as it provided new evidence from the latest technology – computer programmes – in support of the view that the capacities of the natural environment have set limits to human activity. The idea of natural limits has continued to take a central place in Green thinking since the 1974 report and has recently been restated by the Global Greens, a network of Green parties from across the world, who produced a statement of principles in their 2001 Canberra Charter (see box 7.1 on p. 123). These principles are:

- ecological wisdom;
- social justice;
- participatory democracy;
- non-violence;
- sustainability;
- respect for diversity.

Ecological wisdom means accepting the limits argument, that people are part of and limited by the natural world, and recognizing that indigenous peoples have a special knowledge gained from custodianship of the land. It also demands that if knowledge of the consequences of human interventions is not clear, then a precautionary approach should be adopted that puts the onus on developers to demonstrate that their plans will not cause harm. Ecological wisdom can also mean learning lessons about how societies should be organized by exploring the spontaneous organization within nature.

The Global Green Charter links environmental issues with the elimination of *poverty*, stating that, 'there is no social justice without environmental justice and no environmental justice without social justice'. This means tackling international inequalities as a priority and removing the debt burden on developing countries. This strand clearly recognizes the dominant international framework of **sustainable development** (chapter 8). Environmental issues and poverty may appear to be separate matters; after all, labour movements have pursued social justice for more than a century without necessarily linking this to environmental protection. However, Greens argue that unless and until developing countries can achieve a measure of economic development, they will not be in a position to prioritize environmental protection. The industrialized world will undoubtedly have to help with this task.

Participatory democracy entails encouraging citizens to become active rather than passive in society's decision-making processes and this involves devolving decision-making to the local level wherever possible. The Charter also advocates proportional representation (PR) in multi-party electoral systems as the most likely way of producing transparency and accountability. Local democracy is an important issue for Greens because it is the large scale of modern life that causes so many environmental problems. If the organization of social life is to be sustainable, then local democracy is an essential part of this reorganization.

The principle of *non-violence* has been part of the so-called 'new' social movements that have emerged since the 1960s. It is especially important for Green politics because of its historically strong links to peace and anti-nuclear movements. The Charter looks forward to a strengthened role for the United Nations in peacekeeping and conflict management and commits Green parties to a policy of general disarmament.

Sustainability is a key goal for Greens, and is dealt with in more detail in chapter 8. In essence, sustainability requires that human societies live within the limits of the natural environment. In the 1970s and '80s, Greens thought this would require immediate action to halt population growth and reduce the global human population. This was politically controversial, as the highest population growth rates were in the relatively poor, developing countries. The argument also took little account of the environmental damage being caused by mass consumerism in the Northern hemisphere. The 2001 Charter recognizes this, stating that creating sustainability means:

- stopping and reversing the global growth in consumption;
- stopping and reversing global population growth;
- stopping and reversing gross global material inequity.

The Greens' acceptance that population growth should be tackled by reducing levels of poverty, which should then lead to smaller family sizes, has brought them closer to the political left with its focus on social justice and inequality.

Respect for diversity acknowledges the emergence of multicultural societies and promotes a unity through social and ethnic diversity. This may look like a simple recognition of current social realities and, in that sense, no different from the response of other political parties. However, it is more likely that the promotion of social diversity is closely connected to the principle of 'ecological wisdom' outlined above. Some Greens have long argued that if diversity within ecosystems produces more stability and resilience to disruption than uniformity, then the same principle should hold in human society.

As is evident from this discussion, the radical ecological or Green analysis marks a shift away from the mainstream form of managerial reform environmentalism (chapter 6). The main issue for Greens today is to turn their diagnosis and aims into practical actions for change. So far, in the main, the latter have amounted to awareness-raising and educational campaigns. Of course, these are part of any attempt to move societies towards sustainability, but on their own they are not likely to succeed. Many people today *are* already more aware of environmental problems and they *are* better educated about how they have been generated, but it does not follow that people will automatically change their behaviour and actions. People are not entirely free to do as they please because their behaviour takes place within a social context which promotes or constrains their actions and rewards or punishes certain types of activity. Unless this context is also transformed, then those who are educated and environmentally aware of the issues are likely to continue with their environmentally damaging behaviour. It is also important to remember that the radical strand of eco-criticism remains a minority orientation within the much broader environmental movement and has never really been widely adopted by most environmental organizations. The one place we might expect to find ecologism thriving is within the Green political parties, which did set out to transform social life in an ecocentric direction. The next section explores Green political parties and their impact.

The Emergence of Green Parties

Charlene Spretnak and Fritjof Capra's (1984) influential book, *Green Politics*, saw the emergence of Green political parties as one aspect of a new way of looking at reality, produced right in the heartland of the industrialized Northern hemisphere. This new vision was based on seeing the planet in an interconnected and holistic way, which threw light on the unsustainable practices of industrial capitalism that were destroying natural ecosystems. Spretnak and Capra may have been rather optimistic about the pace and extent of this type of social change, but they did set the debate on Green politics into an admirably wide framework. The organizational outcome of this new vision was the formation of Green political parties.

National Green parties

Spretnak and Capra's description of Green party politics brings together many of the elements we have found within ecologism, namely: 'an ecological, holistic, and feminist movement' that 'transcends the old political framework of left versus right'. It also, 'emphasizes the inter-connectedness and inter-dependence of all phenomena' as well as 'the embedding of individuals and societies in the cyclical processes of nature'. Furthermore, Greens 'reject all forms of exploitation – of nature, individuals, social groups, and countries'. They are 'committed to non-violence' and they represent, 'the political manifestation of the cultural shift to the new paradigm (1984: xvi–xvii). As we see, this list puts a lot of pressure on Greens. It also asks them to succeed in political systems, most of which are very difficult for new parties to break into. Existing political systems have presented Green parties with some difficult decisions and in the process of making their choices, they have been forced to make compromises. Some of the opportunities and problems facing Green parties can be drawn out from a comparison of the UK and German Greens, with their very different histories.

Green parties are now part of political systems on every continent and there are regional and international federations and even a global Green organization. But this level of expansion came from very small beginnings. The first recognizable Green political party was the Values Party in New Zealand in 1972, which was formed, like many others, from local citizens' groups. The UK Green Party was the first European Green political party, beginning life as 'People' in 1973, a symbolic reference to the citizens' movements for strengthening local democracy. In 1975, People became the Ecology Party and, in 1985, the Green Party. Foregrounding its ecological concerns allowed the party to distance itself from mainstream environmental organizations and indicated that a more radical politics of nature was emerging. A very similar change in nomenclature took place after the Second World War, when use of the term 'conservation' was slowly overtaken by 'environmentalism' (Hays 1987). Changes of this kind partly reflect generational shifts within the wider nature defence movement. The change of name to the Green Party was made partly to fall into line with other European Green parties, but also to take advantage of the electoral success of the West German Green Party.

UK membership rose from 500 in 1978 to more than 5,000 by 1980, then, as the Green Party, reached a peak of 18,523 in 1990 before falling back to around 4,500 by 1993. The peak membership figure was largely as a result of the party's best electoral performance, achieving 15 per cent of the vote in the 1989 European election. This has been seen as, in part, a protest against the then unpopular Conservative government led by Margaret Thatcher. In the absence of proportional representation in the UK, no Green Party MEPs were elected, despite this excellent result. One year later, the UK Green Party was split when the Scottish Greens effectively broke away to form their own national party. In the 1999 European election, the now England and Wales Greens won 5.8 per cent of the vote and for the first time had two MEPs elected. Also in 1999, the Scottish Greens had one member elected to the newly independent Scottish Parliament and in 2003 bettered this with seven MSPs and 6.68 per cent of the vote. It is not a coincidence that the Greens' best results have been under systems of proportional representation, which provide better opportunities for small parties to succeed.

A major turning point for the UK Green Party came with the factional disputes after the 1989 European Election result, which eventually effectively split the party. The split centred around an 'electoralist' group called Green 2000, which sought to reorganize the party to make it a more effective electoral competitor. This would have meant changing the internal decision-making process and bringing the structure of the party closer to that of the mainstream parties. A second group, the decentralist or anarchist group, argued that electoral campaigns took attention away from grassroots campaigns and extra-parliamentary action and wasted valuable resources for little or no gain. For them, the party's main reason for existing was to campaign on Green issues and raise awareness, not to try to win elections in an unfavourable system. At the 1991 Conference, the Green 2000 grouping won a motion in favour of organizational change, but wrangling between the Executive and the Regional Council led to the resignation of six Executive members, including the well-known electoralist Sara Parkin. In a way, this split is typical of many Green parties, which seem to divide internally along realist electoralists ('realos') and grassroots decentralists ('fundis' or 'fundamentalist') lines (Doherty 1992). The dispute at the heart of this polarization is over what exactly Green parties are for. Are they there to try to win seats and elections or should they stay true to their decentralist roots and work to raise awareness and build grassroots support? The divide can be traced back to the origins of the Greens as a form of 'anti-political politics' (Havel 1988), which did not just introduce new ideas but also refused to adopt the hierarchical organizational form of the mainstream parties. For 'fundis', the idea of reshaping the Green Party in the image of the old 'grey' parties represented failure. For 'realos', it seemed the only way to make electoral progress.

The disagreements and ideological diversity within Green parties has been found to be rather more complicated than just 'realos' versus 'fundis', however. In a 1995 survey of UK party members, Lynn Bennie et al. (1995) found four major groupings within the spectrum of ecologism. One of these was mainly opposed to the Conservative government on the grounds of its extremely poor environmental record, but the other three more significant strands were:

1   *Left-anarchism*, which argues for social justice, party decentralization and non-violent direct action. There seemed to be no centralist and reformist eco-socialist group within the England and Wales Greens. This was unlike the position in, say, the German party, Die Grünen, or Belgium's Green parties, Agalev and Ecolo. Therefore, the possibility of building alliances and political coalitions is much reduced in the UK, though the lack of a proportionally representative system goes some way towards explaining this.

2   *Deep Ecology* or 'biocentrism', which concentrates on individual responsibility for environmental protection. This strand of thought comes close to some American 'New Age' thinking, with its emphasis on personal lifestyles rather than using the state to bring about

social change. Deep ecologists seek to transform the culture of societies and do not restrict their activities to the formal political system.

3 *Electoralists*, who continue to fight for a more 'realistic' electorally based strategy, a stronger organizational structure and a single party leader. Electoralists believe that such changes would promote more media coverage and hence further raise the profile of the party, leading to membership growth.

Bennie's study also showed that the UK Green Party attracted a high proportion of ecocentrics compared to most environmental groups and organizations. One way to assess this is to ask people some clear, ecocentric questions. For instance, around 95 per cent agreed with the statement: 'Plants, animals, streams and mountains, the earth as a whole, have intrinsic value independent of their appreciation by humans.' Agreement with this statement is seen as demonstrating a commitment to ecocentrism. We can see therefore that the main problem facing electoralists in the Green Party is that many other members are solidly opposed to any involvement in the institutional structures of the existing 'grey', lifeless politics, which they fear would mean the assimilation of the Green Party into formal politics with the inevitable loss of its radical edge. Instead, they see the party as a means by which to promote Green values and ideas, not as a serious electoral competitor. All of this means that we cannot really assess the Green Party's achievements in the same way as we can other political parties. There is no point chastising the party for its lack of parliamentary seats or low number of votes if it is not serious about electoral competition. We have to remember, though, that not all national Green parties avoid conventional political activity and some have been quite successful electorally.

In the UK, links between the Green Party and reform environmental organizations are not strong. There are no messages of formal support for the party at election time and the relatively small percentage of votes for the Greens in national elections shows that there is no simple commonality of interest between Greens and the mass environmental movement. Rather than being mutually supportive, Greens and environmentalists have existed quite separately and the Green Party cannot rely on the votes of millions of committed environmentalists. This reinforces the point made earlier, that environmentalists propose practical measures for nature conservation, whilst radicals advocate significant social change. These two things are not easily reconciled into a single strategy for dealing with environmental problems. Rüdig and Lowe's (1986) early research into Green Party membership found that a majority of members had no previous involvement in environmental organizations, while McCormick found that '[t]here is much evidence that many environmentalists have shunned the Greens, and certainly there have been few formal or informal links between the party and the environmental lobby' (1991: 123).

To summarize our findings so far. The UK Greens have had a chequered history with some successes and many failures, but they are still around and their prospects are probably as good or better today than at almost any other time. However, this is not necessarily because they have won all the arguments or changed people's attitudes towards the environment, though they have been partly successful in achieving this. Rather, it is because the UK electoral system may be changing in their favour. In Scotland there is now a Parliament and in Wales an elected Assembly. Plans are also afoot to introduce regional assemblies in England. If these do come into being and do use PR for their elections, then the Green parties may start to make electoral headway and that will put pressure on the organizations to change in order to take full advantage of the new opportunities. The balance between electoralists and decentralists in the party may well change in such circumstances in the same way that the Scottish Greens organized to exploit the newly devolved situation.

By way of contrast, consider the electorally successful German Greens. The German system mixes first-past-the-post (FPTP) and PR elements, which enables the larger parties to win constituency seats under FPTP, but also allows smaller parties to make breakthroughs based on their percentage of the vote. This is possible under PR, as a party's national share of the vote is considered, provided that they cross a 5 per cent threshold. The system consists of a national parliament, the Bundestag, and a federal council, the Bundesrat, consisting of representatives from 16 federal states or *Länder*. The environmental movement grew steadily during the mid-/late 1970s, winning seats in the *Land* parliaments, the Landtag. Die Grünen (the Green Party) was formed in the then West Germany in 1980 and in 1983 the party made a breakthrough, winning 27 seats in the Bundestag with 5.6 per cent of the vote. In 1987, it won 8.7 per cent and took 44 seats. Unlike the UK Greens, therefore, the German party had significant electoral success very early in its history. This early success also proved to be a big incentive and motivation for other European Green parties. The German Greens had grown largely from the combination of local citizens' associations and the anti-nuclear 'new social movement', and its early successes at the local and regional levels provided the stimulus for the Greens' national electoral efforts. The party promoted an anti-economic growth agenda and adopted a strongly anti-nuclear stance as well as demanding withdrawal from NATO. The slogan, 'act locally, think globally' is therefore quite an accurate reflection of the roots of Green parties and their participatory democratic approach to citizenship.

However, following German reunification, in 1990 the West German Greens polled just 4.8 per cent, narrowly missing the 5 per cent threshold, but the new East German party, 'Alliance '90', did better, with 6.1 per cent and 8 seats. In the first all-German election in 1994, the newly merged party, Bündnis 90/Die Grünen, was back on track with 7.4 per cent of the vote and 48 seats and although they polled a reduced 6.7 per cent in 1998, this still gave the party 47 seats. In 2002 the party received 8.6 per cent and 55 seats in the Bundestag, and in 2005 its share of the vote was 8.3 per cent, which gave it 51 seats. This series of good results and continuous parliamentary representation has given the German Greens a presence that the UK Greens have never achieved.

Therefore, from its very early days the German Green Party has been an electorally focused party that has tried to win seats and elections, unlike its UK counterpart. Its 1983 success in crossing the 5 per cent threshold was significant because it brought with it additional state finance and a much higher profile. And although the 'realo'/ 'fundi' division also exists within the German Greens, many 'fundis' left after the 1990 election loss, leaving electoralists firmly in control. This situation is, of course, a mirror image of what happened in the case of the England and Wales Greens. The electoral wing also has good evidence that genuine competition in elections is worthwhile and positive for pursuing a Green agenda and raising awareness. Not least, this is because from 1998 to 2005, the Greens have been part of the governing coalition with the Social Democratic Party of Germany (SPD). Nevertheless, electoral successes and government in the 'red–green coalitions' have proved very difficult for many Greens to live with.

Once Green parties enter political systems, there are pressures on them to conform to existing organizational models and to compromise on their radical policies. The symbolic resignation of socialist and Green activist Rudolf Bahro in 1985 was seen by some as evidence of the incorporation of the party into the political establishment. Bahro thought the party's justification of continued animal experimentation, in particular, gave away its reformist rather than radical character. Since its success in 1998, Bündnis 90/Die Grünen has been forced to negotiate and compromise and has effectively dropped some of its 'ecocentric' demands in the context of the inevitable pressures of governing. The Greens' non-violence position was severely tested when the issue arose of German troops' participation in NATO actions in Kosovo. And in 2001, following the 9/11 terrorist attacks on American targets, German military support for the USA's attack on bases in Afghanistan led to some Green MPs refusing to back the SPD Chancellor. Similar issues of conscience and party direction have occurred around the pace of decommissioning **nuclear power** plants and vivisection. The party has lost members as a result.

What can we learn from this comparison of an electorally unsuccessful Green party and one that has made it into government? First, Green politics is not uniform. Parties around the world have very different experiences and these have been shaped by the national situations they find themselves in. The England and Wales Greens seem to have stuck more closely to Green principles but, of course, they have never been able to test these from a position of power. The German Greens have often found compromise and negotiation difficult, but have been able to exert some influence on environmental as well as the whole range of government policy. To do so, the party has had to become more like the mainstream parties and, for instance, elect a party leader. This issue has long divided the England and Wales Greens. We might say that Greens change societies, but societies also change the Greens. Secondly, the relationship between Green parties and the wider environmental movement is, perhaps surprisingly, not necessarily mutually support-ive. Nature conservationists and environmentalists cannot automati-cally be assumed to share the radical principles of Green party members. We have to remember that the essentially middle-class base of environmental organizations will support 'post-material' but not 'anti-material' policies. Ronald Inglehart propounded the idea of a post-1945 shift towards post-material values during the 1970s (see Inglehart 1977). Post-materialism suggests that, as Western societies became wealthier after the 1950s economic boom, younger genera-tions were socialized into a new set of values in a 'post-scarcity' econ-omy, where thrift and saving were becoming less central as increasing affluence and basic security came to be largely taken for granted. With a more comfortable level of material well-being and a movement towards service-based 'middle-class' employment, many people saw quality of life issues as increasingly important and many of them became part of the environmental movement. This could be one reason why environmentalists do not routinely support radical Green ideas of simple living, voluntary simplicity and reductions in consump-tion. Environmentalists may well support environmental reforms, but may not be keen on revolutionary changes in lifestyles, however gradu-ally they come about.

International and global Green politics

Although, like all other political parties, Green parties are nationally based, they now exist in regional blocs and there are occasional gath-erings of global Greens (see box 7.1). Federations of Green parties exist on every continent. The European Federation of Green Parties consists of 33 national parties, including those in Austria, Belgium, Bulgaria, Cyprus, Denmark, Estonia, Finland, Germany, Hungary, Italy, The Netherlands, Portugal, Russia, Switzerland, Ukraine and the UK. The Asia-Pacific Green Network was founded in 2005 with 13 member parties, including Australia, Japan, Korea, Mongolia, New Zealand, Nepal, Pakistan, Sri Lanka and Taiwan. The Federation of Green Parties of the Americas has 9 national members, including parties from Brazil, Canada, Colombia, Mexico and the United States. The Federation of Green Parties of Africa has 15 member parties, including those in Burkina Faso, Cameroon, Guinea, Kenya, Morocco, Nigeria and South Africa. But what do Greens do at these organiza-tional levels?

Box 7.1

Coordination of Green Party activity at the global level can be traced back to 1990 with the first 'Planetary Meeting' held in Rio de Janeiro in 1992 to coincide with the United Nations Earth Summit being held there. However, the crucial 'global gathering' took place in 2001 when the Charter of the Global Greens was agreed.

The Charter (Global Greens 2001: 2) makes a call for 'fundamental changes in people's attitudes, values and ways of producing and living' in order to achieve a sustainable relationship between human societies and the Earth. Whilst we will have to wait to see what impact global statements of this kind will have, Green politics has moved remarkably quickly through the local, national, regional, international and global levels of coordination, and attempts to connect all of these in a comprehensive way. In this sense, at least in discursive and organizational terms, it is fulfilling some of those extravagant claims we introduced earlier and has taken advantage of the increasingly globalizing communications systems of the modern world.

7.1 In 2001, 800 delegates from Green parties in 70 countries met in Canberra, Australia to agree a Charter of principles and policies for Greens to adopt. Such a move may show that disagreements between Southern and Northern environmentalists need not be a barrier for the global Green movement.

Source: 2001 Global Greens Conference: <www.global.greens.org.au>

The European Federation has existed to promote international communication between parties and coordinate the production of election manifestos for elections to the European Parliament. However, the Federation has lost some of these functions since the formation of the European Green Party in 2004. The European Party effectively organizes 32 national parties, though, given the wrangling and disputes about the future direction of the European Union both outside and within the Green 'family' of parties, this is no easy task. On the other hand, organization at the European level may allow a stronger Green voice to be heard on international issues. An early example was the 2005 common statement on climate change, which focused on the issue of international social justice, making the point that the industrialized countries must bear prime responsibility for global warming and should therefore be prepared to work with developing countries on their energy production needs and responsibilities. Statements from 32 Green parties from across the European Community are likely to carry more weight than those from 32 diverse and sometimes discordant national parties.

Clearly, it is much too early to draw any firm conclusions about whether such supranational bodies can be effective in transforming Green politics in the long term. But at this stage it is still possible to see some of the potential difficulties arising from the very different national histories and international relations between Greens. One specific instance of this is again the tension between the industrialized and developing countries. In 1998 the Federations of Africa and The Americas signed a joint protocol which began with the statement: 'Both federations made a commitment to work together against the global environmental destruction, *caused by the industrialized countries*.' Article 3 also stated: 'Both federations compromised to fight together against the utilization of the poor countries as deposits of toxic waste and dangerous substances, *that come from the industrialized countries*' (my emphasis). This Accord, together with the European Greens' stance on international social justice, shows us how significant is the problem of reaching agreements in a global system so riven with gross inequalities (chapter 9). But at least the Green parties of the world have made a start by recognizing the key issues and openly airing them. And in this, perhaps they will be able to make a contribution to shaping the future of **globalization**.

Conclusion

The politicizing of the relationship between human societies and the natural environment continues to raise serious issues. However, Green political parties are not always the main source of this questioning. In some countries, Green parties have been involved in government coalitions and in many others they remain small parties of apparently permanent opposition. One factor that partly explains this is the fact that when new ideas are introduced into existing political systems the mainstream parties are forced to take account of them, and this usually means incorporating at least some new ideas into their own programmes. When they do this, the mainstreaming of new ideas can then defuse the challenge of the newcomers and, in the process, reduce their support base. Why vote for untried and inexperienced Green parties when the experienced parties and politicians have environmental policies too?

Although there is some evidence that this has happened with some Green parties, a number of sociologists have arrived at the conclusion that there is something peculiarly resistant within Green politics that resists assimilation into the programmes of the mainstream parties. This 'something' is precisely the ecocentric orientation to politics and political decision-making which marks the Greens out as different in the first place. Even though many politicians from other parties might well want to solve environmental problems and mitigate the worst effects of industrial activity on the natural world, they will do this with the direct benefits for human beings in mind. Only within Green political thought is the natural environment protected for its own sake, based on the idea that nature has value in and of itself. This is an important point, because it means that should Green politics give up its ecocentric basis in order to gain wider support, this may well be at the expense of its originality. Without originality, there would be little point in Green political parties. This probably explains in large measure why the disputes between 'realos' and 'fundis' within the Greens have at times been so acrimonious. Compromising with the anthropocentric, grey political system always runs the risk of diluting the Green parties' original message about the natural limits to human activity and there-fore threatens their very reason for existing.

The problem for Green parties, though, is that a majority of the general public does not seem to be ecocentric, and if we wait for the Greens to convert enough of them to be able to make a difference, the environmental problems we currently face may well be beyond repair. Is there really any alternative to working within existing political systems and making compromises with mainstream parties? This dilemma is a thread that runs through the politics of nature and cannot easily be resolved. However, before we give up on Green politics, there is one dominant framework or set of ideas and practices which attempts to combine environmentalism and Green politics within an international social justice agenda. This is the political project of achieving global sustainable development and it is the subject of the next chapter.

Readings

A good place to start coming to terms with Green politics remains with Jonathan Porritt's *Seeing Green: The Politics of Ecology Explained* (1984), which is a clear, accessible introduction. Bill McKibben's *The End of Nature* (1990) is a well-constructed argument covering the 'socializa-tion of nature' and Peter Hay's *Main Currents in Western Environmental Thought* (2002) provides a good overview of the diverse strands of Green and environmentalist ideas.

The origins of Green political parties are explored in Ferdinand Müller-Rommel's *New Politics in Western Europe: The Rise and Success of Green Parties and Alternative Lists* (1989) and Charlene Spretnak and Fritjof Capra's *Green Politics: The Global Promise* (1984). Updated infor-mation can then be found in Neil Carter's comprehensive *The Politics of the Environment: Ideas, Activism, Policy* (2001) or Dick Richardson and Chris Rootes's (eds), *The Green Challenge: The Development of Green Parties in Europe* (1994). The impact of Green parties on UK main-stream politics is examined in Michael Robinson's *The Greening of British Party Politics* (1992). The Global Greens Charter of 2001 can be downloaded from: <www.global.greens.org.au/charter.htm>.

On Green political theory and ideology, the best source remains Andrew Dobson's *Green Political Thought: An Introduction* (4th edn, 2006), though Robyn Eckersley's *Environmentalism and Political Theory: Toward an Ecocentric Approach* (1997) is also worth trying.

8 Sustaining the Environment

Green politics has become established in many political systems around the world but remains a minority orientation at present and has not yet gathered sufficient force to break up longstanding political structures. Nevertheless, Green parties have confounded their critics by showing that they represent more than the short-term fad that some commentators had forecast. While the previous chapter focused on Green ideology, party organization and political platforms, this chapter explores in more detail one central idea of the Greens, namely the concept of **sustainable development**. Sustainable development has become the dominant way of talking about and planning for an improved relationship between societies and the natural environment and, unlike Green politics, it has been taken up by businesses, local authorities, national governments and international bodies such as the United Nations. It also has quite a wide currency amongst ordinary members of society. Everyone who recycles their plastic, paper and glass, conserves water, tries to use their car less frequently or composts their garden waste will probably be aware that they are attempting to put into practice the idea of sustainability. But herein lies the potential problem: sustainable development may be in danger of losing focus, of becoming impossibly broad and promising all things to all people. Still, as we will see in chapter 9, in an age of globalization, sustainable development does represent a concerted attempt to find ways of combining the diverse interests of the relatively rich and relatively poor countries of the world in order to reduce the human 'footprint' on the natural environment. However difficult this may be, it does partly explain why sustainable development has attracted such a wide and receptive audience.

The Idea of Sustainable Development

While governments around the world have become involved in the conservation of natural resources at various times in modern history, most of this involvement has been for specific uses, such as forestry management to establish reserves of timber to be used in construction. Once the environmental movement became a mass social movement of many millions of people, it was no longer possible to see environmental protection as an optional addition to mainstream politics. Instead, environmental issues were being rapidly mainstreamed in society alongside problems of poverty in a global context, which particularly affects the fate of people in developing countries. Set-piece global music events that raise money for famine relief and aid or push for the writing-off of debt in developing countries have attracted huge television audiences across the world. Events such as Live Aid in 1985 and Live 8 in 2005 are just the visible tip of a growing concern with global inequalities and environmental problems. Also, because many of the environmental issues of recent times have a strongly international or global dimension, particularly in their consequences and impacts, international political cooperation has come to be seen as vital if they are to be effectively tackled. It has also become clearer that global environmental problems will not be readily solved in the short or medium term. They are very long-term problems of population growth and of human adaptation to the natural environment.

Environmental issues therefore raise the question of time in human–environment relations (Adam 1996). Finding ways of dealing with global environmental problems will, in all likelihood, take the concerted efforts of many generations of people, most of whom are not yet alive. We cannot know whether future generations will be able or even want to tackle them. Conversely, most people alive today will be long gone before the environmental collapse predicted by some Green catastrophists actually comes about. Why should they be prepared to reduce their own material standards of living for a cause that will not affect them personally? There is no quick fix when the global environment has been damaged and needs long periods to recover. One way to think about environmental problems, then, is to view them as issues of inter-generational equity. People alive today have children, grandchildren and other young relatives. Do they really want to leave them with a deteriorating natural environment and a worse situation than their parents and grandparents left for them? What would their children and grandchildren think of them should they do that? Should they ignore the unremitting poverty and early death faced by many people in developing countries? Would that be fair or just? Environmental issues raise serious questions of an ethical kind about the relevant timeframe involved within interdependent human relationships.

Questions relating to time in environmental issues are also concerned with the issue of long-term social and natural sustainability. Sustainability means developing ways of life in human societies that are less destructive to the natural environment, that will allow human beings and the natural environment on which they depend to survive long into the future. As we have already seen, many environmental campaigners have argued that the industrial way of life is simply *not* sustainable over the long term because it threatens to use up natural resources too quickly for them to be replenished and because the waste and pollution of industrial production methods damage and inhibit nature's capacity for renewal. Edward Goldsmith and his colleagues at the *Ecologist* magazine put this argument starkly in their 'Blueprint for

Survival' (1972: 15): 'The principal defect of the industrial way of life with its ethos of expansion is that it is not sustainable. . . . [W]e can be certain . . . that sooner or later it will end.' Clearly, if you believe that industrial societies have no long-term future, it makes no sense to wait for them to collapse and this is why some Greens want to see a planned de-industrialization of societies. What follows de-industrialization should be smaller forms of social organization in which people will, as the saying goes, 'tread lightly on the Earth' and thereby leave a less obvious ecological footprint. Of course, this is an extremely difficult outcome to achieve with the 6.5 billion people currently populating the planet, let alone the 8 billion that are forecast by 2030. It becomes even more difficult when we factor in the very different lifestyles and economic situations of those people, especially in the high-consumption societies of the industrialized Northern hemisphere, which take so much, so quickly, from the Earth.

As if these problems were not enough, there is also one more (don't despair just yet!). The difficulty of achieving sustainability is compounded by international social inequalities and large-scale, debilitating, absolute poverty in some areas of many developing countries, particularly in parts of Africa. For the relatively wealthy industrialized countries of the North, tackling environmental problems may mean a reduction in economic development and the material *quantity* of life, which many of them may not be prepared to countenance. Encouraging them to accept that quality not quantity is the route to happiness and fulfilment will not be an easy task in an age of mass consumerism. However, for the relatively poor countries of the Southern hemisphere, environmental problems look very different indeed. For instance, water is considered a basic human need; in the affluent North it is literally 'on tap' for a variety of uses. But UNESCO says that 2.2 million people in developing countries died in 2000 from water-borne diseases and drought, whilst the charity WaterAid estimates that 1 billion people do not have access to a safe water supply. These countries want and desperately need more economic development in the form of industrialization, higher levels of production and more international trade if they are to get enough food to stave off shortages and generate improvements in the quality of life for hundreds of millions of people. Their need for development is so urgent that it usually, and you may think quite properly, outweighs the desire for environmental protection and conservation. In the past, this has sometimes brought the environmentalists of the South into dispute with environmentalists in the North over the setting of priorities. It also means that international agreements can be extremely difficult to achieve and sustain.

For a time it really seemed to be a choice between *either* environmental protection *or* economic development. During the 1960s and '70s a whole series of books and articles with titles such as *The Population Bomb* (Ehrlich 1968) or *Too Many* (Borgstrom 1969) informed us that the rates of population growth in the developing world simply could not be sustained. Soils would be rendered infertile, food production would fall and famines and mass starvation were the inevitable consequence. There have certainly been some terrible famines since that time, though these have not been on the scale of the doomsayers' forecasts. Nonetheless, the catastrophists were right about one thing: maintaining historically high levels of global human population without causing irretrievable damage to the natural environment and reducing levels of absolute poverty is proving an extremely difficult problem to solve.

Since the late twentieth century, there has been a much more organized and concerted attempt to bring together North and South through the central concept of sustainable development. This pithy concept is deceptively simple. It tries to combine sustainability (of the natural environment or planetary **ecosystem**) with development (of the economies and societies of the developing countries). Because of this, sustainable development has become the rallying point for all of those who seek to protect the environment and to 'make poverty history' (to quote a catchphrase used in a recent anti-poverty campaign). The British environmental campaigner and former Director of Friends of the Earth, Jonathon Porritt gave a succinct statement of what sustainable development means which remains one of the clearest: 'Green economics is all about *sustainability* and *social justice*: finding and sustaining such means of creating wealth as will allow us to meet the genuine needs of all people without damaging our fragile biosphere' (1984: 126; italics in the original). It sounds so simple when put like that. But as you have probably worked out by now, these two things are not quite as easily reconciled as Porritt's optimistic statement might suggest.

The concept of sustainable development is also remarkably broad and open to conflicting interpretations. Exactly what are those 'genuine needs' Porritt speaks of, for example? What do you *really* need and how would you distinguish these from the things you just want? It has been suggested that there are actually very few real human needs: food, water and shelter, for example. But is this true? What about the very human needs for friendship, emotional support or a sense of belonging? In the 1960s Herbert Marcuse (1898–1979) tried to establish the difference between what he called 'real' and 'false' needs. Real needs were those that arose from human sociability (basically all of those above). False needs were those promoted by the capitalist mass consumer society through advertising and marketing. Once people (literally) bought into these false needs, they became locked into a 'one-dimensional' world which reduced their freedom and stunted their capacity for critical thought. The problem with all such 'needs-based' theories, though, is that they fail to take proper account of the inevitable social creation (or social construction) of human needs. Earlier societies did not discover and use electricity, so it could not be a 'need' for them. But could modern societies exist without electricity? Clearly not, or they would no longer be 'modern' in any real sense. Electricity has become a 'need' for people in particular types of society. Rather than denying this and trying to establish a set of universal *absolute* needs, perhaps a better idea would be to try to balance the *relative* needs of people with their societies at their level of social development. This, indeed, is exactly what sustainable development advocates aim to achieve.

Although the principle seems sound, the actual practices of sustainable development provoke heated disagreements. Despite this, it currently has the highest profile of any set of ideas aiming at the international coordination of environmental and development policies. It has also become part of the normal language of business, national and local government, public agencies and non-governmental actors. It is easy to see why. The combination of environmental sustainability and economic development makes the concept uniquely inclusive. Sustainable development does not pit workers against businesses or environmentalists against governments. Instead, it demands that they all work together to eliminate global poverty and protect the natural environment. Sustainable development is a project to which every one of us is invited to make a contribution.

Now, this remarkable inclusivity is not necessarily a problem in itself, but many sociologists and social scientists believe that it fails to acknowledge some pretty fundamental conflicts of interest which cannot be glossed over or wished away. There is also the nagging feeling that education campaigns and moral argument may not be enough to change the actual behaviour of individuals, corporations and governments. Can a consensus-seeking approach ever be enough, or will it be necessary to challenge some vested interests? If the latter, then which organizations (and perhaps governments) should or will be able to mount such a challenge? To be in a position to arrive at your own evaluation of the sustainable development programme, a brief tour of the history and main themes of the concept is now necessary.

A Brief History of Sustainable Development

One of the fundamental assumptions of modern societies is that economic growth is 'a good thing'. If the economy is growing, then people's standard of living increases and we all become wealthier. Surely that must be good? Through taxation of that increasing wealth, social and health services can then be improved, the public infrastructure can be expanded and the benefits of modern life can be spread to materially poorer groups of people. A steadily increasing Gross Domestic Product (GDP) has long been thought to be the key to a better life, as wealth and prosperity trickle down society's social ladder. Who could be against economic growth? As we saw in chapter 7, however, many radical Greens are against it. They want to question the underlying assumption that living 'a good life' and continuously increasing material standards of living are necessarily one and the same thing. They want to encourage reflection on how we can improve our quality of life and what that would mean in practice. There are some similarities here with the idea of the treadmill of production and consumption (chapter 4). Are we really better off running on the treadmill, rushing to work, working long hours, becoming stressed and getting caught up in the endless status competition of consumerism? Does quantity equal quality? Greens suggest that one key element of the quality of life is the state of the natural environment, so it makes good sense to protect it, even if this means a diminishing quantity of material goods and fewer monetary rewards. Historically, this is not the first time such questions have been posed.

Professor of Political Economy and Modern History, the Reverend Thomas Robert Malthus (1766–1834) worried about the consequences of population growth during the Industrial Revolution in England, which threatened to outstrip the capacity of society to produce enough food to sustain it. He thought the inevitable result would be food shortages and potential disaster. This concern has never really gone away and, statistically, there is a good reason why not. The Italian demographer Massimo Livi-Bacci (1992: 31) estimates that in 10,000 BCE the global population was around 6 million and by the year 0 had risen to 252 million. At the start of the Industrial Revolution in 1750, the global population was around 771 million and by 1990 it had reached 5,292 million. In summary, it took the entire period of human evolution up to the year 1800, more than 100,000 years, for the human population to reach one billion, but just 200 years since 1800 to approach 6 billion – and it is still rising. The potential problem here lies not simply in sheer numbers, but in the 'doubling time' of the population. Livi-Bacci says that in the year 0, the time it would take for the population to double was 1,854 years. By 1750 it was 1,083 years and in 1970 it had fallen to just 116 years. In 1990 the doubling time was a mere 38 years. What level of human population can the planet support? What level of population can the present forms of social organization provide for? There are no easy answers to such questions. After all, Malthus was forecasting possible disaster before the human population had even reached one billion, yet the total collapse of human societies has patently not occurred.

Long before the catastrophist environmentalist writings of the 1970s, some economic theorists had worked on quite radical ideas of a 'steady state' economy that would maintain tolerable levels of production and consumption without the constant quest for expansion. The British utilitarian philosopher John Stuart Mill (1806–73) was one such thinker. Mill saw that human well-being was connected to the condition of the environment and in *Principles of Political Economy* (1848) he bemoaned a future world which had:

every flowery waste or natural pasture ploughed up, all quadrupeds or birds which are not domesticated for man's use exterminated as his rivals for food, every hedgerow or superfluous tree rooted out, and scarcely a place left where a wild shrub or flower could grow without being eradicated as a weed in the name of improved agriculture.

(Cited in Wall 1994: 121)

As we saw in chapter 6, it was sentiments of this kind that motivated the early environmentalists to create the first formal conservation organizations. Mill asked people to consider the benefits of a stationary economy and population: less pressure to work long hours, less stressful lives, more time to become educated or learn new skills. Instead, people could pursue the 'art of good living' rather than becoming slaves to the industrial capitalist machine. Thinking back to chapter 6, you may be noting some parallels between Mill's ideas and those of today's advocates of simple living close to the land. I think you would be right, because although such views failed to alter the direction of nineteenth-century social change, they were back in fashion in the 1970s when environmentalists asked themselves the same question: where are we heading? In the 1970s, though, there was much more evidence of environmental damage and scientific respectability had been added to Mill's moral arguments, not least through research findings from the environmental sciences.

Sustainable development is heavily dependent on an educational approach in which rational, reasonable people can be persuaded to participate in environmental and development initiatives. One influential modelling study stands out in this respect. A team of scientists in the USA led by Donella Meadows was commissioned by a global think-tank, the Club of Rome, to investigate future scenarios linking social changes to natural resource levels and the Earth's carrying capacity. The report was published as *Limits to Growth* in 1974. Its core message was that economic growth could not continue indefinitely because there will always be natural limits to curb it. If the world's societies failed to change, then growth would end anyway through the depletion of resources, food shortages or industrial collapse, sometime before 2100. The research team used computer modelling to explore five global trends:

* accelerating industrialization across the world;
* rapid population growth;
* widespread malnutrition in some regions;
* depletion of non-renewable resources; and
* a deteriorating natural environment. (Meadows et al. 1974: 21)

The programme was then run to test out 12 scenarios, each one manipulated to resolve some of the problems of the previous ones. This process allowed the group to pose questions about what combinations of human population levels, industrial output and natural resources would be sustainable in the long term. The conclusion they drew in

1974 was that there *was* still time to do something about the looming environmental crisis. But if nothing was done, then even if the amount of available resources were doubled, pollution was reduced to pre-1970s levels and new technologies were introduced into the model, economic growth would still end before 2100. Some commentators saw this as a vindication of the radical ecological position that industrial societies were just not sustainable.

Many economists, politicians and industrialists, however, roundly condemned the *Limits to Growth* report. They saw it as unbalanced, irresponsible and, later, when its predictions failed to materialize, just plain wrong. The modelling was largely devoid of political and social variables and was only a partial account of reality. Twenty years later the team then published *Beyond the Limits*, an even more pessimistic report which castigated the world's politicians for wasting the time identified in the first report, arguing that 'overshoot' was already occurring. Then in 2004, their *30 Year Update* was released, arguing that although some progress had been made in environmental awareness and technological developments, much evidence now exists of a world 'overshooting' its natural limits. Increasing poverty, rising sea levels, declining fish stocks, degradation of agricultural land and **global warming** are, they say, signs that the human world is testing the natural limits rather than trying to ensure that it lives within them.

The significance of this 'catastrophist' strand of environmental criticism was evident at the United Nations Conference on the Human Environment in Stockholm in 1972. The UN had commissioned a report on, 'the relationship between man and his natural habitat' in 1971, which was published as *Only One Earth* in 1977. This period marked the beginning of international political concerns about the state of the global environment and set the scene for later developments. However, the concept of sustainable development was not put forward until the International Union for the Conservation of Nature and Natural Resources (IUCN) made it the central aim of their World Conservation Strategy (WCS) in 1980. In practice, though, the focus was on environmental sustainability rather than the plight of the developing countries.

The turning point for sustainable development came in 1987 when the UN President Gro Harlam Bruntland's commissioned report, *Our Common Future* (commonly known as *The Bruntland Report*) was published by the UN Commission on Environment and Development (UNCED). This report contained the now famous, albeit brief, definition of sustainable development as: 'development which meets the needs of the present without compromising the ability of future generations to meet their own needs'. The definition tries to link human needs across generations but is notable for the lack of overt reference to the natural environment, though sustainability is usually linked to the maintenance of environmental quality. The definition is quite properly seen as anthropocentric rather than ecocentric, and this puts it closer to reform environmentalism than to radical ecological politics. The report identified international inequalities between North and South as a major problem because, unless these were tackled, developing countries could not be expected to prioritize environmental protection. And without environmental protection, future generations will not be able to meet their needs. Of course, as we have seen already, all definitions based on 'need' are open to the charge that what some see as 'needs' others see as 'wants'. What are the real needs of people living in relatively rich, post-material cultures? Are these needs at all similar to the real needs of people living in developing countries where food scarcity is commonplace and employment prospects poor? And if these 'real' needs are not similar, then how do we reconcile the two sets of needs in a unified programme of action?

By 1992, sustainable development was the dominant framing at the UN Earth Summit in Rio de Janeiro. This Summit produced Agenda 21 (i.e., an agenda for the twenty-first century), which is a programme for implementing sustainable development at different levels – international, national, regional and local – in all 179 participating countries. A new Commission for Sustainable Development was also created to monitor implementation. With local authorities becoming involved in Local Agenda 21, sustainable development encourages a wide range of social groups and organizations to participate. Not just governments, but also businesses, non-governmental organizations (NGOs) and individuals can be involved. At the 2002 World Summit on Sustainable Development in Johannesburg, the UN reaffirmed the basic concept, linking environmental protection and development, but reported that implementation and meeting targets had been 'uneven'; this is not really surprising given the size of the project. New targets were set for improved sanitation, provision of safe drinking water and restoration of fish stocks, but the frank admission that progress had not matched the expectations raised in the 1992 Rio Summit is significant. The UN report, *The Road from Johannesburg*, admitted that, 'poverty deepened in many areas and environmental degradation continued unabated'. In short, during the previous decade there had been precious little progress towards that utopian state of sustainable development. Because of this, it was decided to strengthen the implementation and monitoring process, naming and shaming inactive governments in order to apply more international pressure for change. Unfortunately, however laudable the report's honesty, it has done little to counter the critics' charge that there is much sustainability talk but not enough sustainable activity.

It is easy to be sceptical about the future prospects for sustainable development. Its aim of finding ways of balancing human activity with sustaining natural ecosystems may look impossible; it is an enormous project and a massive undertaking for national governments to play their part. In practice, sustainable development attempts to find common ground amongst a disparate and often conflictual group of nation-states and other social groups and it connects the world development movement with the environmental movement in a way that no other project has. Sustainable development gives radical environmentalists an opportunity to push for full implementation but, at the same time, moderates can get involved locally and feel they have had an impact. For this very reason, it begins to look too broad and too inclusive perhaps to the point of stagnation. The 2002 Johannesburg Report demonstrates that this is a distinct possibility. So what kinds of practices have flowed from the concept of sustainable development?

Sustainable Development in Practice

As you might expect from the description above, sustainable development initiatives cover the whole range of human activity and social development and it is not possible to cover most of this here. However, a flavour of what is involved can be gleaned from the eight 'millennium development goals' set by the UN in 2000 for achievement by 2015. These are:

1   Eradicate extreme poverty and hunger: reduce by half the 1.3 billion people living on less than $1 a day and the 815 million without enough food to meet daily energy needs.
2   Achieve universal primary education: 115 million children, most in sub-Saharan Africa and Southern Asia, do not go to school. Reduce this number.
3   Promote gender equality and empower women: in three main areas – education, employment and political decision-making.
4   Reduce child mortality: 11 million children die before the age of 5, most from treatable diseases. The aim is to cut this by two-thirds.
5   Improve maternal health: particularly in sub-Saharan Africa, by investing in health facilities, birth attendants and education.
6   Combat HIV/AIDS, malaria and other diseases: an estimated 39.4 million people are living with HIV and malaria kills more than 1 million people per year. The aim is to reduce these numbers significantly.
7   Ensure environmental sustainability: reverse the loss of environmental resources – forests, biological diversity, the ozone layer – and provide safe water, adequate sanitation and affordable housing.
8   Develop a global partnership for development: encourage the North to increase aid to developing countries, to move to fairer trade and cancel the debts of struggling developing countries (in June 2005 it was agreed to cancel $40 billion debt of 18 countries to the World Bank, International Monetary Fund and African Development Bank).

There is a mixture here, then, of clear targets and vague objectives, some of which seem achievable, some well-nigh impossible. There is also a mixture of social and environmental issues to be tackled, with a strong focus on improving the conditions of life for millions of people in the developing world. It may well be possible to get more children into primary schools and reduce child mortality in some developing countries, but will there really be environmental sustainability by 2015? That flies in the face of all the available evidence. In fact, the millennium document itself describes the outlook for achieving this goal as 'grim' – a case of optimism of the will and pessimism of the intellect perhaps?

The body charged with monitoring the implementation of initiatives aimed at achieving these goals is the Commission on Sustainable Development (CSD), which looks for good examples and best practice across the world, reporting on these in the form of case studies. An interesting area to consider is energy production and use, because this clearly links economic and social development with environmental protection. The long-term goal is to move towards production systems that can produce sustainable and reliable energy in developing countries and yet also be sustainable in terms of their consequences for the natural environment. If sustainability can be demonstrated in this key area, then it would go a long way towards answering the critics of such a consensus-seeking international political process.

Energy production and use are fundamental elements of any policy aiming at sustainable forms of development, though debates on the way forward can be extremely confusing and conflictual. In the relatively rich countries of the Northern hemisphere, governments and businesses experiment with renewable energy sources while

Box 8.1

A number of energy schemes and experiments in other countries have been introduced and some have had a measure of success. The Republic of Kiribati introduced 1,710 domestic solar power systems on 18 of its 33 islands in 2003, which has reduced the use of kerosene for lighting, thus improving safety, air quality and sustainability. Children and adults can now study and work into the evenings and the hope is that this will help to keep island communities economically viable. A similar solar scheme was introduced with aid from the USA in the remote rural areas of the Autonomous Region in Muslim Mindanao in The Philippines with some success.

In Uganda, an electrification project was launched to bring reliable power to rural areas, some of which have as few as 3 per cent of households with access to electricity. The aim is to connect 400,000 households to the power grid within ten years by building new hydropower plants. Beginning with environmental impact reports, the first two plants will not involve building dams, which in the past has been a criticism of such schemes. This type of project demonstrates the hopes of sustainable development advocates. If successful, it should increase economic activity, wealth creation and social welfare by creating a reliable source of energy for work and domestic living (development). On the other hand, it should also lead to reductions in the present over-use of diesel-powered generators, wood-burning stoves and open fires, all of which contribute to greenhouse gases (sustainability). It also brings together the two worlds of North and South through creative projects.

Source: US
Department of
Energy, EERE, 2005

8.1 Rooftop photovoltaic cells which power lighting and appliances in the villages of West Bengal, India. A product of collaboration between the US Department of Energy and the West Bengal Renewable Development Agency.

continuing to rely on coal, oil, gas and **nuclear power** for the bulk of their current generation needs. In developing countries, forms of social organization and the urban–rural population balance may be very different, but energy generation remains a thorny problem for a genuinely sustainable policy. Developing countries with large natural reserves of fossil fuels, such as China and India, are likely to use them simply because they are available and relatively cheap to extract and use. However, if this happens in relatively unregulated ways, then all the efforts to restrict greenhouse gases through the terms of the Kyoto Protocol (chapter 9) may be called into question. We only have space here for one example from the developing world and that is the energy situation in India.

India is the second most populous country on Earth (behind China) and it remains heavily dependent on coal reserves for energy generation. Coal makes up around 60 per cent of India's energy generation. Coal is a non-renewable fossil fuel which, when burned, releases carbon dioxide, a greenhouse gas that most scientists accept makes a major contribution to continuing and worsening the problem of global warming. India also generates 24 per cent from hydropower and imports a large amount of crude oil for domestic use. Nuclear power and energy from renewable sources are minimal and one reason for this is the high start-up costs involved, which are beyond not just India, but much of the developing world. However, there is excellent potential for solar energy production, as it is estimated that India receives some 5,000 trillion kilowatt hours (Kwh) of solar radiation per annum. But the cost involved in producing and installing the necessary photovoltaic cells is prohibitive and switching away from existing fossil fuel use may be perceived as putting at risk the economic and social progress achieved so far. This is a good example of how a more systematic policy of North/South technology-sharing could speed up the movement towards sustainable development in developing countries and, in the process, help to tackle global warming. In India's rural areas, electricity has now reached almost 90 per cent of villages and more efficient wood-burning stoves for cooking have been widely introduced. The Indian government is also making efforts at energy conservation, including moving public transport away from diesel to compressed natural gas (CNG).

In rural areas of India, where wood-burning is the norm, the issue of deforestation is recognized as a serious problem, partially remediable by programmes of afforestation to create so-called 'carbon sinks'. Carbon sinks are new forests created specifically to counteract the CO_2 production from fossil fuel use. Trees remove carbon dioxide from the atmosphere; more trees means less CO_2 in the atmosphere, which therefore means a reduction in global greenhouse gases. In this way, carbon sinks may help to provide a better balance against harmful emissions. However, in January 2006 the UK Royal Society of Chemistry reported on some recent research which shows that trees and other plants actually give off millions of tons of methane – another greenhouse gas – every year. Therefore, planting more forests to remove carbon dioxide may not be the straightforward environmental gain previously thought. Even if the net balance of emissions would support more carbon sinks, these will still do nothing to solve the problem of rapidly diminishing natural resources, including fossil fuels.

The case of Indian energy production illustrates the problem of sustainable development quite well. In principle, there are renewable energy resources available to replace coal-burning and the use of gas and oil, but these alternatives are expensive and therefore currently unattractive. The urban–rural population balance in India and elsewhere means that small-scale energy production systems such as domestic bio-gas plants and energy-efficient wood-burning stoves are more likely to fit local energy production practices than attempts at eliminating the national coal-fired thermal power stations and replacing these with solar and wind power. But if, as seems likely, the vast coal reserves available to India (and China) are to be used for energy generation in the future, then these countries will continue to be an overall contributor to global warming. The current pace of change to energy generation patterns will just not be rapid enough to make a significant difference to the global situation. What we see here is certainly very welcome economic 'development', but is it 'sustainable' in environmental terms?

Some of the relatively small-scale initiatives introduced in rural parts of India show that sustainable development can make headway even in some of the most difficult socio-economic and natural environments. The process of introducing them also fulfils the educational aspect of sustainable development by bringing the idea to larger populations, thus making it more likely to survive and grow. I did mention earlier that it was not time to fall into despair just yet! The bigger question is whether such small-scale initiatives will allow for fast enough progress.

If the *Limits to Growth* reports have any salience at all, then the problem is not simply one of a series of good examples, but of how much real progress can be made before global environmental problems become too advanced to be halted and reversed.

Can Societies Become Sustainable?

In 2000, UN Secretary-General Kofi Annan called for a Millennium Ecosystem Assessment (MEA) that would involve experts from around the world to produce an overall evaluation of the state of the global ecosystem in light of the pressures placed on it by human activity. This resulted in a Board Statement in March 2005 entitled *Living Beyond Our Means* (a highly provocative title), which begins with the 'stark warning' that, '[h]uman activity is putting such strain on the natural functions of Earth that the ability of the planet's ecosystems to sustain future generations can no longer be taken for granted'. It suggests that in the quest to satisfy their growing demands, human societies have now 'taken the planet to the edge of a massive wave of species extinctions, further threatening our own well-being'. In one sense, this is something of an indictment of the concept and practice of sustainable development. Almost 20 years of sustainability activity after *The Bruntland Report*, which effectively launched sustainable development as a global goal, the MEA authors and scientists argue that the world has failed to stave off a looming natural crisis and that even more serious efforts will be needed. Despite the damning assessment of the *Limits to Growth* report by its critics in 1972, the MEA exercise also lends some weight to that report's overall conclusion – namely, that worldwide human activity is leading to the overshooting of some of the natural limitations imposed by the natural environment.

Another similarity between the *Limits* and the MEA reports is that the latter ran its own series of future scenarios. Four 'plausible futures' for the next 50 years were constructed, based on differing international approaches. In all four scenarios, some similar themes and increasing pressures on the natural environment came to the fore. First, human population pressure. Global human population is forecast to rise to between 8 and 10 billion by 2050 from just over 6 billion today, and much of the increase will be amongst already poor urban populations in the Middle East, sub-Saharan Africa and South Asia. Population pressure of this magnitude will add increasingly heavy pressure to the natural environment for energy, food, shelter and consumer goods. Secondly, there is an increasing conversion of land to agricultural use leading to a reduction of **biodiversity** and the possibility of large-scale animal and plant extinctions. Thirdly, climate change has a larger impact on economic development, leading to more floods and droughts and making species extinctions more likely.

The MEA report therefore makes four broad suggestions for change that should be more likely to work than any alternative courses of action or those that rely on a single solution. First is the suggestion that *nature* must be placed at the centre of all efforts and activities. This is an important assessment because it effectively privileges the 'sustainable' side of sustainable development and is likely to appeal more to Northern environmentalists than to Southern governments. However, the idea that this might happen is not very realistic unless the real costs of using up natural resources are built into all economic calculations. This would involve businesses and governments moving away from treating the natural environment simply as the backdrop to human life. But what would such a change mean in practice? For a start, it would mean an end to agricultural, fishing and energy subsidies that damage the environment, and payment to landowners who manage natural resources, provided they improve water quality and carbon storage (as in afforestation for instance).

Secondly, local communities should be encouraged to take up conservation activities by making sure they play a proper part in decision-making and share in the benefits that result from their actions. Thirdly, instead of assuming that state environment departments can tackle sustainable development initiatives by themselves, these should be included within *all* of central government's decision-making processes so that nature would really be at the heart of government. Fourthly, businesses should be encouraged and financially enabled to pilot new resource-saving initiatives.

Although such suggestions may well be eminently sensible and have some impact on changing the way that governments, businesses and the public deal with environmental issues, they do seem quite timid when compared to the MEA's conclusion that we are *already* 'living beyond our means'. This raises the question of whether there might not be more rapid but perhaps less consensual ways of realizing sustainable development.

In 1968 an American ecologist, Garrett Hardin (1915–2003), described a scenario which he termed the 'tragedy of the commons' (1968). To illustrate this, Hardin suggested a theoretical pasture (a commons), which was used by several cattle herders. Each herder looks to increase their own yield and sees that the best way to do this is to add to their herd by introducing more animals. For individual herders, this makes good economic sense. But if each adopts the same course of behaviour, then the pasture land itself gradually becomes degraded and less useful to them all. However, the individual advantage of increasing yields remains higher than the smaller disadvantage of overgrazing which is collectively shared. Hardin sees this process as a tragedy because it has a relentless logic as long as the natural environment of land, atmosphere and waterways is treated as 'commons', to be used by all without hindrance. Today, many people consider that oceans, atmosphere and land are, or should, constitute a global commons that have to be protected. But Hardin's argument is that in a finite natural world, with an increasing human population, all of whom gain the same rights of use, the commons will *not* be protected unless deliberate and intentionally instituted restrictions are placed on individual freedoms. In particular, Hardin suggests that we must surrender the 'freedom to breed' and accept some forms of 'mutual coercion' to protect the global commons.

Recent debates on over-fishing are a good example of Hardin's parable. Cod stocks around the UK, especially in the North Sea and Irish Sea, have become so depleted that scientists can no longer give reliable estimates of their numbers. Scientists have been arguing for a blanket ban on cod fishing so that stocks can be replenished. However, such action would have a major impact on employment in the fishing industry and has been consistently resisted. There are parallels with an earlier case of diminishing mackerel and herring stocks. These were also fished in huge quantities until industrial over-fishing reduced their numbers to such an extent that they became commercially unviable. Will the same thing happen to cod? The message from the tragedy of the commons argument is that as long as seas are treated as 'commons', and individuals gain an advantage by fishing without being coerced to stop, then it is likely. In December 2004 the President of the Scottish Association for Marine Science suggested that a system of restricted 'marine reserves', similar to land-based nature reserves, should be considered as a way to allow time for fish stocks to recover. Of course, any such system would also need to be policed, and a measure of coercion would be required if necessary.

Hardin's many critics have pointed out that the 'tragedy of the commons' parable tends to exaggerate the extent of individual freedom, even in capitalist societies, and downplays the effectiveness of educational strategies, which have worked well in Western anti-smoking campaigns and many HIV/AIDS educational health promotions in Africa. It can also be argued that in real-world historical examples, herders and commoners always were well aware of their obligations to the common good and respectful of each other, rather than being driven by unfettered and instrumentally rational individual self-interest. It may not be the 'commons' that is the problem, but a short-sighted self-interest. Dietz et al. (2003) have argued, against Hardin's thesis, that many locally evolved forms of social organization and institutional arrangements successfully sustained resources over long periods of time until rapid social and economic change undermined them. Such evidence clarifies the misplaced assumptions of a universal instrumental rationality and individualistic ethos that underpin Hardin's thesis. Dietz et al. also suggest that dealing with the environmental problems of today, which are multi-levelled rather than simply local as in Hardin's example, will require dialogue, a mixture of institutional types and experimental designs that promote learning and facilitate change. Hence, critics do not accept that the commons tragedy is inevitable, and draw attention to the central sociological concepts of social bonding and social solidarity, which characterize human communities and confound the overly simple idea that self-interest is *always* the prime motivator for people. Nevertheless, the parable still serves as a useful reminder that, should consensus-building sustainable development initiatives fail to make rapid enough progress, then at some point in the future, proposals for harsh coercive measures may start to find a more receptive audience.

Conclusion

Is sustainable development really achievable or is it just a hopeless dream? Is there scope for developing countries to become more industrially advanced without this causing irreparable damage to the global environment? Will the people of the industrialized countries be prepared to consume less of the planet's natural resources so that pressures on the environment are reduced? Will the increasing and historically unprecedented global human population really be able to carry on driving their individual cars, covering billions of air miles and destroying crucially important ecosystems such as rainforests to make way for monocultures and agriculture? These are very difficult questions to wrestle with and answers even more difficult to forecast. Nevertheless, advocates of sustainable development believe that in their concept lies, literally, the hope of the world. They see that it promises to link together the industrialized countries and those in the developing world and to offer every individual, family, community, business and government the chance to participate in that great, but rather ill-defined, utopian project of 'saving the planet'. Every positive action, however small and apparently trivial, can make a contribution to reducing waste, recycling of materials, saving energy and preventing pollution. The undoubtedly positive side of this project is that to become involved in it there is no need for anyone to join a political party or an environmental organization. There is no pressure on them to start a violent revolution or use terrorist methods to achieve their goals. All that is required is for them to consider each and every one of their everyday activities and alter their practices with the single aim of treading more lightly on the Earth whilst doing it. Drive the car less, take the bus and train more often. Use less energy, cut down on water usage and recycle more. Unlimited opportunities exist for people to make a contribution and to feel good about themselves for doing so.

Sustainable development is a global, society-wide project of social, economic, political and natural renewal that potentially has wide appeal, but critics see it as too keen to seek consensus and not keen enough to upset businesses and governments that continue to pollute the environment or that do not change quickly enough. They also see that the perspective carries no theory of exactly *why* some countries are rich and others are poor, nor does it appreciate that it just might be the case that some countries are rich precisely *because* other countries are poor. And if this is true, then implementing genuine sustainable development will mean challenging some very powerful vested interests, which stand in the way of equalizing human life chances and opportunities across the world.

Readings

The *Limits to Growth* reports are probably best approached from the latest one, Donella H. Meadows et al., *Limits to Growth: The 30 Year Update* (2004). The early catastrophist environmentalism is explored in detail in Stephen Cotgrove's *Catastrophe or Cornucopia: The Environment, Politics and the Future* (1982). Barbara Adam's 'Re-vision: The Centrality of Time for an Ecological Social Science Perspective' (1996) gives a short but clear account of the problems of time in environmental sociology.

On sustainable development, a good place to start is with the classic statement by the World Commission on Environment and Development, *Our Common Future* (1987). Then you can move on to two very accessible texts: Andrew Dobson's edited collection, *Fairness and Futurity: Essays on Environmental Sustainability and Social Justice* (1999), and Susan Baker's *Sustainable Development* (2005). Jennifer Elliott's updated *Introduction to Sustainable Development* (2005) is also an excellent account of sustainable development, specifically in developing countries.

The UN's own Millennium Ecosystem Assessment Report, *Living Beyond Our Means: Natural Assets and Human Well-Being* (2005), is very accessible: the 'Statement from the Board' summarizes the findings of the main report. An overview of the Johannesburg Earth Summit can be found in Luc Hens and Bhaskar Nath (eds), *The World Summit on Sustainable Development: The Johannesburg Conference* (2005). Finally, the UN's *Division for Sustainable Development* on the worldwide web is also a valuable source of information and statistics: <www.un.org/esa/sustdev/>.

9 A Global Environment

In this final chapter we look at the way that the interdependent relationships between the peoples of the world are becoming increasingly intertwined through a process currently described as **globalization**. The globalization of social life seems to be creating what some sociologists have called a shared community of fate, one in which the fortunes of people in far-flung parts of the planet are more and more intimately connected. The project of sustainable development described in chapter 8 may be seen in this context as one aspect of the globalizing of human affairs, in its linking together of the developing and industrialized countries across the world. As we saw there, however, sustainable development is a contested concept and the practices inspired by it do not seem to be taking root as quickly as many would like. Although a global orientation may well be developing, altering people's environmentally damaging behaviour is more difficult, given the existence of gross social inequalities around the world.

Globalization is also leading to the redefinition of the natural environment in terms of the planetary ecosystem we call the biosphere or, simply, planet Earth. One reason for this is the scientific identification of a series of global environmental problems that do not respect national political boundaries. Many people across the world will now be familiar with global warming or climate change, ozone layer depletion, acid rain and biodiversity loss. Not only are such problems global in nature, they clearly cannot be solved by any single national government, but require international collaboration and agreement. The chapter ends with a look at some of the many solutions put forward to address global environmental problems.

What is Globalization?

In simple terms, globalization means that the fate of human beings in all parts of the world is rapidly becoming more closely connected. As modern transportation methods allow people to cross the planet more quickly, distance becomes less of an obstacle to mass tourism, migration and commerce. As communication technologies allow us to send emails across the world in seconds and the Internet enables incredibly rapid exchanges of information, it becomes possible to know more about events and peoples than would ever have been possible in previous centuries. Decisions taken in one geographical region can have consequences for people thousands of miles away. Japanese company directors looking to establish their firm's presence in Europe can create many job opportunities for people in Belgium, for example. They can also remove those jobs when things get tough. Wealthy Westerners looking to take honeymoons in 'paradise' locations can generate new economic opportunities that turn the Maldives islands into tourist sites, which at the same time makes them vulnerable to the shifting fashions and fads of the 'tourist gaze' (Urry 2001). Many people are ambivalent about the processes of globalization. Although it brings amazing new opportunities, it can also favour the needs of business, enabling increasingly footloose multinational companies to traverse the globe, avoiding their social and environmental responsibilities.

Over recent years, sociologists have become increasingly aware that the national societies they are used to analysing and trying to understand can no longer be studied in isolation from the wider relationships in which they are enmeshed. Theorists of globalization suggest that the global level of reality may require new methods to capture the main characteristics of the emerging 'world society'. Globalization is therefore not a finished state of affairs but, rather, an ongoing process of change, albeit one with a clear direction. Human relationships are becoming more interdependent and are spreading across the boundaries of nation-states. One way of thinking about this is to divide the discussion into economic, political and cultural forms of globalization (Waters 2000).

Globalization takes place within the economic sphere through global patterns of trade and exchange, the import and export of goods and the migratory flows of workers. Take a look at where the everyday products you use have actually been made and you are likely to find that China, Turkey, Mexico, Malaysia and others are now the major industrial producers of the West's consumer goods. The economies of the world are therefore becoming more closely intertwined, so that decisions taken in one country can affect employment in another. Multinational corporations looking to build manufacturing plant or establish a headquarters need not be tied to their country of origin. Instead, they can now look for sites anywhere in the world, comparing tax rates, government concessions, legislative frameworks and levels of trade union membership and militancy before they make their decision. Modern transportation systems mean that the previous limitations of geography are being slowly overcome.

Globalization also takes place within the political sphere, as international politics tries to keep up with and regulate the global flows of goods and people. Sustainable development initiatives (chapter 8) demanding global political cooperation, collaboration and agreement are a typical example of this. Nation-states, which seek continuing influence over their own affairs, are compelled to take part in international negotiations and agreements or risk losing some of their power chances. This so-called 'pooling' of national sovereignty may feel like a loss of national power, but it is an inevitable part of the emergent global framework. Nevertheless, the political dimension tends to stay at the level of internationalism rather than leading directly to a form of global politics. This is largely because it is still the nation-state that is the main actor and states always promote their own national interests, even within an international system.

Globalization is also a cultural phenomenon, which can be seen in the mixing and communications between people from widely divergent human cultures and societies. The age of mass tourism and travel has enabled a much wider understanding of this diversity and societies are becoming increasingly multicultural, with an amazing variety of foods, clothing styles, religions and practices existing within a single national society. Cultural exchanges tend to promote globalization every bit as much as economic exchanges. This is because, in part, culture is identified by symbols: the sphere of culture is, in part, a symbolic one that involves cultural symbols which are more easily shared around the world. Money is the best example. Once economic exchanges become dominated by monetary tokens, it is easy to convert these into usable information. In this form, monetary exchanges can be moved around more quickly and readily via the virtual world of the Internet. Think about online shopping, for instance, which involves handing over a series of numbers and password codes and can be achieved in a matter of seconds without using physical bank notes, coins or cheques. Many people hardly use physical money at all these days, instead simply carrying credit and store cards. Similarly, stock exchange transactions now involve people working at computers transferring large amounts of 'cash' around the planet for investments and money-speculation (Waters 2000).

In all these ways, the activities of human beings today are more tightly connected to larger numbers of people in all parts of the world. The processes of global transformation (Held et al. 1999) are likely to continue in spite of the protests and resistance by some of those who see globalization as damaging to their interests or as biased in favour of a spreading industrial capitalism. This is likely because globalization is not really a recent development that might end or be easily reversed. A very good argument can be made which suggests that human development over a very long time period, from small-scale hunter-gatherer societies and their settled agricultural successors through to modern industrial societies, should be construed as a gradual process of globalization. This is because, despite some reversals and civilizational collapses during this timeframe, there is a very long-term tendency for human activity to expand across social groups and societies, even if this has very often been through conflicts and wars rather than friendly exchanges and agreements. This realization means that, for the most part, human globalization has been the unplanned outcome of the long-term development of social relations and human activity. Of course, globalization does imply a cultural mixing and sharing of ideas and practices, but it does not necessarily mean that the ubiquitous global brands, such as the McDonald's fast food chain, will produce total uniformity, flattening out all cultural differences and diversity. Roland Robertson (1992) reminds us that the globalizing spread of Western business models and consumer goods very often requires them to be modified to fit the cultures into which they are placed. He describes this process as 'glocalization', which is the creative mixture of globalization and local cultures. This implies that the 'global' and the 'local' will continue to be two elements of the same social process. This is an important qualification, because it shows that the local level of social life is not just a passive recipient of global forces. Local conditions and people can affect the impacts of globalization and this needs to be borne in mind when assessing the latter.

Although globalization is a very long-term social process, since the 1970s there has been a speeding up of the process with an intensified awareness that worldwide relationships are becoming more systematically connected. The Internet and World Wide Web have also helped to create this interconnectedness. Although it has now become commonplace, it remains a source of wonderment, at least to me, that I can send an email communication across the other side of the world and receive a reply within a matter of a few seconds (sometimes). The physical reality of the Earth no longer seems such an obstacle and, in effect, the world just seems smaller, as the time it takes to cross it, both physically and virtually, has been reduced. David Harvey (1989) has described this new situation as the experience of 'time–space compression' – 'the annihilation of space through time' – which others see as leading towards a 'global village' or a world community with a shared destiny. Certainly, the increased interest in the plight of developing countries amongst Westerners and the large-scale relief operations of recent times seem to bear this out. However, as we will see in the case of tackling **global warming**, it is also clear that national interests remain strong and there are no guarantees that a greater awareness of living in a shared global community will inevitably lead to more sympathetic community help and action.

The issue for us in this final chapter, then, is what does this intensified globalization process mean for the natural environment and will it facilitate more or less environmental protection? As we saw in the previous chapter, bringing environmental sustainability together with economic development is the ultimate goal of the United Nations sustainable development programme, but the unplanned outcomes of increasingly global relationships add a new dimension to such efforts. It will be the task of social scientists in the future to understand these relationships better and feed that knowledge back into an assessment of which policy suggestions are realistic or likely to succeed and which are not.

The Biosphere as Environment

As we saw in chapters 6 and 7, early forms of **environmentalism** framed the concept of 'nature' in local and national terms, aiming to defend and protect local environments or the national, natural heritage, as they defined it. But during the twentieth century, a gradual transformation of the meaning of nature occurred which expanded first to the international level and then, from the 1970s, into a much more global version. The *Worldwide* Fund for Nature, *Earth*watch, Friends of the *Earth* and *Earth* First! (my emphasis) are just a few of the household names promoting an expanded, global concept of the natural environment. One reason that these groups were so successful is that both members and potential supporters feel less constrained by their national cultures and in this sense they are both products of and contributors to the process of globalization. Stephen Young says that these new groups had reached the conclusion, perhaps rightly, that 'environmentalism is not possible in one country' (1993: 53). This globalizing phase of environmental movement development mirrors the wider processes taking place.

Some key events and developments have convinced environmentalists of the need for a global version of environmentalism. Obviously, the continued industrialization process has demonstrated that this is not restricted to the Western nations in which it originally emerged. Other states have embarked on planned industrialization to avoid losing status and power and to realize for their people the same levels of material well-being enjoyed elsewhere. This 'catching-up' process has a long way to go yet. Post-1945 **nuclear power** production and nuclear weapons-testing brought home the potential for global catastrophe via nuclear proliferation. This concern led directly into the creation of peace and anti-nuclear movements, which later mutated into environmental organizations. Greenpeace is the best example of this, as the group's name suggests (that is, in favour of a 'green' 'peace').

Also, the scientific discovery of the global environmental problems of global warming, **acid rain**, **ozone depletion** and **biodiversity** loss self-evidently requires international cooperation if these effects are to be effectively tackled. Simply put, no nation-state, however powerful, is capable of dealing with these issues in isolation. Finally, the growing global interest needed a rallying point, somewhere to meet and lobby for change. This was provided in the creation of new international institutions such as the UN Environment Programme and the European Union, which presented fresh political opportunities for exerting influence beyond the level of individual nation-states. Robertson's point is worth repeating here though. Much global environmental activity still takes place in local situations and maintains its basic reformist character, seeking to make small changes that add up to a big difference. To re-use an old slogan invented at the 1972 Stockholm Conference on the Human Environment, in the main, environmentalists still 'think globally but act locally'.

Box 9.1

In 1989 the US *Time* magazine broke with tradition and, instead of announcing a 'person of the year', gave its front-page cover over to the 'planet of the year': 'endangered Earth'. The image *Time* used, of the globe of planet Earth taken from beyond its confines, has had a major cultural impact on people's perceptions of themselves and their place within the Universe. For many, the image brought home how unusual and fragile a living planet was. In an otherwise lifeless known Universe, the Earth, the human 'home planet', seemed miraculous. No one was more impressed or learned such a basic environmentalist message than some of the astronauts who actually experienced it. One former East German astronaut recorded: 'Before I flew I was already aware of how small and vulnerable our planet is; but only when I saw it from space, in all its ineffable beauty and fragility, did I realize that humankind's most urgent task is to cherish and preserve it for future generations' (cited in Kelley 1988: plate 141).

It is interesting to reflect on the fact that manned space flight, the ultimate triumph of scientific knowledge and industrial production and a product of the desire for symbolic demonstrations of national supremacy during the Cold War, produced such potentially globally unifying symbolic imagery. Photographs such as the one shown here (see illus. 9.1) enabled people to understand and appreciate the powerful idea that the Earth behaves like a living entity and seems to have promoted a stronger human identification with it.

9.1 Planet Earth coming into view, as seen from the Moon's orbit, 240,000 miles away. An image taken from the American spacecraft Apollo 8 in 1968 as it orbited the Earth's only significant satellite. Images such as this one have had a profound impact on people's attitude towards the natural environment.

Source: North American Space Agency (NASA) 2002

We saw in chapter 3 that radical ecological or Green thinking demands a shift away from **anthropocentrism** towards an **ecocentric** orientation that puts the natural environment first. Globalization processes are lending support to the reconstruction of the natural environment as an **ecosystemic** whole. This has been called the

biosphere, the ecosphere, Gaia and even just plain old 'Earth', but these all demonstrate a wider understanding of what constitutes 'nature' than has been evident in the past. A significant forerunner of such views was the British independent scientist and inventor James Lovelock, who presented his Gaia Hypothesis during the 1970s and found a wide audience amongst environmentalists. Lovelock argued that the Earth *behaves as if* it were a superorganism (note that he does not say that it *is* an organism). All living things and natural processes act to produce a kind of planetary homeostasis or balance as a result of the self-regulating system, which has maintained the conditions for life since just after life began. Lovelock's ideas were initially seen as eccentric, but as global environmental problems have moved into the scientific mainstream, they no longer seem quite so implausible. However, even the Gaia Hypothesis does not lead us to conclude that the biosphere is fragile and on the verge of collapse as a result of human activity. In fact, Lovelock argues that the system is remarkably resilient and capable of accommodating large-scale changes and environmental damage. But as it adapts to such changes, conditions on the planet may become intolerable for some species, humans included. In short, the planet is not in need of saving, but some human groups may well be. Lovelock has also argued more recently in favour of nuclear power as the only viable solution to global warming, warning in a newspaper article that, 'we have no time to experiment with visionary energy sources' (*Independent*, 24 May 2004). He reaches this conclusion because he is convinced that urgent action, not small changes, is needed to prevent a more rapid global warming. Still, what does unite Greens and the Gaia theory is the view that, in the long run, it is nature and not human societies that is in control. If this is the case, how should societies approach properly global environmental issues?

Global Problems, Global Solutions?

In chapter 5 we reviewed the ideas of Ulrich Beck and Anthony Giddens, both of whom have been interested in problems of risk and trust. Beck in particular is associated with the theory of an emerging 'world risk society' in which environmental issues play a central role. What these sociologists say is that modern risks are increasingly of (potentially) higher consequence, are more far-reaching in their effects and are therefore much more difficult to tackle. A whole series of environmental problems fit this description, including acid rain, ozone depletion, global warming and biodiversity loss. From a globalization perspective, such problems demonstrate the increasing interdependence of human societies and the possibility for activities in one region to impact on geographically distant societies. It is also clear that national governments will have to work together to have any chance of solving these problems. A discussion of global warming should illustrate why.

Global climate change

The environmental issue of climate change or global warming crystal-lizes the arguments of this chapter and perhaps even the whole book. It is the clearest example of a genuinely global environmental problem, because the effects of planetary warming will affect every society on Earth, albeit in different ways. It forces us to see the natural environ-ment in its widest interpretation as the planet Earth itself, because the atmosphere shrouds the entire planet and human activity in any one region will influence conditions in other regions. The problem of global warming cannot be understood without modern science, and sociolo-gists will have to engage with the science of climate change if they are to have useful things to say about its social consequences. Planetary warming will also influence the way we experience our environment as the climate itself becomes a political issue. We can already see this beginning to happen as every extreme weather event produces renewed political debate which usually ends with someone blaming global warming as the ultimate cause. Of course, when weather becomes political, then politicians are likely to get the blame. When New Orleans was flooded in 2005, journalists and commentators were quick to point out that the US government was not doing enough to tackle climate change. Global warming also alerts us to a form of 'pollu-tion' (excessive greenhouse gases) that we never realized existed and it is the focus of and motivation for political campaigns and demonstra-tions around environmental concerns. One effect of this change is that it has speeded up the globalization of environmental politics and helped to redefine 'nature' in planetary terms. Finally, tackling this issue is the foundation for any sustainable future for the human species. And although there are myriad initiatives aimed at promoting sustainable development, the problem of global warming could derail this project. If climate change leads to more fluid migration patterns, more droughts and reduced crop growing capacity and increased expenditure on flood defence systems, then this may change the context of the sustainable development debate. Global warming is now widely recognized as the most significant long-term environmental problem because of such damaging potential effects, and there is an increasingly strong argument which suggests that this issue has to be tackled as an urgent priority if other sustainability projects are to have any chance. Therefore, we need to understand what global warming is and why it is happening.

The **greenhouse effect** refers to the atmospheric warming of the planet and this is an important aspect of life on Earth. Without the warm-ing effect of the planet's atmosphere, the Earth would be too cold to support life, as is the case on Mars, but too much warming could lead to a runaway greenhouse effect with the opposite result. The planet Venus is an example of the latter, which is too hot to support life. Planet Earth's greenhouse effect is therefore quite unusual. 'Global warming' on Earth

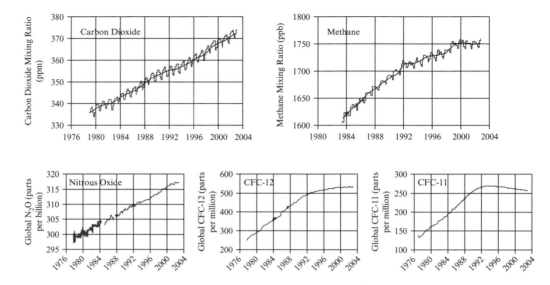

These five gases account for about 97 per cent of the direct climate forcing by long-lived greenhouse gas increases since 1750. The remaining 3 per cent is contributed by an assortment of ten minor halogen gases, mainly HCFC-22, CFC113 and CCI.

Figure 9.1 Global trends in major greenhouse gases, 1976–2003

Source: USA National Oceanic and Atmospheric Administration, 2005

can be considered a natural phenomenon, though evidence from geological and meteorological research also shows that the average planetary temperature has fluctuated in regular cycles: sometimes cooler, sometimes warmer than it is today. Nevertheless, there is an emerging scientific consensus (with one or two exceptions) that the current pattern of warming is enhanced by 'anthropogenic' factors. That means it is enhanced by human activity, particularly since the eighteenth-century Industrial Revolution in Europe. Industrialization processes led to large increases in the group of so-called 'greenhouse gases'. Methane (CH_4) is a greenhouse gas that is generated, for instance, in landfill sites. In the UK alone, landfill contributes around two million tons of methane to the atmosphere. Some journalists have also been amused to find that the large numbers of cattle and livestock in the world (some two billion cattle and sheep for a start) also release large amounts of 'natural methane' in the form of flatulence. The US Environmental Protection Agency says that methane is 21 times more effective at trapping heat in the atmosphere compared to carbon dioxide (CO_2). And though clearly a powerful greenhouse gas, methane's 'chemical lifetime' is only about 12 years and its global warming potential (GWP) is therefore not as great as CO_2, because it is not currently being produced in large enough quantities to persist over long periods of time.

The main greenhouse gas, carbon dioxide (CO_2), is released when fossil fuels such as coal, oil and gas are burned, rising into the atmosphere. In larger concentrations, CO_2 acts to prevent heat energy from the Sun being refracted back into space. Instead, this energy becomes trapped and further warms the Earth's surface. This is of course part of the normal greenhouse effect, but it is widely accepted that human activity is enhancing the natural effect (see figure 9.1), a process sometimes described as 'climate forcing'.

The US National Oceanic and Atmospheric Administration (NOAA) reports that measurements taken from Antarctic ice cores show that the carbon dioxide levels before the industrial period were around 278 parts per million (ppm) and did not vary more than some 7 ppm between 1000 and 1800 BCE. However, evidence from continuous monitoring and measurement at the Mauna Loa observatory atop a volcano in Hawaii clearly demonstrates that atmospheric CO_2 levels have increased every year since 1958, rising from some 315 ppm in 1958 to 378 ppm by the end of 2004. This means that human activity has raised CO_2 levels by 100 ppm (36 per cent) since the year 1000.

Most scientists now agree that over the course of the twentieth century, the average surface temperature of the Earth has increased by around 0.6°C, but the nine warmest years have all occurred since 1980, which strongly supports the thesis of a more rapid process of warming in recent times. The evidence is now much stronger that this increased global warming is in large part due to industrial activity, which produces large amounts of greenhouse gases. What the primary extractive industries effectively did (and still do), was to take the carbon-rich ancient materials which had accumulated over very long time periods, and enable the release of their CO_2 in a very short period, thus rapidly transforming the composition of the Earth's atmosphere. Of course, this process is not yet over, as developing countries look to increase their economic activity rates and need to generate more energy from fossil fuels to do it.

What will be the impact of such an anthropogenic effect? Scientists report that sea levels may well rise. This is because, as temperatures rise, the oceans' water expands. Forecasts of rising sea levels are based partly on this thermal expansion of ocean water, but other causes include the melting of mountain glaciers and the potential for melting of the continental ice sheets such as those in Greenland. The combination of these changes is estimated by an international group of climate scientists to be leading to sea-level rises of between 15 and 34 centimetres by the year 2100. However, there is also a 10 per cent chance of a rise of somewhere between 30 and 65 centimetres. Such rises would lead to more coastal erosion, flood risks and reductions in available agricultural land as a result of the decline in soil quality.

If sea levels are rising – and there is now good evidence that they are – then those land areas closest to sea level will be the first affected. Small islands, such as the Polynesian island nation of Tuvalu and the region of Micronesia in the Pacific Ocean, may provide the first concrete evidence of global warming effects. This is because they are only a few metres above sea level and are at severe risk of flooding. The 11,000 Tuvaluans are already experiencing regular flooding of their gardens and stronger storms which cause more damage. The Foreign

Affairs Minister warned in 2005 that 'our whole culture will have to be transplanted' should the problem continue to worsen. In 2000, it was also reported that some of the land causeways between seven of the inhabited Micronesian islands were water-covered around half the time, when previously, even at high tide, they had remained dry. Around 360,000 people live in the Maldives and many Western tourists see the place as a paradise holiday location. But 80 per cent of the Maldives is no more than one metre above sea level. The capital, Male, is defended against tidal waves by a three-metre-high wall, but even this would be no real defence against permanently raised sea levels. Some pessimistic long-term forecasts suggest that in less than 100 years this Western tourist haven will have to be completely evacuated and, as a functioning nation-state, the country will no longer exist. Depending on the extent of the sea-level rise, even cities such as London will need to improve their defensive fortifications to avoid regular flooding.

Clearly, global warming will be very serious for the human population of the world, changing the seasons and weather patterns. It would also mean more 'extreme weather events' such as tornadoes, heat waves and floods and lead to species extinctions and the reordering of life forms on the planet. That is largely because some species would be eliminated while others may thrive in new conditions, though species may also be forced to move to new environments as well. Agriculture would be severely affected as soil quality deteriorates, and adequate food production may become much more difficult with increasing under-nourishment and famine. Human populations and migration patterns will change as people move to avoid the worst effects, and poorer countries will be least able to adapt to a rapidly changing environment unless advanced technologies from the industrialized world are much more widely shared.

As a result of dire warnings such as these, along with evidence of real negative consequences and amidst a growing scientific consensus, an Intergovernmental Panel on Climate Change (IPCC) was formed in 1988. Its task was to review all the options and make recommendations for the UN General Assembly. When IPCC reported back in 1990, it made a clear statement that the anthropogenic effect was likely to produce 'a rate of increase of global mean temperature during the next century of about 0.3°C per decade . . . this is greater than that seen over the past 10,000 years' (cited in Rowlands 1995: 78–9). Given other possible factors, this would mean a rise of between 1.4°C and 5.8°C by 2100. In effect, this evidence was part of an environmental claim for the issue of global warming. However, there were also 'claims-deniers' and foremost amongst these was the American government, which refused even to use the term 'global warming', preferring its own less clear terminology of 'climate change'. Although technically correct, the latter has been widely seen as an attempt to prevent 'global warming' becoming common currency with its built-in implication that human activity is to blame. This is not really surprising as almost 25 per cent of the global greenhouse gases emitted into the atmosphere are estimated to come from the USA and American oil corporations have a short-term vested interest in challenging scientific evidence which may lead to pressure for change that ultimately affects their profits.

In 1997, many governments around the world, convinced by the accumulating scientific evidence, made an agreement to reduce their greenhouse gas emissions. At the UN Framework Convention on Climate Change, held at Kyoto in Japan, the Kyoto Protocol came into being. You may not be surprised to learn that the Maldives made history by being the first country to sign. The agreement was ratified by the 15 member states of the European Union in 2002 and European governments committed themselves to reducing the EU's emissions of greenhouse gases to 8 per cent below the levels that existed in 1990. Although the Protocol was opened for signatures in 1997, it could not come into force until a certain number of signatures were received and it did not actually come into force until 16 February 2005 following a signature on behalf of Russia.

One notable absentee from the Kyoto Protocol is the USA, whose government has consistently criticized the agreement, which they see as not the best way to achieve reductions in greenhouse gases. The USA did sign, but has not ratified the Protocol and is therefore not bound by its terms and commitments. Australia has also stayed outside the agreement, arguing that it is already working hard to cut emissions and the Protocol would add nothing new, but may cost Australian jobs. In 2003, the USA announced that it would be moving along a 'parallel track' to Kyoto by investing heavily in new energy technologies, promoting voluntary actions and conducting more scientific research on the issue. But these measures are outside the terms of the Kyoto Protocol and, crucially, will not involve placing any cap on CO_2 emissions. Clearly, the global problem of climate change will be severely hidebound if the country with the highest national emission levels – the USA – effectively opts out of international attempts to cap greenhouse gas emissions.

The Kyoto Protocol was also controversial in a number of areas for the developing countries of the Southern hemisphere. Let's take just one. The Protocol took 1990 greenhouse emission levels as its starting point for planned reductions. But this starting point was seen as benefiting the industrialized countries, because it fails to take into account their 'historical responsibility' for the current greenhouse gas emissions problem. In short, the Kyoto Protocol failed to take into account which countries are to blame for the current global warming. Although Kyoto did take account of the currently far lower greenhouse gas contributions of developing countries, by allowing them to opt out of reduction commitments, there is uncertainty about when and on what basis they will enter the Kyoto regime. Will it allow for their inevitably higher emission levels as their economic development catches up with the industrialized world, for example? If it does not, then it will undoubtedly be seen as unfair and will probably be unworkable in practice. What many developing countries have argued is that there is a whole world of difference between 'luxury emissions' – most of those discharged in the industrialized North – and 'survival emissions' – those that will be required to bring about an adequate standard of living in the developing South – which will need to be taken into consideration (Najam et al. 2003).

The issue of global warming tells us quite a lot about the prospects for sustainable development. The fact that 156 nation-states have now ratified the Protocol perhaps shows that there is a will to make international agreements to solve global environmental problems. Of course there will be continual difficulties ahead, not least the accession of developing countries into the main framework, which will mean limiting their emissions. However, the refusal of countries such as the USA and Australia to ratify the Protocol demonstrates that there is no effective means of getting them to do so. We may well be living through a process of globalization, but politically and militarily, the nation-state remains a powerful actor in the global system as there simply is no global government or global authority that would be capable of bringing states into line.

Modernization critique

In this section, I want to introduce and explore an interesting perspective, which claims to be targeted at providing solutions to environmental problems at all levels of social organization. This perspective is **ecological modernization**. It emerged around the same period that advocates of sustainable development were formulating their own position and came directly from the work of a small group of German, Dutch and British academics. Joseph Huber is credited with inventing the concept, which David Sonnenfeld describes as, 'industrial restructuring with a green twist' (2000: 236). At root, these researchers sought to preserve a commitment to the modernization project by turning it in an ecological direction so that instead of modernization being the villain of the piece, in its ecological form it may turn out to be the hero and saviour. Before we look more closely at this, let us face the issue of why modernization has been considered villainous.

In the mid-nineteenth century, Karl Marx encouraged people to marvel at the incredible wonders of the modern world, which, in Marx's time, had been created in the short period of just over a century. Steel bridges spanning huge rivers, massive factories producing more goods than have ever been seen in human history, metal ships sailing across vast oceans and mountains quarried for rocks and minerals to use in construction. Marx saw that these feats not only put the wonders of the ancient world in the shade, but also, and more importantly, were merely the start of an expanding process that promised to give modern societies much more control over the natural environment than in any previous age. Most adults alive today who have access to a television set will probably have seen many more spectacular feats of engineering such as rocket launches into space, sending people into orbit around the Earth, and NASA's space shuttles landing on runways in the manner of commercial aircraft, after a trip to the International Space Station. Older generations would remember the televised images from manned space flights to and landings on the Moon in the 1960s and '70s. Such impressive human achievements demonstrate spectacularly just how unique the modern era really is.

As we saw in chapter 4, industrialization, urbanization and capitalist economics combined to set the modern world on this impressive but environmentally disruptive modernizing path. The Soviet Union and communist societies adjusted the formula, replacing free-market capitalism with state-sponsored direction and central planning, but in most other respects they pursued a modernizing policy framework. For environmentalists, both forms of modernization have signally failed. They have delivered much wealth and material success but at the cost of massive environmental damage which can no longer be managed and sustained. Why did this happen? James C. Scott (1998) gives us some clues.

Scott argues that some of the grandest modernist projects, the ones launched with great fanfare and optimism of improving the lot of humankind, turned into inglorious failures. And in studying the failures, we can often learn more than studying the success stories. Scott describes four features which, when combined, have tended to produce pernicious outcomes. First, the normal simplifications involved in administering the business of the modern state. Nation-states try to bring order to the natural environment and to society so as to be able to plan for the future. But in doing so, their simplifications often miss out on the crucial small details of life. A simple example is the 'cadastral map', an overview of a geographical area showing boundaries and natural features such as may be found in a road atlas. Clearly these maps are useful for some purposes, but in order to be useful, a myriad of small details has to be omitted. Secondly, Scott identifies what he calls a 'high modernist' ideology. This refers to the Enlightenment ideals of the human mastery of nature through scientific understanding and the rational ordering of society, alongside the self-confident belief in the modern 'project' of meeting human needs by manipulating nature: not science or scientific practice as such, but the *ideology* of what science can and should be used to achieve. Thirdly, Scott argues that an 'authoritarian state' is required to turn high modernist visions and ambitions into reality. Such a state can muster the resources and the will to force through the dream, even against opposition and inertia. The fourth and final feature identified by Scott is a weak civil society – that range of voluntary groups, social organizations and collective institutions that make up the tissue of everyday social organization – which is therefore unable to mount any effective resistance to the plans. When these four elements coalesce, there is the potential for social and environmental disasters on a large scale, and Scott provides a wide range of examples. The 1920s modernization of agriculture by forced collectivization of farming in the Soviet Union produced state and collective farms, but also led to a lack of food and starvation for millions of peasants. Tanzanian compulsory 'villagization' from 1967 was aimed at bringing order to the existing scattered settlements by resettling householders into larger villages. By 1975, some 75 per cent of the population lived in the new villages. However, the previous form of agriculture known as 'shifting cultivation' had allowed pastoralists to move around to find new land, allowing periods of fallow for land to recover. In this way the system as a whole was quite balanced. But with villagization the population became centralized and expanded, which left previously cultivated areas to revert to bushland. Livestock concentration led to damage from over-grazing, while concentrated water usage led to a falling water table and poorer soils. Villagization created many environmental and agricultural problems, despite being introduced as a solution to such problems. Finally, the planned modernist city of Brasilia (1956–60), which was meticulously designed and implemented in the shape of a cross or aeroplane, was to be the centrepiece new capital city of Brazil. The city's architects aimed to eliminate slums, crime, disease and traffic jams. But in the process of creating a city to a rational and aesthetically coherent design, they also removed the street corners and public places that create the vibrant heart of many other modern cities. Those moving into the new Brasilia often complained that 'it is a city without crowds' (Scott 1998: 125). Scott's discussion provides detailed explanations of why these schemes failed, but we can focus on one central issue here.

What Scott suggests is missing from all of these examples is what might be called 'practical knowledge' and flexibility – learning on the job, as it were. That is, the kind of knowledge that peasant farmers in the Soviet Union, pastoralists in Tanzania and voluntary groups in Brasilia already had, but which was devalued as common sense or unscientific, and thus ignored. Sometimes, though, this kind of practical knowledge can prevent bad mistakes from becoming worse by providing the real-world experience of people who are able to evaluate what might work and, crucially, what will not. It was this type of knowledge that was missing from all the schemes just mentioned, which were centrally planned from above with little room for creative modification during implementation. Without practical knowledge, a whole range of ideas and suggestions rooted in practice rather than planning theory and grand ambition were simply lost, as the schemes just did not allow for the kinds of compromise or continuous modification that potentially could have rescued them.

What we might learn from Scott's study is that 'saving the planet' probably will not be achieved through some grand, all-encompassing plan or scheme directed from on high. If it is to have any chance of success then it has to take advantage of the large amount of practical knowledge held by people with experience in various social, political, cultural and geographical contexts around the world. Sustainable development initiatives delivered through local Agenda 21 at least seem to recognize that the old slogan, 'think globally, act locally', has a little more mileage left in it. But the recent ideas of ecological modernization theorists may also have a key contribution to make.

Ecological modernization

Ecological modernization theorists recognize that 'business as usual' is not possible given the current set of environmental problems we face. But they also reject radical Green decentralist and de-industrializing solutions. Instead, they focus on technological innovation and the use of market mechanisms to bring about environmentally benign outcomes, especially in transforming production methods and reducing pollution at source. Ecological modernizers see huge potential in some leading European industries to reduce the usage of natural resources *without* this affecting economic growth. This is an unusual position to take, but it does have a certain logic. Rather than simply rejecting continuing growth, as in the radical ecological reading of the *Limits* reports, it is argued that an ecological form of growth is theoretically possible. An example would be the introduction of catalytic converters and emission controls for motor vehicles, which has been delivered within a short period of time and shows that advanced technologies may potentially make a big difference to greenhouse gas emissions. Of course, if environmental protection really can be achieved in this way, then the radical Green critique simply melts away. What ecological modernizers also argue is that, if consumers demand environmentally sound production methods and products, then market mechanisms will be forced to try to deliver them. In the UK, for example, supermarkets have not stocked or pushed the supply of genetically modified foods, because large numbers of consumers have made it clear that they will not buy them.

The theory of ecological modernization suggests that five social and institutional structures have to be ecologically transformed: science and technology – to work towards the invention and delivery of sustainable technologies; markets and economic agents – to introduce incentives for environmentally benign outcomes; nation-states – to shape market conditions which allow this to happen; social movements – to put pressure on business and the state to continue moving in an ecological direction; and ecological ideologies – to assist in persuading more people to get involved in the ecological modernization of society (Mol and Sonnenfeld 2000). Science and technology have a particularly crucial role to play by working for preventative solutions, building in ecological considerations at the design stage to change currently polluting production systems.

Critics have seen ecological modernization as being too reliant on technological fixes and ignorant of cultural, social and political issues and conflicts. But, in response, Hajer (1995) argues that ecological modernization is really a form of 'cultural politics', in so far as the drive for new ways of taking the modernization process forward actually comes from citizens' action groups and social movements, which is where the growing environmental consciousness has emerged.

By the mid-1990s, three new areas of debate had entered the ecological modernization perspective. First, research began to expand to the developing countries of the South and this significantly challenged the original position. Ecological modernizers had based their ideas on the social institutions with which they were familiar in Western democratic societies, namely:

- a democratic and open political system;
- a legitimate and interventionist state with an advanced and differentiated socio-environmental infrastructure;
- widespread environmental consciousness and well organized environmental non-governmental organizations (NGOs) that have the resources to push for radical ecological reform;
- intermediate or business organizations that are able to represent producers in negotiations on a sectoral or regional basis;
- experience with and tradition in negotiated policy-making and regulatory negotiations;
- a detailed system of environmental monitoring that generates sufficient, reliable and public environmental data;
- a state-regulated market economy that dominates production and consumption processes, covering all the edges of society and strongly integrated in the global market;
- advanced technological development in a highly industrialized society. (Frijns et al. 2000: 258)

But these plainly do not exist in this form outside some of the relatively wealthy countries, and major modifications would have to be made to accommodate the diverse range of countries in the developing South. Secondly, once ecological modernizers started to think beyond the West, ideas of globalization became more relevant to them and there is now research seeking to link globalization and ecological modernization (Mol 2001). Thirdly, ecological modernization has started to take account of the sociology of consumption and of consumer societies. This has led to some interesting studies exploring the ecological modernization of domestic consumption as well as production. These studies look at the ways in which consumers can have an impact on the ecological modernization of society, but also on the environmental impact of different lifestyles and the way that domestic technologies might be improved to reduce energy consumption, save scarce resources such as water and contribute to waste reduction through recycling.

Unlike other perspectives, ecological modernization is less concerned with global inequality and more interested in businesses, individuals and non-state actors. This makes it different in important respects to the discourse and practice of sustainable development. Ecological modernizers also take an interesting position on capitalism. If the capitalist economic system can be made to work for environmental protection, then capitalism will continue, but, if it can't, then something different will have to emerge. This is because ecological modernization is also an evolutionary theory of social development. In this guise it is argued that Western societies have passed through several 'industrial revolutions', each of which has brought about significant changes in technologies and production. But the latest of these, the one they see themselves contributing to, is an ecological version.

Although critics are probably right to say that ecological modernization is, at root, a form of technological optimism rather than a fully worked-out theory of how to get from here to a future sustainable society, the one thing that might just be in their favour is exactly the thing that Scott found missing in the high modernist schemes he examined. That is, many of the examples they produce are fairly small-scale, practical suggestions for change that could collectively make a big difference, especially if ways can be found to make them financially viable in developing countries. But they will probably not succeed unless they are introduced in conjunction with the kind of international agreement that characterizes the Kyoto process, which might ensure the spread of best practice and knowledge of what works.

Conclusion

It is always difficult to know how best to bring books to an end, so let us finish with a somewhat unusual example. In 1986, the city authorities of Philadelphia in the USA ran out of landfill space and sent 15,000 tonnes of ash from waste incineration by ship to an island in the Bahamas for disposal. The Bahamian government rejected it and the ship set off to find a country that would take it, but none did. On its travels, most of the ash cargo was simply illegally dumped in the oceans (two shipping company officials were jailed as a result) and a smaller amount was dumped on a Haitian beach. After local protests, the remaining 2,500 tonnes was again collected up and finally found a resting place, 16 years after it had been shipped out, back in the USA in Pennsylvania, just 100 miles from where it had set off. When it arrived back in the USA, people were amused by the wild flowers and 10-foot-high pine trees that were growing out of the ash. It seems that whilst human beings debated, dumped, argued and protested about the environmentally polluting ash, nature simply went back to work doing what James Lovelock suggests it does best: adapting to changing circumstances. Of course, Lovelock's perspective provides cold comfort for all of us human beings. It suggests that life in the planetary ecosystem will change and adapt to arrive at a new equilibrium, but this new balanced state may well bring extraordinary and terrible consequences for human societies and populations. The natural environment will continue to develop, but unless they make some necessary and difficult changes very rapidly, many existing human societies may not.

Our conclusion takes us back to the sociological perspective of the book, because we cannot avoid the conclusion that environmental problems *are* social problems. They engage, concern, frighten and are ignored by human beings who argue and make claims and counter-claims about them. The tale of waste disposal above tells a story that involves social attitudes towards nature, risk-awareness, waste-disposal policies, national identities, deviance and rule-breaking and environmental protest. I hope that at this stage you recognize that these are all clearly *sociological* issues, not simply matters pertaining to the natural sciences. If we want to understand and explain environ-mental issues satisfactorily, then we *do* need to know something of the natural scientific evidence involved. It is plainly impossible to under-stand climate change without knowing something about the physical and chemical properties of greenhouse gases and their function within the atmosphere. But at the same time, it is just as absurd to believe that global warming is simply a problem of the natural environment with no relationship to industrial production, consumer behaviour, busi-ness activity, state policies and social movement campaigns.

As sociologists came to the environmental issue relatively late, they have had a fair bit of catching up to do. However, it seems to me that this has now been achieved and it is time to move forward. There are some hopeful signs that this is beginning to happen in the works of, for exam-ple, Dickens, Hannigan, Irwin, Macnaghten and Urry, Yearley and others (see References), all of which take the sociological study of envi-ronmental issues that bit further.

Perhaps the next stage will see more interdisciplinary collaborations between sociologists and natural scientists to ensure that both the social and the natural are represented within a more inclusive **envi-ronmental sociological** enterprise. An example of what this might look like can be found in Bert de Vries and Johan Goudsblom's (2002) edited collection, which adopts a long-term 'socio-ecological' perspec-tive, bringing together evidence and theories from both the natural and the social sciences. The global environmental issues discussed here certainly seem to call for more collaborative research of this kind, though with the present set of bounded scientific disciplines, this may be much more difficult in practice than I have made it sound in theory, however desirable. Nonetheless, I hope that some readers will be inspired to take up the challenge.

Readings

Two very good books on globalization are Malcolm Waters's *Globalization* (2000), a short but highly engaging read, and, for a more involved and systematic treatment, David Held et al.'s *Global*

Transformations: Politics, Economics, Culture (1999). A series of critical commentaries can be found in Alan Scott's edited collection, *The Limits of Globalization* (2001).

On globalization and environmental issues, Steven Yearley's *Sociology, Environmentalism, Globalization: Reinventing the Globe* (1996) is one of the best accounts, while Michael Redclift and Ted Benton's selections in *Social Theory and the Global Environment* (1994) bring social theories and environmentalism into contact. Gert Spaargaren et al.'s edited collection, *Environment and Global Modernity* (2000) explores modernity's impact on the environment and covers ecological modernization and risk theory. Arthur Mol's *Globalization and Environmental Reform: The Ecological Modernization of the Global Economy* (2001) views globalization from the standpoint of ecological modernization.

Riley Dunlap and William Michelson's (eds) *Handbook of Environmental Sociology* (2001) is a very useful general resource, though sadly only available in hardback, which may be rather too expensive for a student budget. Although not focused directly on environmental issues, James C. Scott's *Seeing Like a State: How Certain Schemes to Improve the Human Condition Have Failed* (1998) is a brilliant and wide-ranging survey of high modernist schemes to 'tame' the environment as well as people. Finally, Bert de Vries and John Goudsblom's impressive synthesis is entitled *Mappae Mundi: Humans and their Habitats in a Long-Term Socio-Ecological Perspective, Myths, Maps and Models* (2002).

Glossary

Acid rain: rain that has become more acidic than normal due to sulphur dioxide and nitrogen oxide; these react with water to form sulphuric and nitric acids which then fall with rain. Seen as an environmental problem because of the contribution of high sulphur content coal-burning by human populations.

Anthropocentrism: any form of thinking about the world that values humans above other animals or puts the interests of human beings at its centre. Widely seen by environmentalists and Greens as a root cause of environmental damage.

Biocentrism: the belief that all life is of equal value and human beings are not superior to the rest of the natural world. A basic tenet of Deep Ecology.

Biodiversity: literally, biological diversity, or the diversity within nature. Refers either to a particular region or to the whole of nature. Usually seen as deserving of preservation, for either human instrumental reasons or as an end in itself.

Biosphere: that part of the planet in which life exists, including land, surface rocks, water and air.

Bovine Spongiform Encephalopathy (BSE): a fatal, neurodegenerative disease of cattle, discovered in the late twentieth century. Also known as 'mad cow disease' because of the symptoms displayed by infected animals. BSE occurs only in cattle.

Chlorofluorocarbons (CFCs): chemical compounds consisting of chlorine, fluorine and carbon, widely used as a propellant in aerosols. Led to ozone layer damage when chlorine was released into the atmosphere, thereby destroying stratospheric ozone.

Conservation biology: a branch of biology concerned with the study and preservation of habitat in order to conserve genetic diversity in plants and animals. A 'crisis discipline' that linked natural scientific methods to the political goal of conservation.

Critical realism: a philosophy of science and method, which assumes the reality of an objective world as the basis for scientific investigation. Critical realism seeks out the mostly invisible, underlying causal mechanisms which give rise to observable phenomena. In environmental sociology, critical realism has provided an alternative to social constructionism.

Deep ecology: a way of thinking that begins from the position that the natural environment has value in itself – intrinsic value – which is independent of human valuations. Deep ecology is also a form of practice based on the principle that human activity must not compromise the integrity of natural systems.

Ecocentrism: a mode of thought or way of thinking which puts the Earth's natural ecosystems at the centre of concern, both living and non-living. Ecocentric philosophy underpins many Green and radical ecological proposals for social change.

Ecofeminism: various forms of feminist theory that take the relationship between women and nature as their main theoretical interest. Essentialist, social, socialist, liberal and cultural ecofeminism are the main variants. Because of the way it raises and answers questions about the link between women and nature, essentialist ecofeminism remains controversial amongst more mainstream feminist theorists.

Ecological (or environmental) citizenship: rights of access to and duties towards the preservation of the natural environment emerging from a recognition that human beings and societies are part of the planetary ecosystem on which all life depends. Ecological or environmental citizenship can be seen as extending earlier ideas of citizenship beyond the human or social world to take in other animals and the wider natural environment.

Ecological modernization: an initially academic perspective promoting research into the thesis that high-technology solutions are the most likely to resolve environmental dilemmas. However, ecological modernization also seeks to change social institutions and carries an evolutionary theory of long-term development of societies through a series of industrial revolutions, the latest of which is the current 'ecological revolution'. In the latter sense, it is an ecologically oriented form of modernization theory.

Ecological self: the natural or ecological aspect of the human self. Green activists argue that this aspect needs to be cultivated and developed because of its current suppression in industrial capitalist societies. Theorists of ecological selves believe that all human beings can become aware of the ecological aspect of selfhood through practice and intuition as well as being convinced of its existence by rational argument.

Ecologism: a political ideology that comprises a set of ethical ideals and principles concerning the relationship between human societies and the natural environment. Also includes a blueprint for creating a new social order that would be less damaging to nature.

Ecology: a subdiscipline of biology that studies the relationship between organisms and their environments. Invented by Ernst Haeckel in 1866, it has, like ecosystem, been appropriated for Green politics, as it is argued that natural ecology has things to teach societies about how they can best be organized.

Ecosystem: a functional biological system consisting of a community of living organisms and their interrelated physical and chemical environment.

Environmental sociology: a type of sociology that takes the relationship between societies and the natural world as its main research focus. In its strong versions, rather than being another subdiscipline of sociology, environmental sociology seeks to reorient the entire discipline of sociology around the nature–society problem.

Environmentalism: a political ideology that informs activity aimed at preventing damage to the natural environment by working in consensual ways. Environmentalists work with business, governments and the public, seeking to raise awareness of environmental issues, campaigning and lobbying to apply political pressure for change. Most forms of environmentalism draw on scientific knowledge and are reformist in orientation, seeking to tackle environmental issues through mainstream channels.

Genetic modification (GM)/genetic engineering: the science and practice of manipulating the natural DNA of a plant or animal to produce desirable characteristics. It remains controversial, and some Greens see it as experimenting with nature when the consequences are not known and are potentially harmful.

Global warming: a form of climate change in which the average surface temperature of the planet increases over time. Usually associated with 'anthropogenic' – human created – causes, as distinct from the regular cycles of naturally occurring cooler and warmer periods in a geological timescale.

Globalization: the social, economic, political and cultural processes that create more intense and far-reaching human interdependencies across national boundaries. Generally recognized as gathering speed in the second half of the twentieth century, though this trend can be said to have begun much earlier in the history of human development.

Green politics: a body of political ideas that insists on the need for radical social change to solve environmental dilemmas and create a sustainable relationship between human societies and the natural environment. Green politics is pursued through Green political parties and other organizations. Greens draw on the political ideology of 'ecologism' and are distinct from environmentalists, who tend to reject many of the Greens' prescriptions for radical social change.

Greenhouse effect: the warming of the surface temperature of the Earth caused by gases in the atmosphere, including carbon dioxide, methane, nitrous oxide, ozone and chlorofluorocarbons. The greenhouse effect is essential for life on the planet as, without it, surface temperatures could not sustain life. This meaning is distinct from the potential 'runaway' greenhouse effect that is thought to be occurring as anthropogenic activities enhance the natural greenhouse effect.

Human Exemptionalist Paradigm (HEP): the assumption that human beings are exempt from the laws of nature which limit the activities of all other animals. A concept invented by William Catton and Riley Dunlap (1978) to characterize the main problem in moving to an ecologically sustainable society.

New Ecological Paradigm (NEP): the perspective that human societies are dependent on and have to live within the same natural laws as all other animals, therefore the social sciences, particularly sociology, should revise their theoretical base to take this into account. The NEP was Catton and Dunlap's attempt to show how far the HEP had to change to become sustainable.

Nuclear power: energy generated using heat produced by an atomic reaction. Nuclear power has been used as part of mixed-fuel energy policies in numerous countries, but remains controversial because of the problems of dealing with nuclear waste and the link between nuclear power and nuclear weapons development.

Ozone layer: a thin stratum of ozone (O^3), the gas that surrounds planet Earth and absorbs much ultraviolet solar radiation. The ozone layer effectively acts as a barrier to excessive ultraviolet radiation, penetrating the atmosphere and causing damage to life.

Secularization: the gradual loss of influence of religions in the beliefs, practices and means of orientation within societies. Secularization theories were popular during the twentieth century, especially in

Europe, but have recently been challenged in the wake of the rise of Islam and the emergence of new religious movements.

Smog: originally, a combination of smoke and fog which, when mixed with water vapour, can cause health problems. Today, smog usually refers to poor air quality with restricted visibility due to a variety of pollutants including vehicle exhaust gases and industrial smoke.

Social constructionism: an approach to the study of social problems and sociology more generally, which investigates the way that social groups partly create their own reality. Social constructionists begin from the premise that social problems are the end product of problem claims and that some claims succeed while others do not. Investigating the relative ranking of social and environmental problems in society is an important focus of constructionist analysis.

Sociology of the environment: the investigation of environmental issues using existing sociological theories and methods. Sociology of the environment also connects mainstream sociological subjects such as social class and wider inequalities to environmental issues, leading to an interest in environmental justice and the relative risk positions of social groups.

Sociology of knowledge: a form of analysis that explores the ways that knowledge is produced and validated. Although relatively little empirical work has been produced in the sociology of knowledge, its fundamental ideas have been very influential in the sociology of scientific knowledge and, hence, in the study of environmental problems.

Symbolic interactionism: a sociological approach that takes the symbolic world of human communication as its core concern. Symbolic interactionists have tended to investigate the human world and its symbolic creations rather than the natural environment.

Sustainable development: an approach to tackling environmental problems that links these directly to issues of social justice and poverty reduction in developing countries. This is because unless ways are found to raise the living standards of the poor, then the push for development will create more pollution, more risks and a degraded global environment. Sustainable development has been promoted by the United Nations as the central feature of its environment programme under the brief definition: 'Development that meets the needs and aspirations of the current generation without compromising the ability to meet those of future generations.'

Treadmill of production and consumption: an approach to studying environmental dilemmas that draws on Karl Marx's theory of capitalist development. Profit-seeking companies are forced to produce as efficiently as possible to compete and this usually means neglecting environmental protection and pollution control. In addition, modern consumer behaviour based on a cycle of desire–purchase–use– renewed desire leads to a high turnover of products and more environmental damage. On some accounts this approach is viewed as producing a basic contradiction in society as the natural environment from which production draws its raw materials is used up or polluted, thus reducing profits and potentially threatening the continuance of the system (see O'Connor 1998).

References and Further Reading

Adam, B. 1996. 'Re-vision: The Centrality of Time for an Ecological Social Science Perspective', in S. Lash, B. Szerszynski and B. Wynne (eds), *Risk, Environment and Modernity: Towards a New Ecology*, London: Sage: 84–103.

Albrow, M. 1992. 'Globalization', in T. Bottomore and W. Outhwaite (eds), *The Blackwell Dictionary of Twentieth Century Social Thought*, Oxford: Blackwell Publishing: 248–9.

Anderson, A. 1997. *Media, Culture and the Environment*, London: Routledge.

Ashton, J. and Seymour, H. 1988. *The New Public Health: The Liverpool Experience*, Milton Keynes: Open University Press.

Bagguley, P. 1992. 'Social Change, the Middle Class and the Emergence of New Social Movements: A Critical Analysis', *The Sociological Review*, 40(1), February: 26–48.

Baker, S. 2005. *Sustainable Development*, London: Routledge.

Baker, S., Kousis, M., Richardson, D. and Young, S. (eds) 1997. *The Politics of Sustainable Development: Theory, Policy and Practice within the European Union*, London: Routledge.

Beck, U. 1992. *Risk Society: Towards a New Modernity*, London: Sage Publications.

Beck, U. 1999. *World Risk Society*, Cambridge: Polity.

Beck, U. 2002[1995]. *Ecological Politics in an Age of Risk*, Cambridge: Polity.

Bell, M. M. 2004. *An Invitation to Environmental Sociology, Second Edition*, Thousand Oaks, CA: Pine Forge Press.

Bennie, L. G., Franklin, M. N and Rüdig, W. 1995. 'Green Dimensions: The Ideology of the British Greens', in W. Rüdig (ed.), *Green Politics Three*, Edinburgh: Edinburgh University Press: 27–39.

Benton, T. 1991. 'Biology and Social Science: Why the Return of the Repressed Should Be Given a Cautious Welcome', *Sociology*, 25: 1–29.

Benton, T. 1994. *Natural Relations: Ecology, Animal Rights and Social Justice*, London: Verso.

Blaikie, P., Cannon, T., Davis, I, and Wisner, B. 2003. *At Risk: Natural Hazards, People's Vulnerability and Disasters*, London: Routledge.

Blocker, T. J. and Eckberg, D. L. 1997. 'Gender and Environmentalism: Results from the 1993 General Social Survey', *Social Science Quarterly*, 78(4), December: 841–58.

Bookchin, M. 1986. *The Modern Crisis*, Philadelphia: New Society Publishers.

Borgstrom, G. 1969. *Too Many*, New York: Macmillan Press.

Bottomore, T. B. and Rubel, M. (eds) 1990. *Karl Marx: Selected Writings in Sociology and Social Philosophy*, London: Penguin.

Bramwell, A. 1989. *Ecology in the Twentieth Century: A History*, London: Yale University Press.

Braun, B. and Castree, N. (eds) 1998. *Remaking Reality: Nature at the Millennium*, London: Routledge.

Brulle, R. J. 2000. *Agency, Democracy and Nature: The US Environmental Movement from a Critical Theory Perspective*, Cambridge, MA: MIT Press.

Burningham, K. and Cooper, G. 1999. 'Being Constructive: Social Constructionism and the Environment', *Sociology*, 33(2), May: 297–316.

Buttel, F. H. and Taylor, P. 1994. 'Environmental Sociology and Global Environmental Change: A Critical Assessment', in M. Redclift and T. Benton (eds), *Social Theory and the Global Environment*, London: Routledge: 228–55.

Callenbach, E. 1978. *Ecotopia: A Novel About Ecology, People and Politics in 1999*, London: Pluto Press.

Campbell, C. 1992. *The Romantic Ethic and the Spirit of Modern Consumerism*, Oxford: Blackwell Publishing.

Carmin, L. 1999. 'Voluntary Associations, Professional Organisations and the Environmental Movement in the United States', *Environmental Politics*, 8(1): 101–21.

Carson, R. 1962. *Silent Spring*, Boston, MA: Houghton Mifflin.

Carter, N. 2001. *The Politics of the Environment: Ideas, Activism, Policy*, Cambridge: Cambridge University Press.

Catton Jr., W. R. 2002. 'Has the Durkheim Legacy Mislead Sociology?', in R. E. Dunlap, F. H. Buttel, P. Dickens and A. Gijswijt (eds), *Sociological Theory and the Environment: Classical Foundations, Contemporary Insights*, Oxford: Rowman and Littlefield: 90–115.

Catton Jr., W. R. and Dunlap, R. E. 1978. 'Environmental Sociology: A New Paradigm', *The American Sociologist*, 13: 41–9.

Chapman, G. 1997. *Environmentalism and the Mass Media: The North/South Divide*, London: Routledge.

Clapp, B. W. 1994. *An Environmental History of Britain Since the Industrial Revolution*, London: Longman Group UK Ltd.

Clayre, A. (ed.) 1979. *Nature and Industrialization: An Anthology*, Oxford: Oxford University Press.

Coates, P. 1998. *Nature: Western Attitudes Since Ancient Times*, Cambridge: Polity.

Cotgrove, S. 1982. *Catastrophe or Cornucopia: The Environment, Politics and the Future*, Chichester: John Wiley and Sons.

Cowen, N. 2001. *Global History: A Short Overview*, Cambridge: Polity.

Dalton, R. J. and Kuechler, M. (eds) 1990. *Challenging the Political Order: New Social and Political Movements in Western Democracies*, Cambridge: Polity.

Demeritt, D. 1998. 'Science, Social Constructivism and Nature', in B. Braun and N. Castree (eds), *Remaking Reality: Nature at the Millennium*, London: Routledge: 173–93.

Dessler, A. E and Parson, E. A. 2006. *The Science and Politics of Global Climate Change: A Guide to the Debate*, Cambridge: Cambridge University Press.

Devall, B. 1990. *Simple in Means, Rich in Ends: Practising Deep Ecology*, London: Green Print.

Diamond, I. and Orenstein, G. F. (eds) 1990. *Reweaving the World: The Emergence of Ecofeminism*, San Francisco: Sierra Club Books.

Dickens, P. 2004. *Society and Nature: Changing Nature, Changing Ourselves*, Cambridge: Polity.

Dietz, T., Ostrom, E. and Stern, P. C. 2003. 'The Struggle to Govern the Commons', *Science*, 302(5652): 1907–12.

Dobson, A. (ed.) 1999. *Fairness and Futurity: Essays on Environmental Sustainability and Social Justice*, Oxford: Oxford University Press.

Dobson, A. 2000. *Green Political Thought: An Introduction*, 3rd edn, London: Routledge.

Dobson, A. and Bell, D (eds) 2006. *Environmental Citizenship*, Cambridge, MA: MIT Press.

Doherty, B. 1992. 'The Fundi–Realo Controversy: An Analysis of Four European Green Parties', *Environmental Politics*, 1(1): 95–120.

Doherty, B. 2002. *Ideas and Actions in the Green Movement*, London: Routledge.

Doyle, T. 2000. *Green Power: The Environment Movement in Australia*. Sydney: University of New South Wales Press Ltd.

Doyle, T. 2004. *Environmental Movements in Majority and Minority Worlds: A Global Perspective*, Piscataway, NJ: Rutgers University Press.

Dryzek, J. 1987. *Rational Ecology: Environment and Political Economy*, Oxford: Blackwell Publishing.

Dunlap, R. E. 2002. 'Paradigms, Theories, and Environmental Sociology', in R. E. Dunlap, F. H. Buttel, P. Dickens and A Gijswijt (eds), *Sociological Theory and the Environment: Classical Foundations, Contemporary Insights*, Oxford: Rowman and Littlefield: 329–50.

Dunlap, R. E and Michelson, W. (eds) 2001. *Handbook of Environmental Sociology*. Westport, CT: Greenwood Press.

Dunlap, R. E., Buttel, F. H., Dickens, P. and Gijswijt, A. (eds) 2002. *Sociological Theory and the Environment: Classical Foundations, Contemporary Insights*, Oxford: Rowman and Littlefield.

Eckersley, R. 1997. *Environmentalism and Political Theory: Towards an Ecocentric Approach*, London: University College London Press.

Eder, K. 1990. 'The Rise of Counter-Culture Movements Against Modernity: Nature as a New Field of Class Struggle', *Theory, Culture and Society*, 7(4), November: 21–48.

Eder, K. 1996. *The Social Construction of Nature: A Sociology of Ecological Enlightenment*, London: Sage Publications.

Ehrenfeld, D. 1981. *The Arrogance of Humanism*, New York: Oxford University Press.

Ehrlich, P. 1968. *The Population Bomb*, New York: Ballantine Books.

Elias, N. 1987. *Involvement and Detachment*, Oxford: Blackwell Publishing.

Elias, N. 2000[1939]. *The Civilizing Process: Sociogenetic and Psychogenetic Investigations*, Oxford: Blackwell Publishing.

Elkington, J. and Hailes, J. 1988. *The Green Consumer Guide*, London: Gollancz.

Elliott, D. 2003. *Energy, Society and Environment, Second Edition*, London: Routledge.

Elliott, J. 2005. *Introduction to Sustainable Development, Second Edition*, London: Routledge.

European Opinion Research Group. 2002. *The Attitudes of Europeans Towards the Environment, Eurobarometer 58.0*, EORG.

Evans, D. 1992. *A History of Nature Conservation in Britain*, London: Routledge.

Faber, D. (ed.) 1998. *The Struggle for Ecological Democracy: Environmental Justice Movements in the United States*, New York and London: Guilford Press.

Foreman, D. and Haywood, B. (eds) 1989. *Ecodefense: A Field Guide to Monkeywrenching*, Tucson, AZ: Ned Ludd Books.

Fox, W. 1995. *Towards a Transpersonal Ecology: Developing New Foundations for Environmentalism*, New York: State University of New York Press.

Frijns, J., Phung Thuy Phuong and Mol, A. P. J. 2000. 'Ecological Modernisation Theory and Industrialising Economies: The Case of Viet Nam', *Environmental Politics*, 9(1), Spring: 257–92.

Gaard, G. (ed.) 1993. *Ecofeminism: Women, Animals, Nature*, Philadelphia: Temple University Press.

Gellner, E. 1986. *Nations and Nationalism*, Oxford: Blackwell.

Gibbs, L. 2002. 'Citizen Activism for Environmental Health: The Growth of a Powerful New Grassroots Health Movement', *The Annals of the American Academy*, AAPSS 584, November: 97–109.

Giddens, A. 1990. *The Consequences of Modernity*, Cambridge: Polity.

Giddens, A. 1991. *Modernity and Self Identity: Self and Society in the Late Modern Age*, Cambridge: Polity.

Giddens, A. 1994. 'Living in a Post-Traditional Society', in U. Beck, A. Giddens and S.

Lash, *Reflexive Modernization: Politics, Tradition and Aesthetics in the Modern Social Order*, Cambridge: Polity: 56–109.

Giddens, A. 1999. *Runaway World*, London: Profile Books.

Gilig, A. W. 1981. 'Planning for Nature Conservation: a Struggle for Survival and Political Responsibility', in R. Kain (ed.), *Planning for Conservation*, New York: St Martin's Press: 97–116.

Global Greens. 2001. *Charter of the Global Greens*. Canberra: Global Greens.

Golby, J. M. (ed.) 1986. *Culture and Society in Britain 1850–1890*, Oxford: Oxford University Press.

Goldblatt, D. 1996. *Social Theory and the Environment*, Cambridge: Polity.

Goldsmith, E. 1988. T*he Great U-Turn: De-Industrializing Society*, Hartland, Devon: Green Books.

Goldsmith, E., Allen, R., Allaby, M., Davoll, J. and Lawrence, S. 1972. 'A Blueprint for Survival', *The Ecologist*, 2(1), January: 1–43.

Gorz, A. 1994. *Capitalism, Socialism, Ecology*, London: Verso.

Goudsblom, J. 1992. *Fire and Civilization*, London: Allen Lane, The Penguin Press.

Griffin, S. 1978. *Woman and Nature: The Roaring Inside Her*, New York: Harper and Row.

Grove, R. 1994. *Green Imperialism*, Cambridge: Cambridge University Press.

Guha, R. 2000. *Environmentalism: A Global History*, Harlow and New York: Longman.

Hajer, M. A. 1995. *The Politics of Environmental Discourse: Ecological Modernisation and the Policy Process*, Oxford: Clarendon Press.

Hannigan, J. A. 1995. *Environmental Sociology: A Social Constructionist Perspective*, London: Routledge.

Hardin, G. 1968. 'The Tragedy of the Commons', *Science*, 162: 1243–8.

Harvey, D. 1989. *The Condition of Postmodernity: An Enquiry into the Origins of Cultural Change*, Oxford: Blackwell Publishing.

Harvey, D. 1993. 'The Nature of Environment: The Dialectics of Social and Environmental Change', *The Socialist Register*: 1–51.

Havel, V. 1988. 'Anti-Political Politics', in J. Keane (ed.), *Civil Society and the State: New European Perspectives*, London and New York: Verso Press: 381–98.

Hays, S. P. 1987. *Beauty, Health and Permanence: Environmental Politics in the US, 1955–85*, Cambridge: Cambridge University Press.

Hay, P. 2002. *Main Currents in Western Environmental Thought*, Bloomington: Indiana University Press.

Hayward, T. 1998. *Political Theory and Ecological Values*, Cambridge: Polity.

Held, D., Goldblatt, D. and Perraton, J. 1999. *Global Transformations: Politics, Economics, Culture*, Cambridge: Polity.

Hens, L. and Nath, B. (eds) 2005. *The World Summit on Sustainable Development: The Johannesburg Conference*, Dordrecht: Springer.

Horigan, S. 1989. *Nature and Culture in Western Discourses*, London: Routledge.

Huber, P. 1999. *Hard Green: Saving the Environment from the Environmentalists: A Conservative Manifesto*, New York: Basic Books.

Hunter, R. 1980. *The Greenpeace Chronicle*, London: Picador, Pan Books Ltd.

Inglehart, R. 1977. *The Silent Revolution: Changing Values and Political Styles Among Western Publics*, Princeton: Princeton University Press.

Irwin, A. 2001. *Sociology and the Environment, A Critical Introduction to Society, Nature and Knowledge*, Cambridge: Polity.

Joseph, L. E. 1990. *Gaia: The Growth of an Idea*, London: Penguin Books.

Jütte, R. 2005. *A History of the Senses: from Antiquity to Cyberspace*, Cambridge: Polity.

Kelley, K. W. (ed). 1988. *The Home Planet: Images and Reflections of Earth from Space Explorers*. London: Macdonald, Queen Anne Press.

Landes, D. S. 1969. *The Unbound Prometheus: Technological Change and Industrial Development in Western Europe from 1750 to the Present*, London: Cambridge University Press.

Lash, S., Szerszynski, B. and Wynne, B. (eds) 1996. *Risk, Environment and Modernity: Towards a New Ecology*, London: Sage.

Leader, S. H and Probst, P. 2003. 'The Earth Liberation Front and Environmental Terrorism', *Terrorism and Political Violence*, 15(4), Winter: 37–58.

Lewis, M. W. 1994. *Green Delusions: An Environmentalist Critique of Radical Environmentalism*, Durham, NC, and London: Duke University Press.

Light, A. 2000. 'What is an Ecological Identity?' *Environmental Politics*, 9(4), Winter: 59–81.

Livi-Bacci, M. 1992. *A Concise History of World Population*, Oxford: Blackwell Publishing.

Lomborg, B. 2001. *The Skeptical Environmentalist: Measuring the Real State of the World*, Cambridge: Cambridge University Press.

Lovelock, J. E. 1988. *The Ages of Gaia: A Biography of our Living Earth*, New York: Norton.

Lupton, D. 1999. *Risk*, London: Routledge.

Macnaghten, P and Urry, J. 1998. *Contested Natures*, London: Sage.

Martell, L. 1994. *Ecology and Society: An Introduction*, Cambridge: Polity.

Mathews, F. 1994. *The Ecological Self*, London: Routledge.

McCormick, J. 1991. *British Politics and the Environment*, London: Earthscan Publishers Ltd.

McCormick, J. 1992. *The Global Environmental Movement: Reclaiming Paradise*, London: Bellhaven Press.

McNeill, W. H. 1979. *A World History*. Oxford: Oxford University Press.

McKibben, B. 1990. *The End of Nature*, London: Viking, Penguin.

Meadows, D. H., Meadows, D. L., Randers, J. and Behrens III, W. 1974. *The Limits to Growth*, London: Pan Books.

Meadows, D. H., Rander, J and Meadows, D. L. 2004. *Limits to Growth: The 30 Year Update*, White River Jct, VT: Chelsea Green Publishing Company.

Melucci, A. 1989. *Nomads of the Present: Social Movements and Individual Needs in Contemporary Society*, London: Hutchinson Radius.

Merchant, C. 1982. *The Death of Nature: Women, Ecology and the Scientific Revolution*, London: Wildwood House.

Merchant, C. 1992. *Radical Ecology: The Search for a Liveable World*, London: Routledge.

Mennell, S. 1992. *Norbert Elias: An Introduction*. Dublin: University College Dublin Press.

Millennium Ecosystem Assessment Board. 2005. *Living Beyond Our Means: Natural Assets and Human Well-Being: Statement from the Board*. Washington: Island Press.

Mies, M. and Shiva, V. 1993. *Ecofeminism*, London: Zed Press.

Mol, A. P. J. 2001. *Globalization and Environmental Reform: The Ecological Modernization of the Global Economy*, Cambridge, MA: MIT Press.

Mol, A. P. J. and Sonnenfeld, D. A. 2000. 'Ecological Modernisation Around the World', *Environmental Politics*, 9(1), Spring: 3–14.

Müller-Rommel, F. 1989. *New Politics in Western Europe: The Rise and Success of Green Parties and Alternative Lists*, Boulder, CO: Westview.

Murphy, R. 1997. *Sociology and Nature: Social Action in Context*, Boulder, CO: Westview.

Naess, A. 1973. 'The Shallow and the Deep, Long-Range Ecology Movement, A Summary', *Inquiry*, 16: 95–100.

Naess, A. 1985. 'Identification as a Source of Deep Ecological Attitudes', in M. Tobias (ed.), *Deep Ecology*, San Diego, CA: Avant Books: 256–70.

Naess, A. 1986. 'Self-Realization: An Ecological Approach to Being in the World', *The Trumpeter*, 4(3): 35–42.

Naess, A. 1989. *Ecology, Community and Lifestyle*, Cambridge: Cambridge University Press.

Najam, A., Huq, S. and Sokona, Y. 2003. 'Climate Negotiations Beyond Kyoto: Developing Countries Concerns and Interests', *Climate Policy*, 3(3): 221–31.

Noorman, K. J. and Schoot, T. (eds) 1998. *Green Households? Domestic Consumers, Environment and Sustainability*, London: Earthscan.

O'Connor, J. 1998. *Natural Causes: Essays in Ecological Marxism*, New York: Guilford Press.

Parkin, S. 1989. *Green Parties: An International Guide*, London: Heretic Books.

Pearce, F. 1991. *Green Warriors: the People and the Politics Behind the Environmental Revolution*, London: Bodley Head.

Pepper, D. 1996. *Modern Environmentalism: An Introduction*, London: Routledge.

Perrow, C. 1984. *Normal Accidents*, New York: Basic Books.

Plumwood, V. 1993. *Feminism and the Mastery of Nature*, London: Routledge.

Ponting, C. 1993. *A Green History of the World: The Environment and the Collapse of Great Civilizations*, London: Penguin Books.

Porritt, J. 1984. *Seeing Green: The Politics of Ecology Explained*, Oxford: Blackwell Publishing.

Porritt, J. and Winner, D. 1988. *The Coming of the Greens*, London: Fontana Paperbacks.

Purdue, D. A. 2000. *Anti-genetiX: The Emergence of the Anti-GM Movement*, Aldershot: Ashgate Publishing Ltd.

Redclift, M. and Benton, T. (eds) 1994. *Social Theory and the Global Environment*, London: Routledge.

Repcheck, J. 2003. *The Man Who Found Time: James Hutton and the Discovery of the Earth's Antiquity*, London: Simon and Schuster.

Richardson, R. and Rootes, C. (eds) 1994. *The Green Challenge: The Development of Green Parties in Europe*, London: Routledge.

Robertson, R. 1992. *Globalization: Social Theory and Global Culture*, London: Sage.

Robinson, M. 1992. *The Greening of British Party Politics*, Manchester: Manchester University Press.

Rootes, C. (ed.) 1999. *Environmental Movements: Local, National and Global*, London: Frank Cass Publishers.

Rootes, C. (ed.). 2003. *Environmental Protest in Western Europe*. Oxford: Oxford University Press.

Rootes, C. 2005. 'A Limited Transnationalization? The British Environmental Movement', in D. della Porta and S. Tarrow (eds), *Transnational Protest and Global Activism*, Lanham, MD: Rowman and Littlefield.

Roszak, T. 1981. *Person/Planet: The Creative Disintegration of Industrial Society*, St Albans: Granada.

Rowlands, I. H. 1995. *The Politics of Global Atmospheric Change*. Manchester: Manchester University Press.

Rüdig, W. and Lowe, P. 1986. 'The Withered Greening of British Party Politics: A Study of the Ecology Party', *Political Studies*, XXXIV: 262–84.

Rüdig, W., Bennie, L. G. and Franklin, M. N. 1991. *Green Party Members: A Profile*, Glasgow: Delta Publications.

Salleh, A. 1997. *Ecofeminism as Politics: Nature, Marx and the Postmodern*, London and New York: Zed Books.

Sandilands, C. 1999. *The Good-Natured Feminist: Ecofeminism and the Quest for Democracy*, Minneapolis: University of Minnesota Press.

Sargisson, L. 2001. 'What's Wrong with Ecofeminism?', *Environmental Politics*, 10(1), Spring: 52–64.

Schnaiberg, A. 1980. *The Environment: From Surplus to Scarcity*, New York: Oxford University Press.

Schnaiberg, A. and Gould, K. 1994. *Environment and Society: The Enduring Conflict*, New York: St Martin's Press.

Schumacher, E. F. 1973. *Small is Beautiful: A Study of Economics as if People Mattered*, London: Abacus Books.

Scott, A. (ed.) 2001. *The Limits of Globalization*, London: Routledge.

Scott, J. C. 1998. *Seeing Like a State: How Certain Schemes to Improve the Human Condition Have Failed*, New Haven and London: Yale University Press.

Scottish Environment Protection Agency. 2006. *Preventing Household Waste in Scotland: A Consultation Paper*, Edinburgh: Scottish Exceutive.

Shiva, V. 1988. *Staying Alive: Women, Ecology and Survival in India*, London: Zed Books.

Singer, P. 1975. *Animal Liberation: A New Ethics for our Treatment of Animals*, New York: Avon.

Smil, V. 2005. *Energy at the Crossroads: Global Perspectives and Uncertainties*, Cambridge, MA: MIT Press.

Smith, M. J. 1998. *Ecologism: Towards Ecological Citizenship*, Buckingham: Open University Press.

Sonnenfeld, D. A. 2000. 'Contradictions of Ecological Modernisation: Pulp and Paper Manufacturing in South-East Asia', *Environmental Politics*, 9(1), Spring: 235–56.

Spaargaren, G., Mol, A. P. J. and Buttel, F. (eds) 2000. *Environment and Global Modernity*, London: Sage.

Spretnak, C. and Capra, F., with Rüdiger L. 1984. *Green Politics: The Global Promise*, London: Hutchinson and Co. Ltd.

Starhawk. 1999. *The Spiral Dance: A Rebirth of the Ancient Religion of the Great Goddess*, San Francisco: Harper.

Strydom, P. 2002. *Risk, Environment and Society: Ongoing Debates, Current Issues and Future Prospects*, Buckingham: Open University Press.

Sturgeon, N. 1997. *Ecofeminist Natures: Race, Gender, Feminist Theory and Political Action*, New York: Routledge.

Sutton, P. W. 2000. *Explaining Environmentalism: In Search of a New Social Movement*, Aldershot: Ashgate Publishing.

Sutton, P. W. 2004. *Nature, Environment and Society*, Cambridge: Palgrave Macmillan.

Szasz, A. 1994. *EcoPopulism: Toxic Waste and the Movement for Environmental Justice*, Minneapolis: University of Minneapolis Press.

Tester, K. 1991. *Animals and Society: The Humanity of Animal Rights*, London: Routledge.

Thomas, K. 1984. *Man and the Natural World: Changing Attitudes in England 1500–1800*, London: Penguin Books.

Turnock, D. 2001. 'Environmental Problems and Policies in East Central Europe: A Changing Agenda', *GeoJournal*, 55: 485–505.

Urry, J. 2001. *The Tourist Gaze*, 2nd edn, London: Routledge.

Visgilio, G. R. and Whitelaw, D. M. (eds) 2003. *Our Backyard: A Quest for Environmental Justice*, Oxford: Rowman and Littlefield.

Vries, B. de and Goudsblom, J. 2002. *Mappae Mundi: Humans and their Habitats in a Long-Term Socio-Ecological Perspective, Myths, Maps and Models*, Amsterdam: Amsterdam University Press.

Wall, D. (ed.). 1994. *Green History: A Reader in Environmental Literature, Philosophy and Politics*, London and New York: Routledge.

Wall, D. 1999. *Earth First! and the Anti-Roads Movement: Radical Environmentalism and Comparative Social Movements*, London: Routledge.

Wall, D. 2005. *Babylon and Beyond: The Economics of Anti-capitalist, Anti-globalist and Radical Green Movements*, London: Pluto

Ward, B. and Dubos, R. 1972. *Only One Earth: The Care and Maintenance of a Small Planet*, New York: W. W. Norton and Co. Ltd.

Waters, M. 2000. *Globalization*, 2nd edn, London and New York: Routledge.

Watts, M. 1997. 'Black Gold, White Heat: State Violence, Local Resistance and the National Question in Nigeria', in S. Pile and M. Keith (eds), *Geographies of Resistance*, New York: Routledge: 33–67.

White, Jr., L. 1967. 'The Historical Roots of Our Ecological Crisis', *Science*, 155, March: 1203–7.

Wilson, A. 1992. *The Culture of Nature: North American Landscape from Disney to the Exxon Valdez*, Cambridge, MA: Blackwell Publishing.

World Commission on Environment and Development. 1987. *Our Common Future*, Oxford: Oxford University Press.

Worster, D. 1985. *Nature's Economy: A History of Ecological Ideas*, Cambridge: Cambridge University Press.

Wynne, B. 1996. 'May the Sheep Safely Graze? A Reflexive View of the Expert–Lay Knowledge Divide', in S. Lash, B. Szerszynski and B. Wynne (eds), *Risk, Environment and Modernity: Towards a New Ecology*, London: Sage Publications: 44–83.

Yearley, S. 1991. *The Green Case: A Sociology of Environmental Issues, Arguments and Politics*, London: HarperCollins Academic.

Yearley, S. 1996. *Sociology, Environmentalism, Globalization: Reinventing the Globe*, London: Sage Publications.

Young, S. C. 1993. *The Politics of the Environment*, Manchester: Baseline Book Company.

Zonabend, F. 1993. *The Nuclear Peninsula*, Cambridge: Cambridge University Press.

Index

Bold page numbers refer to illustrations

acid rain, 29, 30, 31, 164
acts of God, 10, 13
Adam, Barbara, 143, 127
Afghanistan, 121
African Development Bank, 135
Agenda 21, 134, 159
agriculture, *see* farming
AIDS, 135, 141
air pollution, 73
aircraft, 84
Albert, Prince, 3
alienation, 47–8
Amoco Cadiz (oil tanker), 78, 79, 80
anarchism, 105, 118
Anderson, Alison, 36–7
Animal Liberation Front, 105
animals
    animal rights, 16, 27
    cloning, 113
    cruelty to, 6, 7
    dual attitudes to, 9
    farm, 32–6
    pets, 9
    representations, 18
Annan, Kofi, 139
Annan, Thomas, **61**
Antarctica, 153
anthropocentrism, 46, 47, 149, 164
anti-globalization movements, 99
Argentina, 45, **66**
artificial environments, 14–16, 112
Asia-Pacific Green Network, 122
Association for the Preservation of
    Rural Scotland, 99
astrology, 2
Atlantic Empress (oil tanker), 78
Australia
    dams, 101–2
    environmentalist associations, 96, 97,
        99, 101, 103
    Great Barrier Reef, 41

and Kyoto Protocol, 155, 156
    Royal National Park, 96

Bacon, Francis, 22, 23, 25, 85
Bahamas, 161
Bahro, Rudolf, 121
Baker, Susan, 143
bear-baiting, 6
Beck, Ulrich, 81, 82, 90, 93, 112,
    150
Bell, Derek, 52, 54
Bell, Michael, 32, 68, 71, 105
Bennie, Lyn, 118–19
Benton, Ted, 37, 163
Bible, 10, 19, 20, 24, 25, 70
biocentrism, *see* deep ecology
biodiversity, 28–9, 30, 31, 33, 164
Biodiversity Convention, 31
biosphere
    as environment, 148–50
    industrialization, 62
    meaning, 164
Birdlife International, 98
birds, 14–15
Black Environmental Network, 103,
    105–6
Black Sea, 74
Blaikie, Piers, 12, 17
Bookchin, Murray, 67
Borgstrom, G., 128
Bovine Spongiform Encephalopathy,
    see BSE
Braer (oil tanker), 78
Brasilia, 66, **102,** 158
Brazil, nuclear power, 100
Brower, David, 70, 71
Brundtland Report, 133–4, 139
BSE, 34–5, 82, 164
Buddhism, 19
Buenos Aires, **66**
Bush, George W., 11

Campbell, Colin, 69
Canada, 31, 57
Canberra Charter, 114–15, 123
capitalism
    alienation and, 47
    environmental effect, 67
    industrialization, 59
    Marxist model, 81
    treadmill of production and
        consumption, 67–70, 168–9
Capra, Fritjof, 116, 125
carbon dioxide, 77, 152–3, 155
carbon sinks, 138
Carpenter, Edward, 49
Carson, Rachel, 14–15, 113–14
Carter, Neil, 125
Catton, William, 47, 167
CEE countries, pollution, 75, 89
CFCs, 83, 84, 85, 152, 164
Chernobyl accident, 75, 82, 86–7, **87**
children
    mortality, 135
    and natural world, 38, 39
    social identifications, 45
China
    consumer goods, 145
    e-waste recycling, 89
    early cities, 57, 64
    earthquakes, 10
    industrialization, 60, 68, 76
    rivers, 57–8
Christianity, 19–21, 24–5
CITES, 28
cities, *see* urban environments
citizenship
    categories, 52
    ecological citizenship, 52–3, 165
civil society, 157, 160, 161
Clapp, Brian, 71
class, 105–6
Clayre, Alasdair, 17
climate change, *see* global warming
cloning, 113
Club of Rome, 132
Coal Smoke Abatement Society, 74, 97
Coates, Peter, 17
cock-fighting, 6
Cold War, 75, 149
Commission on Sustainable
    Development, 136
Committee for Environmental
    Conservation, 99
Commons Preservation Society, 96, 97

commons, tragedy of the, 140–1
communist countries, pollution, 20, 75
community, 65
computers, 62
Concorde, 84
conservation biology, 29, 164
Conservation Society, 99
consumerism, 68–70
contaminated land, 73
Copernicus, Nicolaus, 21
Cotgrove, Stephen, 143
Council for Nature, 99
Council for the Preservation of Rural
    England, 99
Couturié, Bill, 71
Cowen, Noel, 57, 71
creationism, 24, 25
Creutzfeldt-Jacob Disease (CJD), 34; *see
    also* vCJD
Critical Mass, 99, 102
critical realism, 32–6, 165
Crocodile Dundee (film), 65–6
culture
    cultural ecofeminism, 51
    and gender, 23
    globalization, 146–7
    versus nature, 3–4, 16
Czech Republic, 75
Czechoslovakia, 75

Dalton, R. J., 100
dams, 58, 101, 136
Danube river, 74
Darwin, Charles, 25
DDT, 14
debt cancellation, 135
deep ecology, 48–9, 92, 118–19, 165
Defoe, Daniel, 42
deforestation, 138
deism, 25
democracy, participatory, 114, 115
Dessler, A. E., 89–90
Devall, Bill, 46, 54
developing countries
    biodiversity loss, 30, 31
    e-waste recycling, 89
    environmental protection, 115
    experience of development, 40
    industrialization, 59, 76
    Millennium Goals, 135–6
    poverty, 128, 134
development, *see* sustainable
    development

deviance, 29
Diamond, I., 54
Dickens, Peter, 37, 162
Dietz, T., 141
dinosaurs, 10
direct action, 44, 102
disasters, natural, 10–13
diversity, 114, 115
division of labour, 65
Dobson, Andrew, 52, 54, 113–14, 125, 143
dog-fighting, 6
Doherty, Brian, 102, 108, 118
Doyle, Timothy, 102, 108
Dunlap, Riley, 47, 163, 167
Durkheim, Emile, 65

Earth First!, 99, 101, 103, 105, 108, 148
Earth Liberation Front, 103, 104–5
earthquakes, 10, 12, 13
Earthwatch, 148
Eckersley, Robyn, 125
ecocentrism, 46–9, 63, 113, 119, 125, 149, 165
ecofeminism, 50–2, 82–3, 165
ecological alienation, 47–8
ecological citizenship, 52–3, 165
ecological footprints, 48
ecological modernization, 94, 156, 159–61, 165
ecological selves, 47–9, 165
ecological wisdom, 114
ecologism, 111–16, 166
ecology
    meaning, 166
    New Ecological Paradigm, 47, 167
    social, 67
    transpersonal, 48
Ecology Party, 111, 117
economic growth, 114, 132–3, 139, 143, 159
eco-socialism, 113
ecosphere, 150
ecosystems, 92, 166
Eder, Klaus, 108
Egypt, 57, 64
Ehrlich, P., 128
Elias, Norbert, 6, 17, 36
Elliott, David, 90
Elliott, Jennifer, 143
energy
    environmental effect, 55–6
    renewable, 77

sustainable development, 136–8
    see also nuclear power
Engels, Friedrich, 61
Enlightenment, 23–5, 67, 110, 157
environment
    biosphere as, 148–50
    changing attitudes, 16, 91–4
    fear of, 10
    and globalization, 144
    historical perspectives, 5–7
    human powers over, 7–14
    and industrialization, 5–7, 18
    meaning, 4–5, 15
    natural versus artificial, 14–16
    versus culture and society, 3–4, 16
    see also nature
environmental changes, 55–71
    industrialization, 57–64
    social development, 55–8
    treadmill of production and consumption, 67–70, 168–9
    urbanization, 64–7
environmental citizenship, 52–3, 165
environmental realism, 32–6, 165
environmentalism, 91–107
    19th-century associations, 97
    20th-century associations, 95, 99
    campaigning methods, 101–2
    changing attitudes, 91–4
    class, 105–6
    definition of nature, 15
    development, 99–106
    doomsayers, 70, 132–3
    ecological identifications, 45, 46
    environmental justice, 105–6
    meaning, 166
    members, 102–5
    new, 103, 104
    objectives, 100
    organizational forms, 100–1
    origins, 95–9
    reformists and radicals, 93–4, 101
    terminology, 117
    women, 50
    see also Green parties
Erika (oil tanker), 78, 79
European Environmental Bureau, 103, 123
European Federation of Green Parties, 122
European Green Party, 123
European Union, 148
Evelyn, John, 74

evolution theory, 25
experience of environment, 38–53
  ecological identifications, 44–52
  Lake District, 41–4
  senses, 38–40
Exxon Valdez (oil tanker), 78, **79,** 80

Faber, D., 105, 108
Falklands War, 45
famines, 11
farming
  agricultural revolution, 57
  agricultural societies, 57
  factory, **33**
  modern methods, 32–6
  Soviet Union, 158
  Tanzania, 158
Federation of Green Parties of Africa,
  122, 124
Federation of Green Parties of the
  Americas, 122, 124
fell-walking, 43
feminism, 23, 50–2, 82–3, 110, 165
fire, 8
fish, 27–8, 141
floods, 10, 11
flu pandemic 1918, 11
foot and mouth disease, 82
Fox, Warwick, 48
fox-hunting, 6
France
  1789 Revolution, 23, 110
  Amoco Cadiz oil spill, 80
  Concorde, 84
  early environmentalists, 96, 97
  Enlightenment philosophers, 23
Friends of the Earth, 99, 103, 148
Frijns, J., 71, 160

Gaia, 92, 150
Galileo Galilei, 21
gardens, 9, 15, 38
Gellner, Ernest, 70
Gemeinschaft, 65
gender
  ecofeminism, 50–2, 82–3, 165
  environmental justice, 106
  masculinity, 51
  promotion of equality, 135
Genesis, Book of, 70
genetic modification, *see* GM crops
geocentrism, 21
geology, 23–5

Germany, Green Party, 117, 120–2
Gesellschaft, 65
Gibbs, Lois, 105
Giddens, Anthony, 15, 36, 59, 64, 65, 71,
  81–2, 90, 112, 150
Glasgow, **61**
Global Greens, 114–15, **123,** 125
global inequality, 59, 106, 128, 160
global warming
  awareness, 84–5, 113
  effect on development, 139
  global solutions, 151–6
  greenhouse effect, 151–2, 167
  greenhouse gases, 77, 138, 152–3
  meaning, 166
  measurement, 153
  prehistoric climate change, 10
  scientific research, 113
  social construction, 31
globalization
  cultural phenomenon, 146–7
  global climate change, 151–6
  global solutions, 150–61
  and localities, 147, 148
  meaning, 144–7, 166–7
  process, 146–7
  redefinition of natural environment,
    144, 148–50
  world society, 145
GM crops, 29, 100, 112, 113, 159, 166
Goldsmith, Edward, 15, 62, 63, 64, 71,
  111, 127–8
Gottlieb, Roger, 107
Goudsblom, Johan, 8, 17, 162, 163
Gould, K., 71
Green 2000, 118
Green parties
  ecological thinking, 92
  emergence, 82, 110–13, 116–24
  Germany, 117, 120–2
  Global Greens, 114–15, **123,** 125
  international parties, 122–4
  national parties, 116–22
  New Zealand, 117
  policies, 107
  success, 111, 126
  United Kingdom, 117–20, 122
Green Party (UK), 111, 117–20, 122
greenhouse effect, 151–2, 167
greenhouse gases, 77, 138, 152–3
Greenland, 153
Greenpeace
  Brasilia nuclear power, **102**

non-renewable resources, 77
non-violence, 114, 115
nuclear power, 29, 56, 73, 82, 85–8, 100,
    102, 137, 148, 167
nuclear tests, **75**
nuclear weapons, 58, 75, 85, 148

oceans, 16
O'Connor, J., 169
oil, 16, 63, 80, 137, 138
    spills, 73, 74, 76–80
Oil Pollution Act (1990), 80
ontological security, 36
Orenstein, G. F., 54
ozone depletion, **83,** 83–5, 88, 167

pagans, 19
Pakistan earthquake 2005, 12
Parson, E., 89–90
participatory democracy, 114, 115
pesticides, 73, 114
philanthropy, 19th-century, 44–5,
    95–6
Philippines, 60, 136
photovoltaic cells, **137**
plagues, 11
Planet Earth, **149**
Plumwood, Val, 51
poetry, 42, 91–2
Poland, 75
Polanyi, Karl, 64
politics, 109–25
    ecologism, 111–16
    left and right, 110, 111
    of nature, 109–13
    political environment, 1
    see also environmentalism
pollution, 72–89
    awareness, 80–8
    inevitability, 73
    significance, 73–80
    types, 72–3
Pompeii, 10
population growth, 128–9, 131, 139
Porritt, Jonathan, 111, 125, 129
post-industrial societies, 62
post-materialism, 122
poverty
    developing countries, 128, 134
    Millennium Goals, 135
    social justice, 114
precautionary principle, 53
Prestige (oil tanker), 78

Pripyat, 86, **87**
Project Creation, 25
proportional representation, 115, 117
psychology, 8, 45
Purdue, D. A., 108

radical Greens, 93–4, 101
radioactivity, 56, 73, 82, 86
rainforests, 30
Ramblers Association, 99
realism, critical realism, 32–6, 165
Reclaim the Streets, 99, 102, 103
Redclift, Michael, 163
religions, 19–21, 23, 24–5
renewable energy, 77
Repcheck, J., 24
Richardson, Dick, 125
Rio Earth Summit 1992, 31, 123, 134
risk societies, 72, 81, 150
risks
    awareness, 80–8, 91
    gender differences, 82–3
    nuclear power, 85–8
    ozone depletion, 83–5, 88
    and politics, 112–13
    'runaway world,' 81–2, 90
    sun rays, 39
river diversion, 57–8
road issues, 29–30
Robertson, Roland, 147, 148
Robinson, Michael, 125
rock patterns, **24**
Romania, 75
romanticism, 42
Rootes, Chris, 101, 106, 108, 125
Rowlands, Ian, 84, 89, 154
Royal Society for the Protection of Birds
    (RSPB), 104
Rüdig, W., 119
'runaway world', 81–2, 90
Ruskin, John, 42–3

Sandilands, Catriona, 52, 54
Sargisson, Lucy, 54
Saro-Wiwa, Ken, 106
Schnaiberg, Alan, 67, 71
science
    critical realism, 32–6
    disaster control, 11
    and ecological modernization, 159
    effect on view of nature, 7, 13
    global warming, 113
    knowledge of environment, 18–26

modernity, 19
new priesthood, 85
objectives, 157
and religions, 19–21
scepticism, 36
scientific revolution, 22–6
textbooks, 18–19
Scotland
  Enlightenment, 23–5
  Glasgow slums, **61**
  Parliament, 117, 120
  Scottish Greens, 117
  Scottish National Trust, 97
  water pollution, 74
Scott, Alan, 163
Scott, James C., 157, 158, 161, 163
Scottish Greens, 120
scrapie, 34
Sea Empress (oil tanker), 78
sea levels, 153–4
secularization, 167–8
Sellafield, 86
senses, 38–40
Seoul, 66
Serengeti National Park, 41
Shell, 106
Siccar Point, 24
Simmel, Georg, 65
simple living, 132
Singapore, 68
Slovakia, 75
slums, **61**
Smil, Vaclav, 90
Smith, Mark J., 52, 54
smog, 73, 74, 95, 168
social constructions
  acid rain, 29, 30, 31
  assembling, 28–9
  biodiversity loss, 28–9, 30, 31
  contesting, 30–1
  contextual constructionism, 28
  deviance, 29
  human needs, 129–30
  meaning, 168
  and nature, 26–32
  presenting, 29–30
  strict constructionism, 27–8
social ecology, 67
social justice, 114, 129
social movements, 99, 107, 108, 110
social status, 68–9
socialism, 106, 111, 113
society

sociological perspective, 5
versus nature, 3–4, 16, 112
world society, 145
Society for Conservation Biology, 29
Society for the Preservation of Birds,
  97
socio-ecological perspective, 162, 163
sociology
  and environment, 26–7, 162, 166,
    168
  of knowledge, 168
solar radiation, 137
solar system, 21
Sonnenfeld, David, 156, 159
South Africa, 97
South Korea, 66, 68
Soviet Union
  environmental policies, 20
  farming modernization, 158
  industrialization, 76, 157
  nuclear power accidents, 86
  pollution, 75
  supersonic aircraft, 84
Spaargaren, Gert, 163
space, 43
space flight, 149, 157
Spain, 78
Spretnak, Charlene, 116, 125
Stabiae, 10
Starhawk, 51
Stockholm Conference on the Human
  Environment 1972, 29, 133, 148
Sumatra, **13**
supersonic aircraft, 84
'surrogate world', 62–3, 64
sustainable development, 126–43
  Canberra Charter, 114, 115
  concept, 126–30
  development of concept, 130–5
  economic growth, 132–3
  feasibility, 139–42
  meaning, 168
  orthodoxy, 126
  practice, 135–9
  World Summit on Sustainable
    Development, 134, 135, 143
Sweden, 97
Switzerland, 97
symbolic interactionsim, 168

Taiwan, 60, 68
Tanzania, 41, 158
television, 18

Tester, Keith, 6, 27
Thatcher, Margaret, 117
Thomas, Keith, 5–6, 17
Thoreau, Henry David, 49, 91–2
Three Mile Island, 86
Tokyo, 66
Tönnies, Ferdinand, 65
Torrey Canyon (oil tanker), 78
tourism, 16, 145
towns, *see* urban environments
traditional knowledge, 23
tragedy of the commons, 140–1
transfer of technology, 137–8
transpersonal ecology, 48
treadmill of production and
    consumption, 67–70, 168–9
tsunami (Asia, 2004), 12–13, **13**
Turkey, 145
Turnock, David, 89
Tuvalu, 153–4

Uganda, 136
Ulster Society for the Preservation of
    the Countryside, 99
UNCED, 133
UNEP, 148
UNESCO, 128
United Nations
    and climate change, 154–6
    environmental concerns, 98
    environmental conferences, 28–9
    Millennium Ecosystem Assessment,
        139–40, 143
    Millennium Goals, 135
    Only One Earth, 133
United States
    20th-century environmentalist
        groups, 99
    Apollo 8, 149
    and Biodiversity Convention, 31
    and climate change, 151
    conservation biology, 29
    creationism, 25
    early conservation, 7, 96
    environmentalist associations, 97, 99,
        103, 105
    greenhouse gas emissions, 155
    Hurricane Katrina, 11, **12,** 151
    and Kyoto Protocol, 155, 156
    Love Canal community, 105
    New Age, 118–19
    nuclear power, 87
    nuclear power accidents, 86

    nuclear tests, 101
    nuclear weapons, 85
    Oil Pollution Act, 80
    Sierra Club, 96, 97
    supersonic aircraft, 84
    toxic waste location, 105, 161
    urbanization, 65
urban environments
    artificial environments, 15, 63
    environmental justice, 106
    first cities, 57, 64
    meaning, 1
    and natural processes, 49
    sustainability, 66
    urbanization, 64–7
    versus natural environment, 5–7
Urry, John, 34, 42, 43, 44, 53–4, 145,
    162
Ussher, Archbishop James, 10, 24

vCJD, 34–5
Venus, 151
Vesuvius, 10
Vietnam War, 99
volcanic eruptions, 10–11, 72
voluntary associations, 65
Vries, Bert de, 162, 163

Wales, 120
Wall, Derek, 17, 99, 102, 108, 132
Wallace, Alfred Russell, 25
war, industrialization, 98
waste
    cities, 67
    e-waste, 89
    ocean, 16, 161
    radioactive, 86
    toxic waste location, 105, 161
water pollution, 73
Waters, Malcolm, 145, 146, 162
weather reports, 40, 43
whaling, 100, 101
White, Lynn, 19, 36
Wilson, Alexander, 36
Windscale, 86
witches, 23
women
    devaluation, 22–3, 51
    ecofeminism, 50–2, 82–3, 165
    and environmental risk, 82–3
    feminist movements, 110
    and nature, 50–2
Wordsworth, William, 42

World Bank, 135
World Commission on Environment
    and Development, 143
World Conservation Union, 98
World Cultural and Natural Heritage
    Convention 1972, 28
World Heritage Sites, 41
World Nuclear Association, 87
world risk society, 81, 150
world society, 145

World Summit on Sustainable
    Development 2002, 134, 135, 143
Worldwide Fund for Nature, 99, 104,
    148

Yearley, Stephen, 84, 89, 162, 163
Young, Stephen, 148

Zonabend, Françoise, 90
zoos, 16